Powershop 2
New Retail Design

VOLUME 1: FASHION

FRAME PUBLISHERS AMSTERDAM

Contents
Volume 1

LIVING THE BRAND

LISA HASSANZADEH
SENIOR PROJECT ARCHITECT
AT CONCRETE ARCHITECTURAL
ASSOCIATES, AMSTERDAM,
THE NETHERLANDS.

The days when trading two apples for a loaf of bread was all there was to retail are clearly over. So are the days when collecting a bunch of products and displaying them randomly in a corner shop was sufficient. Even specializing shops and dedicating them to certain brands no longer satisfies the modern consumer. People today are not leading lives but lifestyles, which are strongly connected to certain brands most of the time. The places where they connect to such brands - retail environments - must clearly represent the brand in question in all ways, while offering an exciting experience. Here lies the new challenge for architects and designers within retail design.

This book presents 200 of the latest well-designed retail environments and explains how the designer in each case translated a brand identity into a shop interior. In addition, the book offers a theoretical chapter that focuses on different aspects of retail as examined by various professionals in the field.

Identity and Total Branding
Nowadays, all aspects of life are branded. Brands function literally as labels representing the attitude or lifestyle that an individual has chosen. In this sense the brand store - virtual or physical - serves as the source of a lifestyle and its ultimate representation. Therefore, brand stores need to offer much more than products for sale. They have to sell an identity which the customer can literally make his own by buying a particular product. This identity is taken home not only in the form of purchased items but also as amenities that come with the products: recognizable packaging (which functions as a billboard announcing one's identification with the brand) and the brand-store experience, which is based on its interior design. People who are strongly connected to a brand talk about the brand store as if it were their second home or the home of a very good friend (as exemplified by the Apple Store). In some cases, the analogy goes so far that only 'really good friends' are privy to the location of a shop: the addresses of guerrilla shops (such as Comme des Garçons), which appear and disappear on the city map are not known to everyone. This temporary store concept can give a brand exclusivity.

Experience
A unique shopping experience is part of the identity challenging every architect commissioned to lend shape to a brand shop. The more closely the concept - and thus the design - of the shop mirrors the very essence of the brand, the more accessible and recognizable a brand and its products become. This statement has already been proved by a number of well-designed logos. One famous example is the Nike logo, which shows the brand's essence in a single 'swoosh'. People internalize and are most attracted by things they can understand. The shop design needs to overwhelm the customer but not over-strain him. This is one reason why reduction to the essence plays a big role in selling identities and brands. Another rather simple reason is that a strong shop design that hits the core values of a brand can live much longer than the commonly expected five years, which means nothing less than more profit for the owner. Then, too, a unique experience is often achieved by combining retail functions with other forms of entertainment. Nowadays, bookshops also function as libraries, computer shops as cafés, fashion shops as living rooms. The act of buying becomes almost secondary when a customer has the opportunity to read, drink, chat.

Challenges
A brand store can be the home of a single brand that is connected to a lifestyle or the home of a lifestyle that includes several matching brands (Colette, Paris, France). It can be a stand-alone store or a shop-in-shop. It can be the place where an individual buys 'homemade' bread, flashy sneakers, a new car or an iPod. In all cases, the task of the designer in charge of the retail environment goes far beyond designing a functional space. The brand store is often - along with its products - the only materialization of a brand. If you take only the products out of the shops of any average shopping centre or shopping street, you will no longer recognize which shop has been located where. This gentrification of shop design is a lost chance for every brand.

>>

01-02   Comme des Garçons Guerilla Stores pop up at various locations around the globe. Each shop is open for a limited time only. Shown here is the Los Angeles store.

01

02

PEOPLE TODAY ARE NOT
LEADING LIVES
BUT LIFESTYLES

The shop designs of brand stores (especially flagship stores), which are nothing less than 3D advertisements, need to become a platform on which the brand's identity and the lifestyle connected to it are communicated and can be experienced. It is crucial, of course, for shops to be designed as functional retail spaces as well, but this aspect stays in the background. One example is the retail concept of the Apple Store, which communicates the feeling that customers are part of one big global family. This feeling and brand identity are the real products sold in the shop. In fact, Apple does not care if you buy its products in the shop or later, via internet. If you have a good experience in the world of Apple, this feeling will be strongly connected to the brand and will make you a loyal customer. Consequently, brand stores are becoming more and more part of the entertainment sector in the same way that shopping has become a highly attractive leisure activity.

Home Base

As the brand and its products become a crucial part of the customer's lifestyle and identity, the 'home of the brand' - the shop - becomes the home of the customer. Within this reversal of circumstances, the private sphere moves into the public domain after the brand has penetrated the private sphere. The customer no longer enters the shop and looks at products in an objective way. Instead he enters the 'home base' of his lifestyle, where he becomes an active part of a brand experience that can be 'sold' to fellow customers in turn. Contemporary retail design is not about making a public interior but about creating a space that is more and more private with every passing day.

APPLE DOES NOT CARE IF YOU
BUY ITS PRODUCTS IN THE SHOP
OR LATER, VIA INTERNET

Photography: Marcus Jackson-Baker, Kozo Takayama and Brett Westfall

|||||||||||||||||||||||||||||||||||||||||||||||||

NOWADAYS, BOOKSHOPS ALSO
FUNCTION AS LIBRARIES,
COMPUTER SHOPS AS CAFES,
FASHION SHOPS AS LIVING
ROOMS

|||||||||||||||||||||||||||||||||||||||||||||||||

06

03   Parisian multi–brand
store Colette features a glass–
and–steel 'T-shirt Box'.

04   Japanese firm Wonderwall
redesigned Colette in 2008, giving
the store its current look. In that
same year, the design studio's
second monograph was published
and launched at Colette.

05   A huge glass cube forms
the entrance of the Apple flagship
store on 5th Avenue in New York
City. Stairs lead down to the
retail area.

06   View of the first–floor gallery
at Colette and part of the ground–
floor area devoted to streetwear
culture.

BEHIND RETAIL DESIGN

EIGHT ESSAYS ON RETAIL DESIGN TODAY AND IN THE FUTURE

CONTENTS

THE STORE AS HOME OF THE BRAND

ERICA BOL

FROM THE MOMENT *HOMO SAPIENS* LIT THE FIRST FIRE, PEOPLE HAVE BEEN CONCERNED WITH THE LARGER MEANING OF LIFE - WHO ARE WE AND WHY ARE WE HERE? THIS IS NOT AN EASY QUESTION TO ANSWER, AND EVEN IF ONE FINDS AN ANSWER, HOW LONG WILL IT BE SATISFYING? LIVES CHANGE; PEOPLE ARE IN A CONTINUOUS PROCESS OF DEFINING A SENSE OF WHO THEY ARE AND WHAT THEY BELIEVE IN. 'THEY ARE CONSTANTLY BUILDING AND REARRANGING THEIR MOSAIC OF THE SELF,' IS HOW DENNIS HAHN APTLY PUTS IT.[1] SO HOW DOES A PERSON, IN THIS BIG MULTICULTURAL WORLD WITH ALL ITS CHOICES, FIND AN IDENTITY? THIS IS WHERE BRANDS CAN COME IN - AND CAN TAKE ON A NEW AND INTRIGUING ROLE.

< Photography: Petrovsky & Ramone
Designed by Tejo Remy, this model of the Rag Chair is made of denim remnants supplied by fashion label Kuyichi. The concept is completely in line with the brand's pursuit of sustainable design.

Creating a Sense of Identity

What people stand for and what they believe in used to be issues which were largely defined by the culture in which they were raised: family, local environment, education and religion influenced the way they saw themselves. The local culture provided them with the symbolic tools needed to create a sense of identity. In the current global environment, people are no longer limited to traditional choices offered by local cultures. The world has opened up. The internet and all its possibilities form a whole new digital world, while the ease of travel makes physical distances appear shorter. For the European, talking with a Chinese friend through Skype or visiting a sister who lives in the USA is possible in the current day and age. Globalization is giving people the possibility to see what is 'out there', and one result is a broadening of interests among people (consumers). They have become more open to different cultures and are able to relate to various lifestyles. It has also resulted in a growth of cross-cultural contacts and in the realization of a global market. Experiences are no longer determined completely by local environments; the world is the playing field. Roots will continue to define people, but the exposure to new experiences will provide them with different perspectives. As part of this process, traditional lifestyles start to lose authority and choices enter the picture.

Connecting to a Brand

The search for personal identity helps define what is important and what you need to know to gain self-esteem, approval and recognition. People like to belong, to be part of something bigger than themselves. One way to define yourself is to connect to a brand and its culture. Consumers no longer buy products only because of their functional qualities; they like buying a brand that stands for something. Something to connect and relate to, something - or, even better, someone - they can be a part of. As Elliot and Davies point out, 'In a consumer culture, people no longer consume for merely functional satisfaction, but consumption becomes meaning-based . . . .'[2]

ONE WAY TO DEFINE YOURSELF IS TO CONNECT TO A BRAND AND ITS CULTURE

Do you want to walk through life with a clear conscience? Kuyichi is a fashion brand that invites everyone to take a peek behind the scenes. You can see that the clothes are all produced in an environmentally friendly way and that the brand takes human rights into account. Their unique track-and-trace system shows the journey made by jeans or sweaters before they end up in your closet - from harvesting the cotton to sewing the fabric to shipping the finished garment. Open and transparent, the message ensures respect for all parties involved. The brand's conscious lifestyle inspires and motivates lots of people. Kuyichi believes in creating a positive change. Customers wear the products to inspire others - not only to *look* good, but also to *do* good. DJ Tiësto, for example, made a deliberate choice to wear Kuyichi for his appearance at Dance4Life in 2006.

Functional and Emotional Brand Elements

Although the functional elements of a brand - the 'what' - are important to its success, these elements are easily copied by competitors. A brand needs to find another way, therefore, to differentiate itself from the competition. It needs to connect with the consumer. This can be done by creating emotional elements. The emotional side of the brand, the personality - the 'who' - helps people connect to the brand. The premise here is that brands can have personalities in much the same way as people do. It is the brand's personality that defines a brand in terms of human characteristics. It creates a basis for the feeling that has to be transferred to the consumer if the

> Photography: Rosminah Brown
and Think Tank Creative
(Jacki Silvan)
The aim at Dean & DeLuca,
a gourmet-food chain, is to offer
the best food selected from
sources worldwide. Supporting
this goal is the brand's style of
presentation: food is displayed
in a natural context, without
plastic packaging. The product
itself is what it's all about.

desired - and valuable - emotional connection is to be made.
Three specific points must be kept in mind when developing
a brand personality strong enough to forge this vital link.

1. Metaphorically speaking, a brand personality suggests
a certain type of relationship. This relationship is modelled
after person-to-person contact and thus provides a quick
and effective indication of what can be expected of the
relationship.
2. A brand personality provides a vehicle for the expression
of a customer's personal identity. Self-expression is usually
more vivid in the case of a brand with a strong personality
3. A successful brand personality conveys functional benefits and product attributes effectively.

In brief, a brand personality makes a brand more interesting
and memorable for the consumer. It forms the foundation of
the complete culture around a brand, to which people can
connect in order to identify themselves.

Holistic Branding Concepts
Branding is a holistic concept. In his explanation of holism in
the *Metaphysics*, Aristotle writes that 'the whole is more than
the sum of its parts'. If all pieces of the puzzle match, the image is complete. Branding is about total appearance. Every
step taken needs to be authentic and consistent. Developing a brand has to do with the way people act, smell, taste,
sound, feel and look. Only by being aware of how to communicate the brand inside and outside the company in question can brand-makers be truly successful. One key part of
the puzzle - and one often overlooked during the assessment of the consistency of the various elements of brand
culture - is design. If brand-related design is to be functional and successful, it has to be based on brand personality. It should not only be aesthetically appealing, but also
correspond to the overall brand culture. On its own, a nice
image is not going to cut it any more. If there is a disconnect
between the image and the message, people get confused.
Victoria's Secret, a lingerie brand, is a good example of a
label currently dealing with a disconnect. The design of its

ON ITS OWN, A NICE IMAGE IS NOT GOING TO CUT IT ANY MORE

stores does not match its message. The brand has
become too sexy for its own good. 'Lusty mannequins' in the
stores and massage oil on the shelves do not match the
ultra-feminine message of hiding sexuality as a woman's
little secret. This disconnect has also been acknowledged
by the chief executive of Victoria's Secret, Sharen Turney.[3]
Victoria, a proper 'to-the-manor-born Londoner' whose
'lacey underthings' were her little secret, gradually turned
into the lusty Vicky, who has 'no qualms about flaunting her
sex appeal'.

Matching the Store to the Message
Your store should be seen as the home of your brand. It
should be aesthetically appealing while also conveying the
message behind your brand personality. Dean & DeLuca,
a USA-based gourmet-food store, is a good example of a
retailer that matches the design of the store to its message.
Dean & DeLuca opened its first store on a busy corner in
SoHo, New York. The store is an inspiration for people who
want to be identified as creative and knowledgeable when
it comes to the attributes of quality food. Dean & DeLuca's
aim is to serve organic food from all over the world to a
creative audience. The brand offers customers a sumptu-
ous celebration of food and a place to experience all of
the pleasures that cooking and eating can bring. Food is
prepared on the spot so that people can see how to use the
products and can taste the results. Vegetables are sprayed
to keep them fresh. And, as much as possible, food is
shown in its natural context (without boxes and plastic) and
stacked in an artisanal way. The merchandizing and design,
both distinctive and elegant, are based on the minimalist

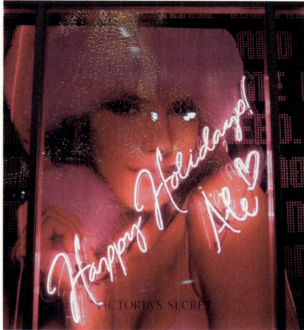

^ Photography: Erica Bol and
Sachit Butail
Display window of Victoria's Secret,
a fashion label whose identity
gradually evolved into something
sexier than the original intention,
thanks to the way in which the
brand image was communicated
to the public.

PEOPLE LIKE TO BELONG, TO BE PART OF SOMETHING BIGGER THAN THEMSELVES

principle 'form follows function'. Like the products for sale,
materials used in the store are natural and of high quality.
The store is a place where people come together and want
to be seen, a place where they can express their love for
the beauty of food. When one Dean & DeLuca customer was
asked why he walked an additional four blocks to have coffee at the store, the answer was, 'It's my family here. This is
where I belong.'

Finding an Identity
In search of a personal identity, people look for ways to
define themselves. Connecting with a brand and its culture
is one way of doing this. Only brands with personalities can
create a culture and a meaning to which consumers can
relate. A brand culture and all it involves should be
authentic and consistent - only then can a true belief system emerge. And the design of the store, which is the home
of the brand, should transcend aesthetics to convey, in a
clearly visual way, a personality that matches the culture of
the brand. True fusion of portfolio, brand and design inten-
sifies the brand culture and reinforces the visual impact of
the brand and everything it stands for.

[1] Dennis Hahn, 'Give Them Something to Believe In:
The Value of Brand Culture', iD Branding,
www.idbranding.com/brand-culture, 2008 (accessed 23 December 2008).

[2] Richard Elliot and Andrea Davies, 'Symbolic brands and authenticity
of identity performance', Brand Culture, Routledge, New York, 2006.

[3] Ylan Q. Mui, 'Victoria's Revelation', Washington Post,
Business Section, 29 February 2008, D01.

COMMERCIAL CHARITY

MARTIJN FRANK DIRKS

WE'RE SEEING THE APPEARANCE OF MORE AND MORE COMMERCIAL CHARITY WORLDWIDE. COMPANIES AND BRANDS ARE DONATING PARTIAL PROCEEDS OF THEIR SALES TO SOCIALLY BENEFICIAL CAUSES AND PROJECTS. A FEW EXAMPLES THAT INSTANTLY SPRING TO MIND ARE SALES OF M·A·C COSMETICS' VIVA GLAM LIPSTICK FOR THE SUPPORT OF PEOPLE LIVING WITH AIDS; THE PROMOTION OF CANCER RESEARCH THROUGH THE SALE OF LANCE ARMSTRONG'S YELLOW LIVESTRONG WRISTBANDS; A PROGRAMME RUN BY THE VALUE AGENCY, PART OF MVO (DUTCH ORGANIZATION PROMOTING CORPORATE SOCIAL RESPONSIBILITY), WHICH COMPENSATES FOR EVERY DROP OF WATER USED AT ITS SPECIAL BAR O BY INVESTING IN WATER PROJECTS FOR DEVELOPING COUNTRIES; AND THE RED INITIATIVE LAUNCHED BY BONO AND BOBBY SHRIVER, IN COLLABORATION WITH AMERICAN EXPRESS, TO ELIMINATE AIDS IN AFRICA WITH THE HELP OF VARIOUS BRANDS THAT MARKET SPECIAL RED PRODUCTS AND DONATE 10 PER CENT OF THE PROCEEDS TO THE CAUSE.

|||||||||||||||||||||||||||||||||||||||||||

RETAIL HAS THE POWER
TO TRANSFORM ETHICAL
INDICATORS INTO VISUAL IMAGES

|||||||||||||||||||||||||||||||||||||||||||

Branding and Marketing
Following the marketing of companies, brands and products - not to mention people and countries - the 'branding and marketing' duo has also brought charity to the attention of the modern consumer. This double whammy is a successful instrument, not only as a way of attracting attention and enticing consumers to donate, but also as a way of getting them to recognize the unique identity and *raison d'être* of a particular organization. Because besides economic concerns, strong social interests are also part of branding and marketing today. No longer is branding merely the key function in marketing for generating sales, a goal achieved by putting a face on a company, brand, product, country or person; branding is also a factor in building long-term social and public relations with consumers, employees, shareholders and their environments.

Retail Features
Having enjoyed temporary sales success, commercial charity has reached a point at which it's time to think long term. A logical follow-up to the branding of charity and the sale of products via diverse channels is the 'retail of moral and emotional concern' that is tied to a unique store formula. After all, retail has the power to transform ethical indicators into visual images. It also boasts a number of universal features and possibilities that can be of essential significance in persuading and acquiring customers, in communicating a brand's message and *raison d'être*, and in creating long-term social and public relationships. Several of these features are of extreme importance in the area of commercial charity.

1. NONVERBAL COMMUNICATION
One of the greater strengths of retail lies in its capacity for universal nonverbal communication. Wherever in the world people may be, spending money has never presented much of a problem. The universal nonverbal language of retail contains a sizable arsenal of gimmicks for seducing consumers to buy. Many companies like to enhance the reality surrounding the supply of products or services with banners or narrowcasting, for instance, or to equip fitting rooms with flattering lighting. And supermarkets tend to position the most expensive A-brands at eye level, making it easy for shoppers to toss these items straight into their trolleys. When it comes to charity-related retail, such gimmicks are unsuitable, however. In light of the background and objectives involved, what's needed here is an unforced, honest and transparent approach combined with complete clarity regarding sales, profits and goals.

2. THEMED ENVIRONMENT
A second way to convey a message to consumers is by creating a themed retail environment. This is done by gearing colours, materials and design to one another to produce an unambiguous image of what a specific brand, company or product stands for. Commercial examples are Apple stores, which communicate the brand's contemporary style; Diesel stores, which represent the lifestyle of the fashion label worldwide; and Ferrari's retail formula, which corresponds to the automaker's corporate identity. A themed retail environment can reveal, for example, the essence of a charity and its goals in a simple-to-understand way.

∧ Photography: Will Femia
Interior of the Diesel 'Planet' flagship store, which occupies three floors of a building on 5th Avenue, a prime retail location in New York City.

|||||||||||||||||||||||||||||||||||||||||||||

WHEREVER IN THE WORLD PEOPLE MAY BE, SPENDING MONEY HAS NEVER PRESENTED MUCH OF A PROBLEM

|||||||||||||||||||||||||||||||||||||||||||||

It can also form an outline of the charitable world in general and, in so doing, create a link between two worlds that makes it easy for customers to feel the seriousness of the situation and the need for this particular charity.

3. ENTERTAINMENT
A third potential success factor is retail entertainment, introduced some time ago in Disney stores. For years entertainment has exercised a positive attraction for consumers and been a dynamic force within retail. Telecom provider Orange, for example, allowed MTV to broadcast a show from its flagship store in Rotterdam, which led to the regular appearance of pop bands on the premises; the average Barnes & Noble book store has a coffee bar or sandwich shop; and CNN operates a store next to its TV studios in New York.
Although the validity of entertainment remains a controversial topic within the 'world of good causes', the principle that entertainment has a favourable effect on the perception of a charitable project has never been a serious point

of debate. Turning the reality of a charity into entertainment not only leads to positive attraction, but also ensures that this reality does not become overly oppressive. Then, too, when entertainment fulfils an educational role, it can convey essential information in a pleasant manner.

4. SIZE AND LOCATION
A final matter of crucial importance is the size and location of the store. There are department stores, boutiques, shopping arcades, stores with a variety of brands (multi-brand stores) and stores representing only one brand (single-brand stores). A flagship store is the most exclusive type of single-brand store. The primary focus of a flagship is not to sell products but to persuade customers to adopt the brand's lifestyle.
Consequently, a single-brand or flagship store is a suitable retail environment for commercial charity, for the persuasion and acquisition of customers, and for the expression and presentation of an individual charity's *raison d'être*, missions and objectives.

Stores Devoted to Good Causes
In the meantime, products emerging from the commercial-charity sector are being sold in diverse multi-brand stores, and this is a good thing. It is possible that in the long term the sale of these products can generate more money and prove to be more persuasive than periodic door-to-door collections or charity bank accounts. There's no denying that today's society revolves largely around consumption, a fact that offers a cornucopia of opportunities - one of which is commercial charity.

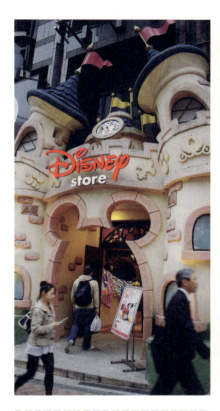

< Photography: Jeff Weston
The brand's Mohican logo
covers the black steel façade
of the Diesel store, which
represents the lifestyle of
the fashion label.

^ Photography: Emma Dupont
Disney Store in Shibuya, Tokyo.
Disney makes sure that people
who visit its stores are entertained
and experience a genuine
'Disneyland feeling'.

Examples of new retail formulas aimed strictly at good
causes do exist, of course, but for the most part this is
a new area of business. A themed single-brand or flagship store forms the ideal environment for communicating
matters such as *raison d'être*, core concern, goals and the
world of the charity in question. In light of the nature of
the business, the sales aspect should be unforced, honest
and transparent. Entertainment can assume a major role in
attracting customers and in conveying essential information
in a light-hearted way.
In closing, commercial charity offers companies, brands,
entrepreneurs and retail designers the chance to do something positive. A retail designer who can increase the
popularity of brands and companies with an eye to boost-
ing sales can do the same for good causes and for socially
responsible brands and companies.

COMMERCIAL CHARITY OFFERS
COMPANIES, BRANDS,
ENTREPRENEURS AND RETAIL
DESIGNERS THE CHANCE TO DO
SOMETHING POSITIVE

RETAIL RESEARCH

KATELIJN QUARTIER

THE APPROACH TAKEN BY THE POPULAR MEDIA TO INTERIOR
ARCHITECTURE AND RETAIL DESIGN IS USUALLY BASED ON
AESTHETICS. THUS THE NEED FOR RESEARCH INTO RETAIL DESIGN
IS NOT A FOREGONE CONCLUSION. WHAT'S MORE, A CULTURE
OF RESEARCH IS, IN PRACTICE, QUITE LIMITED IN THE CASE OF
RETAIL DESIGNERS. BUT THE COMPLEXITY OF THE DISCIPLINE AND
THE RAPIDLY ADVANCING DEVELOPMENTS MARKING THE RETAIL
LANDSCAPE INTENSIFY THE DESIRE FOR SCIENTIFIC KNOWLEDGE
BASED ON FUNDAMENTAL RESEARCH.

^Photography: Katelijn Quartier
The Retail Design Research Lab,
a scientific facility with a focus
on the interior design of stores,
is used by students attending the
Provinciale Hogeschool Limburg
(PHL University College).

A Changeable Industry

Research is a quest for reliable information. But what does this mean within retail design? Because the daily act of shopping is virtually inseparable from society, it is also strongly affected by changes and trends, often coupled with a high turnover rate. Consequently, research into retail design is not a sinecure. Even more so because scientific research entails a much slower process and, unlike retail design, aspires to durability, endeavours to rest on a foundation of fixed values and can prove itself only by documenting repeated findings. Moreover, scientific research can occur only against the background of a theoretical framework developed on the basis of literature or empirical research. A reconciliation between retail design, subject to change, and solid scientific research is not, therefore, a given.

In recent decades, developments in the consumer's shopping behaviour have been widening the gap between retail design and research. The consumer has changed from a functional 'buying creature' into something more of a creature that shops recreationally and thus spends much more time shopping. His demands have increased as well, since he wants to enjoy himself during the time he spends shopping. He wants to have more fun, on the one hand, but also to be comfortable while shopping, a crucial aspect that requires a retail environment that both provides an experience and is functional. Changes in shopping behaviour are caused not only by the consumer but also by the growing supply of products. Thanks to this increase, the consumer more frequently faces difficult choices. At the same time, the retailer must work hard to distinguish himself within a product supply that is becoming more and more uniform. The confluence of the aforementioned developments forms the foundation of the origin and evolution of research into retail design. A brief historical summary clarifies this situation.

Research Disciplines

The relatively short history of research within the field of retail design emerges from three disciplines: marketing, environmental psychology and architecture. Although the line of approach can differ greatly, the desired result is the same: an increase in sales. A marketeer would call it 'customer relations', a psychologist would be more likely to approach it by pursuing the customer's notion of an ideal retail environment, and an (interior) architect would talk about 'an image–enhancing store design'. In any case, a satisfied shopper in an image–enhancing retail interior is good for customer relations, and the result is an increase in sales. Down through history, these three disparate points of view have also led to three analogue channels in the published output: journals with a focus on marketing, journals with a focus on environmental psychology, and popular specialist architecture publications.

|||||||||||||||||||||||||||||||||||||||||||||

THE OVERALL EXPERIENCE IS ALWAYS LARGER THAN THE SUM OF ITS VARIOUS PARTS

|||||||||||||||||||||||||||||||||||||||||||||

The literature shows that marketeers tend to divide a retail space into a number of - individually researched - zones, such as point of display and point of sale. In addition, the interior and its specific characteristics are scrutinized as separate components. Research on the influence of sensory stimuli such as smell, sound, colour and temperature exemplifies such fragmentation.[1] Although the results of such studies do provide an indication of how customers react to an isolated factor, they have little validity in terms of a complete store with an endless number of factors, each of which has an impact on the customer. Nor is the research method used always valuable, as many of these studies are based on images or are even carried out with the use of spatial descriptions. Only a few research projects of this type have taken place in actual retail environments. Despite the fact that methods which rely on images or spatial descriptions have proved useful in other disciplines, in the case of retail design the results are problematic. The reason is quite simple: the experience of a space is a holistic event that cannot be broken up into separate components. The overall experience is always larger than the sum of its various parts.

Here the second line of approach, that of environmental psychology, becomes relevant, since studies in this discipline are more likely to focus on the experience of the space as a whole. Various models developed within this field are aimed at predicting consumer behaviour on the basis of emotion.[2] Although the space and the customer's reaction can be better understood with the use of such models, it is difficult to attribute a certain reaction to one specific factor. The third line of approach is taken by investigative (interior) architects, who do have a long tradition of developing knowledge through a holistic perspective, but only as yet to a negligible degree in the area of retail design. One reason for this is that not until recently has the worth and perception of a retail environment/interior been assessed at its true value.

Interdisciplinary Collaboration

Channels of international scientific publications barely reach (interior) architects, who - as precisely the people partially responsible for the success of retail concepts - would find them beneficial. Scientific articles are not easily accessible, because (interior) architects invariably approach a problem, such as the design of a space, as an entity and not as a number of facets. Then, too, neither marketeers nor psychologists have yet to translate successfully the results of a study into practicable guidelines for architects. In a certain sense, the three disciplines mentioned here exist side by side, certainly in the area of research. A following stumbling block impeding accessibility is the secrecy surrounding information. A lot of research is carried out or supported by retailers or brands. Hence the information gathered often remains within the company in question until the moment at which it is no longer useful.

Burgeoning interest in scientific research worldwide has been a factor in the scientification of retail design. Further support for such scientification is the demand for research results made more usable for a broader target group. The rising need for well–founded information represents a third force. And the growth of a sound research culture within the discipline is bound to accelerate the developmental process even more.[3]

The increasing complexity of consumer demand, society and branding has necessitated cooperation among experts with an eye to getting the most out of these developments. As a result, the clear–cut separation of the three disciplines has made way for interdisciplinary collaboration. Marketeers and psychologists had worked together before, but their teamwork lacked an approach to the space as a whole. What the (interior) architect can contribute, therefore, is the holistic approach, augmented by a greater accessibility of research results. Furthermore, a blurring of the various design–related disciplines has led to a conjugation of (interior) architects with designers involved in other creative endeavours. The scientification of retail design has produced sufficient opportunities for designers from various fields to become part of a multidisciplinary team.

The Power of Scientific Research

Depending on the type of research, findings can provide concrete guidelines, parameters or a design. Such research concentrates primarily on the practical aspect of retail design and often displays an empirical orientation. It is referred to as research into retail design. But the desired result can also be a theoretical pursuit in which research assumes a more observant nature. This type of research, which delves into what occurs within the retail experience, is called research on retail design. Included in this method of gathering information is the hypothesized anticipation of where retail design is headed and not only where it's been. In concrete terms, this means that research *into* and *on* retail design takes into consideration the holistic character of architecture and is able to make a place for itself within the spirit of the times, as well as within a well-founded theoretical framework. An example of how scientific research can aid the practice of design is the limitation of risk-taking, made possible by preliminary studies concerning the potential impact of certain factors on the consumer. For a manufacturer of products, interiors or lighting, such information can be very useful. Scientific research can also provide a theoretical basis for policy advice or even be used to underpin the development of new trends.

Certainly in times of economic uncertainty, research into retail design can demonstrate its power. When retailers and brands find themselves in a situation with more limited financial resources, scientific research can reveal, for example, how budget-friendly modifications of a retail environment can entice the consumer into making a purchase.

Retail Design Research Lab

In-depth research into and on retail design is happening at the Retail Design Research Lab, the first scientific research laboratory for the interior design of stores, established by the Provinciale Hogeschool Limburg (PHL University College). Here, the development of a methodology applied to research into retail design is based on the aforementioned lines of approach. To approximate the holistic shopping experience, the research is carried out within what is considered to be the ideal framework: a three-dimensional space. The modular lab built to represent this space is able to simulate any retail environment; the requirements of the current study determine its character. Within this environment, specific aspects can be isolated, without removing them from their holistic context. From this perspective, it is important to know how the interior of a retail space functions: think of it as a molecule whose structure can be altered completely by modifying a single atom. But when this happens in a controlled manner, the process can be followed and described. By manipulating the environment (researchers use the term 'stimulus'), the reaction of the participant in the study can be analysed with the use of video images, questionnaires and interviews, all aimed at getting a good picture of how the participant feels and behaves (purchasing behaviour, shopping habits and approach-avoidance behaviour). Research projects are developed, supervised and analysed by an interdisciplinary team made up of designers, psychologists and statisticians. Most important of all, the analysed results are translated into useful information for everyone involved in the design process of a retail concept. Although studies are conducted in an extremely specific context, the information can still be translated into other retail environments, often preceded by validation within an actual retail setting.

The Need for a Solid Foundation

More than ever, retail design is a multidisciplinary field of study. This is evident not only in the area of scientific research but also in the collaboration and amalgamation that occurs among design studios, communication specialists and marketing firms. Scientific research can assume the

||||||||||||||||||||||||||||||||||||||||||||||||||

CERTAINLY IN TIMES OF ECONOMIC UNCERTAINTY, RESEARCH INTO RETAIL DESIGN CAN DEMONSTRATE ITS POWER

||||||||||||||||||||||||||||||||||||||||||||||||||

role of fully fledged partner here as well. After all, cross-pollination involving industries and universities can enrich all parties involved. Not enough crossover takes place in practice, however, where it seems at the moment that research doesn't dribble the ball close enough and practical experience is sometimes wide off the mark.

Nevertheless, the evolution of the retail landscape requires the making of more well-founded choices during the process of designing a retail concept. In fact, the very recognition of this need has set in motion the evolution of research into retail design, thus heralding the promise of a dynamic era for such research.

[1] L.W. Turley and Ronald E. Milliman, 'Atmospheric Effects on Shopping Behavior: A Review of the Experimental Evidence', *Journal of Business Research*, Vol. 49, No. 2, 2000, 193–211.

[2] R.J. Donovan and J.R. Rossiter, 'Store Atmosphere: An Environmental Psychology Approach', *Journal of Retailing*, Vol. 58, 1982, 34–57; A. Mehrabian and J.A. Russell, *An Approach to Environmental Psychology*, The MIT Press, Cambridge, MA, 1974; J.A. Russell and G. Pratt, 'A Description of the Affective Quality Attributed to Environments', *Journal of Personality and Social Psychology*, Vol. 38, No. 2, 1980, 311–322.

[3] M. Davis, 'Why Do We Need a Doctoral Study in Design', *International Journal of Design*, Vol. 2, No. 3, 2009, 71–79.

DIGITAL REALITY: THE PLACE OF COMPUTERS IN RETAIL DESIGN

JONAH GAMBLIN

IT IS EASY TO DISMISS THE RECENT VOGUE IN RETAIL DESIGN FOR CURVY SHAPES AND OTHER TYPES OF NONLINEAR FORM AS MERELY THE LATEST FASHION TAKING ITS TURN ON THE STAGE. THE NEW FORMS ARE CERTAINLY NOVEL, ENCHANTING IN THEIR COMPLEXITY, AND SUGGEST THE INCREASING TRIUMPH OF TECHNOLOGY OVER MATTER AND SPACE - ALL POPULAR QUALITIES FOR RETAILERS LOOKING TO DIFFERENTIATE THEIR PRODUCTS AND BRANDS IN AN INCREASINGLY SATURATED WORLD. AT THE SAME TIME, THESE NEW FORMS CAN ALSO BE SEEN AS THE SIGN OF A MUCH DEEPER YET RELATIVELY UNEXAMINED TREND: THE EMERGING DOMINANCE OF THE COMPUTER OVER THE DESIGN AND CONSTRUCTION OF RETAIL ENVIRONMENTS.

||||||||||||||||||||||||||||||||||||||||||

FOR THE YOUNGER GENERATION OF ARCHITECTS AND DESIGNERS TODAY, THE COMPUTER IS NO LONGER OPTIONAL

||||||||||||||||||||||||||||||||||||||||||

Introduction of Digital Technology

Computers are by no means necessary for curvy and unusual shapes. Mid-20th-century modern architects experimented with complex nonlinear forms, frequently derived from geometry found in nature, using little more than paper, pencil and cardboard models. Many of these projects were conceived as reaction against the dominance of technology and the increasing mechanization of society. Complex, non-orthogonal buildings, such as Eero Saarinen's TWA Terminal in New York and John Utzon's Sydney Opera House, were designed and constructed in a traditional labour-intensive, hand-based process. For the TWA building, workers carefully constructed elaborate concrete formwork based on a huge number of conventional 2D drawings from Saarinen's office. The building is effectively a massive, bespoke craft-object.

Subsequent architects continued to explore nonlinear, organic forms and introduced digital technology to assist in the technical refinement and construction of these designs. Frank Ghery, most notably, pioneered the use of 3D modelling in architecture with CATIA, a program originally developed for the design of military aircraft, which is used to digitize physical models and then fabricate building components using computer-controlled machinery. Ghery's projects would be prohibitively expensive to build without the help of computers, although their design evolves from a much more conventional design process.

Use of the Computer Today

For the younger generation of architects and designers today, the computer is no longer optional. All aspects of the design process are assisted by software. Concept design, presentation and simulation rely on 3D-modelling programs such as Rhino, Maya and 3ds Max. CAD programs are used for nearly all 2D drafting. Parametric building information modelling programs like Revit and NavisWorks manage construction and project operating costs. Environmental-systems simulation is possible with Ecotec and VE-Ware. CAM systems such as laser cutters and CNC milling machines manufacture building materials - from structural steel to façade claddings - using digital files created by the programs above.

We have crossed a point today to where this software is not merely helpful but essential, regardless of a designer's formal predilection. In a typical office, there are no drafting tables or cyanotype machines. Clients will not accept hand-drawn technical drawings. Coloured-pencil sketches on competition boards look antique beside animations and photorealistic renderings. The speed with which these new tools have been adopted makes it difficult to fully appreciate their effect on the design process. Digital simulation is an integral part of architectural design and production, although it has been assimilated, in large part, without serious consideration of its effect.

Tendencies of Computer Designs

The relationship between a tool and the things produced by that tool is complex and ambiguous. Simply having a hammer and nails to build a house, and a pencil to sketch the design of that house, does not tell us much about what that house will look like.

^ Photography: Amanda Levete Architects
Future Systems designed the Selfridges department store in Birmingham, UK. The curvy 'blob' landmark contrasts with the architecture cf the ancient Saint Martin's Church opposite.

v Photography: Amanda Levete Architects
Escalators at Selfridges department store exemplify the emerging dominance of the computer in the design and construction of retail environments.

With computers, this relationship appears all the more abstract because computers are advertised as essentially universal machines. Alan Turing, an early theorist of computing, defined computers as machines that could transparently simulate any other symbol-processing machine - typewriters, pencils, even human brains - so the effect of working on the computer should be no different than working with any of these machines.

The reality of designing with computers suggests something different. In the incredible volume of work now produced by and with computers, it is, in fact, possible to see certain recurring tendencies.

There are certain details, forms and strategies which are surprisingly common, and which often appear unrelated to the primary architectural direction of a building. These tendencies are an expression of the inner logic of digital space. They hint at the ultimate effect that the total computer design office will have on the built environment.

To explain this effect more clearly, three of the more significant tendencies are considered below.

1. OBJECTS

The first tendency of digital design is a preference for independent objects, typically freestanding and sculptural, over a more holistic concern with environments. A good example of this is the Carlos Miele flagship store in New York (2003), designed by Asymptote Architects, one of the more vocal advocates for the use of computers in design.

The store is located in a converted 280-m² industrial space in New York's Meatpacking District. Behind a minimally detailed, ultra-clear low-e glass façade, nearly everything is bright and white and has an immaterial, otherworldly feeling. The floor is a white epoxy matrix, the ceiling stretched white plastic, and white-lacquered cabinets, mostly empty, line the walls. In the centre of the volume is the main event: a massive sculptural volume that snakes from the front door to the fitting rooms in the back. This shape, called the 'altar' by the architects, alternately serves as a display mount, seating areas and a room divider. Its form is curvy and voluminous, then suddenly hard and angular. It was designed entirely on the computer, using software in which the digital matter could be stretched and modelled with infinite plasticity until a pleasing shape was found. The altar was fabricated using computer-controlled milling machines off-site before being trucked to the store in pieces and assembled inside.

The use of computers by Asymptote in this process was both liberating and strangely constricting. It was liberating in the sense that the architects could create any form imaginable for the altar; it was constricting in the sense that these forms could be realized only by a specific machine, independent of the construction site. Because the project was a renovation, any interface between the digital creation and the existing space required very detailed information on the existing conditions to be put into the computer. On a typical job site, workers can resolve conflicts between a design and the existing conditions on the spot. When the computer prefabricates components, these adjustments have to be worked out completely in advance by the designer on a computer. By choosing to design a freestanding object, Asymptote avoided this issue. With current technology, it is difficult to interface the virtual space of computer design software and the real space of a construction site. Asymptote's design is an example of the incentives created by this difficulty. Digital design and its products tend to be kept independent of the more conventional handmade aspects of the project.

2. SURFACES

The second tendency of digital design is a preference for thin surfaces over thicker, more solid elements. Most architectural design software represents all elements as a set of points. The architect creates points on screen which the computer then connects into 2D lines or 3D elements composed of triangular polygons. For more complex forms - in particular, forms that curve in more than one direction - software programmers developed spline-based modellers which add control points to a line, allowing for much smoother representations of curved forms. In the computer, however, these smooth forms are infinitely thin despite their potential complexity. They are simply a surface without depth. A sphere in the computer is more like an eggshell than a ball of clay.

|||||||||||||||||||||||||||||||||||||||||||||||||||||

COLOURED-PENCIL SKETCHES ON COMPETITION BOARDS LOOK ANTIQUE BESIDE ANIMATIONS AND PHOTOREALISTIC RENDERINGS

|||||||||||||||||||||||||||||||||||||||||||||||||||||

Spline-based modellers were used by Los Angeles-based architect Greg Lynn in the design of a showroom concept for PrettyGoodLife.com (1999), a Swedish furniture retailer. The design allows for showrooms of various sizes and shapes to be configured from an undulating wooden wall system. Like the Asymptote project, the system was fabricated using a computer-controlled milling machine and has a textured, rippling surface possible only with the help of such a machine. The undulations of the surface provide for the display of objects, either nesting in niches or resting on its projections. The system is flexible and beautiful, and is a good example of the new forms enabled by computer-based design and construction. At the same time, it is very awkward in its physical presence. Much attention has been given to the contours of the wall surface, but these contours are no more than skin deep. The depth of the wall is arbitrary. The computer was able to design the outside only, leaving the inside to be worked out by someone else, with less care and attention. The material reality of the wall is an afterthought and clearly the result of a certain blindness created by Lynn's digital process.

3. CONTINUITY

The third tendency of digital design, and perhaps most significant for future work, is a recurring preference for continuity over difference. Negotiation of difference has arguably been the basis of architectural design since the origin of architecture as a profession. A majority of the design work by architects, and much of what is simply referred to as 'architecture' (as independent from construction), has been dedicated to resolving transitions between unlike things: the joint between an opaque wall and a transparent window, a vertical support (column) and a horizontal support (floor), a building and a landscape. These sorts of differences cannot be represented very well in digital space, because everything is part of the same abstract geometrical point set. The joinery of wall and floor does not need to be articulated in the computer. A line must simply be drawn from point (a,b,c) to point (x,y,z).

The Selfridges store in Birmingham, (2003), designed by British architecture firm Future Systems, is one of the more extreme examples of the emphasis on total architectural continuity encouraged by the computer. The store appears to be the result of a bizarre biological experiment, in which a big blob of undulating blueness was grated to a relatively conventional shopping mall. The blob has neither top nor bottom in any conventional sense, nor any perforations in the façade. The fact that it stops at the ground is a surprise. At its top, the blob appears to turn inside itself, like a doughnut, creating a large daylight atrium crossed by a dazzling sequence of fibreglass escalators, which integrate all levels and programmes of the building. In its form, and in the experience of its form, this Selfridges store seems to operate more like an organism, in a biological sense, than a building, in a conventional sense. It is apparent that much effort was spent in integrating all components of the building into a systematic whole. The elements of the building seem to be mutations of a single substance rather than a composition of individual parts.

The design reflects an awareness of a dominant school of thought in architecture today that uses biological metaphors to explain the possibilities offered by the computer. Architecture, in this theory, acquires animation. It is no longer a static, passive recipient of forces, programmes and people but a participant immersed in dynamic flows. Many of the forms created on the computer are also seen to have biological referents. Façades become 'skins', internal volumes are 'organs' and circulation is called 'flow'.

The attraction of biology for digital architects relates to architecture's long-standing effort to negotiate different elements in construction. Biological unity is an ambitious goal for someone cursed to work with bricks and mortar. With the computer, however, there is a sense that this vision may at last be achievable, given the sheer volume of intelligence available. Anything can now be imbued with computational ability. Computer chips are in airbags and toasters.

As the computer seeps deeper into the practice of architecture, from aiding in the design process to generating mechanical systems and even building materials, there is a growing continuity between architecture and all the other forms of networked, intelligent activity. Why can't a brick be a smart brick? Buildings could acquire an awareness of their internal condition, and perhaps even of their inhabitants. Systems adjust automatically. There is an opportunity for a dynamic, biological-like metabolism in architecture, as is hinted at in the continuity and the total integration of Future Systems' design.

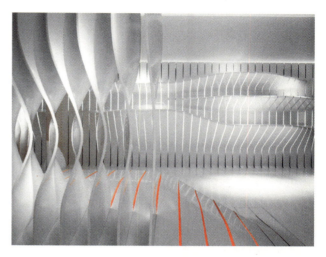
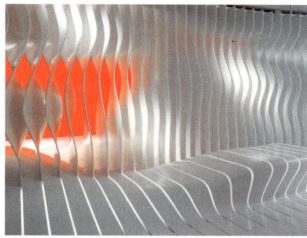

^ Photography: Leo Torri for DuPont™ Corian®
The design of the Corian Lounge, made completely of the 'solid surface' material itself, was inspired by the ripple effect created when a drop of water falls on the still surface of a pool. Amanda Levete Architects' dynamic space represents the transition between passivity and activity.

WHY CAN'T A BRICK BE A SMART BRICK?

Retail as Testing Ground

It is no accident that the first realization of new digital design is predominantly in retail. Shopping has long been a testing ground for experimental architecture and has often provided the general public with the first experience of emerging architectural trends, from early Art-Nouveau department stores to current collaborations between high-fashion brands and star-architects. There also appears to be an unusual affinity between the sorts of tendencies and preferences of computer-assisted architecture and some of the main strategies of retailers. In the emphasis on smoothness, on continuity, on the integration of component parts, digital design echoes the efforts in retail to create cohesive 'experiences' between brands and consumers, to lubricate the in-store encounter with products, to stimulate desire, and to smooth the point of sale and exchange of money for product. This collaboration is still in its early stages. There is much more development to come. As computing leaves fixed terminals and begins to be dispersed into the world, there will be an inevitable interface between the digital design of architects and the broader digital domain of retailers. CAD systems and RFID tags, bar codes and CNC milling machines, merge to become an intelligent and integrated digital reality.

RETAIL AS RELATIONSHIP PLATFORM

MAAIKE VAN LEEUWEN

THE CONSUMER IS CONSTANTLY ON THE MOVE ON THE INTERNET, AND FIGURES SHOW THAT THE NUMBER OF PURCHASES MADE THROUGH THIS VIRTUAL CHANNEL CONTINUES TO SHOW STRONG GROWTH. THE INTERNET IS THE PLACE TO FIND OUT ABOUT PRODUCTS AND TO COMPARE PRICES. EXCHANGING EXPERIENCES WITH OTHER CUSTOMERS HELPS THE INTERNET USER TO EVALUATE POSSIBILITIES AND TAKE DECISIONS. THE CONSUMER HAS BECOME THE REAL OWNER OF THE BRAND. THE BUYER'S DEGREE OF COMMITMENT TO A BRAND IS WHAT LARGELY DETERMINES ITS SUCCESS. TODAY'S CONSUMERS ARE NOT INTERESTED IN STANDARDIZED AND PREPROGRAMMED SOLUTIONS PRESENTED TO THEM THROUGH THE 'PUSH METHOD'. IT USED TO BE THE MANUFACTURER WHO TEMPTED THE CUSTOMER, SOMETIMES WITH THE HELP OF SUBSTANTIAL MARKETING BUDGETS, BUT THESE DAYS THE ROLES HAVE BEEN REVERSED. THE POTENTIAL BUYER REALLY WANTS SOLUTIONS THAT SUIT HIS OR HER INDIVIDUAL PREFERENCES. WHAT'S MORE, THEY DECIDE THEMSELVES WHAT SATISFIES THEIR NEEDS, WHICH FEATURES THEY REQUIRE IN A SERVICE OR PRODUCT, AND WHICH BRAND SUITS THEIR PERSONAL PHILOSOPHY OR LIFESTYLE.

Online Knowledge and Experience–Sharing

These articulate, curious consumers find one another on the internet. Everyone has access to an extensive network through Twitter, LinkedIn or MySpace. Every day, new communities are formed on internet, based on common or shared values, interests and/or concerns - and it's all completely voluntary. Communities play an important role in assessment and information–gathering with regard to the product or service being considered for purchase. Knowledge and experience is exchanged among consumers online. Price and quality are examined carefully; nothing is missed. Keywords for retailers that want to keep their positions and survive in this world are 'transparency', 'involvement' and 'authenticity'.

Online content is generated increasingly by the users themselves. Originally, internet was more of a 'reading' medium; these days anyone can produce content. Internet has become an interactive 'reading and writing medium'. On YouTube, eBay and Lulu.com, individuals can present themselves, share ideas and provide input. Lulu.com is a digital marketplace where writers and teachers, video–makers and musicians, companies and non–profit–making organizations, professionals and amateurs are offered the opportunity to create their work and present it directly to the public. In this way, they can make their books, videos, CDs, DVDs, calendars or reports available to a worldwide audience consisting of as many or as few people as they choose, and they earn 80 per cent of the royalties. The potential and strength of an 'open source' setup is enormous. The Linux computer-operating system, which evolves continuously through the enormous amounts of knowledge and experience shared by active users all over the world, is another good example of the extent to which users are involved. The system has become a standard and the collective effort invested by its users invaluable.

^ Photography: Roger Harris
This summer shop window is part of a NikeiD awareness campaign created by design agency Rosie Lee. A gigantic swatch book featuring three iconic NikeiD trainer silhouettes in colours from the latest iD palette communicates the core principle of sneaker customization.

The challenge for the retail industry lies in the creation and organization of opportunities to bring together the individual wishes and requirements of critical consumers and to translate these into concrete products and services. And, in so doing, to make the most of globally available potential.

|||||||||||||||||||||||||||||||||||||||||||||||||

EVERYONE HAS ACCESS TO AN EXTENSIVE NETWORK THROUGH TWITTER, LINKEDIN OR MYSPACE

|||||||||||||||||||||||||||||||||||||||||||||||||

Knowing the Needs of Consumers

Traditionally, the retailer fulfils a bridging function between consumer and producer. The local shopkeeper assumes a central role in the neighbourhood. He knows his customers personally and is up to date on the latest developments within the neighbourhood and the community. He knows exactly when there is a demand for certain products and who wants them. He provides a tailored solution that even gives his customers the opportunity to buy now and pay later. Theirs is a reciprocal relationship based on trust and shared history. However, most traditional shopkeepers have become large retailers, conceptual superpowers. As a result, the gap between consumer and retailer has widened; what exists today is one-way traffic, originating from the superpowers. The customer has little influence and has no access to the processes involved. Anonymity predominates, and the relationship with the customer has been reduced to a minimum. Without this relationship, competition is fierce in a world where the consumer has every possibility at his disposal to make his own choices and to compare everything on offer.

Nonetheless, in order to retain an understanding of consumer requirements, use is made of CRM systems, loyalty cards and charge cards. These provide insight into the consumer's buying patterns, allowing special offers to be made at the right moment. The virtual sales channel plays an increasingly important role in this area, but too often the process takes place separately from existing CRM systems. The real challenge for the retail industry is to link operational information, virtual channels and CRM systems, so that knowledge can be brought together and integrated. Multi-channelling becomes cross-channelling, whereby the customer's choice predominates.

Customer Loyalty

Besides acquiring new customers, retailers pay attention to customer relations and the retention of existing customers by means of loyalty programmes and savings schemes. Think of the frequent-flyer programmes offered by airlines, for example, or supermarkets; we all have loyalty cards in our wallets. Where the main aim is to gain a price reduction, programmes like these are not sufficient to develop client loyalty and to build up a mutually satisfactory relationship between retailer and customer. A company cannot buy a consumer's loyalty; it has to be earned. Trust and the beginning of a reciprocal relationship ensure that the customer keeps coming back. To achieve this, the retailer must be a good example and deliver added value. KLM has created a customer-centric online community to strengthen its relationship with customers. The Dutch airline has launched passenger-driven communities for clients who do business in China and Africa. Participation is by invitation only, which guarantees a certain exclusivity. In this way, KLM offers its valuable customers a platform on which like-minded entrepreneurs can network and exchange experiences.

The virtual channel plays an important role in bringing (potential) clients together and offers a superior opportunity to involve them in the development of services and products. Generation Benz (Mercedes) has created an exclusive community in which a well-defined target group, in this case young people, is invited to collaborate with teams at Mercedes-Benz. The participants' opinion is paramount, and they are told that they can help co-create the future of the brand. An important aspect of cooperation is that both parties are genuinely open and that the input provided is actually integrated into the product or service involved, for this is the only way to create a real relationship between the two.

Tailored Solutions

In addition, the virtual channel offers extensive opportunities to present and buy products and services in a globally (cost-) efficient and effective way. NikeiD and mi-adidas invite customers to create shoes that are tailor made to their own wishes. You can custom-order groceries at e-tailer Fresh-Direct. On request, products are sliced and freshly packaged in the desired quantities. Here the keywords are 'sustainability', 'quality' and 'freshness'. The diverse product lines range from four-minute meals to organic, kosher and local food. Each customer's products are assembled individually and packed in a special box. Refrigerated trucks that run on biodiesel deliver the orders directly to the customer or to a collection point if preferred. Flexibility and speed allow stocks to be kept to a minimum, and efforts are made to reduce waste. Refrigerated vehicles take the place of storage space. The relationship with the community and the environment is central, and this is evident, for example, in the supply of regional products and support for local projects and initiatives.

|||||||||||||||||||||||||||||||||||||||||||||||||

MOST TRADITIONAL SHOPKEEPERS HAVE BECOME LARGE RETAILERS, CONCEPTUAL SUPERPOWERS

|||||||||||||||||||||||||||||||||||||||||||||||||

Bridge Between Consumer and Producer

The challenge for retailers is to take advantage of the opportunities by organizing themselves in such a way that they fulfil a bridge function and by become the connecting factor between consumer and producer. The communities, feedback groups and testing panels that offer customers the chance to try out products and exchange experiences are sources of inspiration. The involvement of customers in the development of services on offer and the realization of a transparent and efficient manufacturing process require a completely new integral approach.

The retail industry has the chance to develop into a platform that offers people the possibility to create together, to share, and to further extend knowledge and experience. In this way, we can achieve supported solutions in areas such as (market) innovation, logistics, resource deployment and time-to-market advantage. And, ultimately, customers will become satisfied ambassadors of their own brand.

^ Photography: Adrian Duckett
Online grocery store FreshDirect -
popular for its selection of organic
foods - delivers freshly packed
groceries in desired quantities
straight to the customer's door.

RETHINKING THE RETAIL ENVIRONMENT

KAI VAN HASSELT

VARIETIES OF COMMERCIAL SPACES - SHOPS AND THE LIKE - ARE USUALLY IN CLOSE PROXIMITY TO ONE ANOTHER, ACCOMMODATING CUSTOMER–TO–CUSTOMER AND CUSTOMER–TO–RETAILER INTERACTION. THEY VARY FROM VERY PRIVATE TO COLLECTIVE SPACES, BUT THEY NEVER LOSE THEIR CONNECTION WITH THE LARGER PUBLIC DOMAIN, THUS PROVIDING BRAND POCKETS WITHIN THE CONTINUOUS PUBLIC SPHERE. HOW UTTERLY STRANGE IT MUST BE, THEREFORE, TO STUMBLE UPON A HIGHLY DESIGNED PRADA BOUTIQUE IN THE DESERT NEAR MARFA, TEXAS. ON SEEING IT, YOU MIGHT WONDER JUST HOW EXTENSIVE THE REACH OF GLOBAL BRANDS IS THESE DAYS, OR HOW INCREDIBLY WEALTHY THE INHABITANTS OF THIS TEXAN DESERT MUST BE. BUT DON'T PONDER TOO LONG. THIS PARTICULAR PRADA SHOP IS AN INSTALLATION DESIGNED BY ARTISTS MICHAEL ELMGREEN AND INGAR DRAGSET.

Photography: Daniel Hsu
Seemingly out of place in this
remote location, the Prada shop
in Valentine, Texas, was not
designed to cater for customers
looking for a new pairs of shoes.
It is an art installation created
by artists Michael Elmgreen
and Ingar Dragset.

||||||||||||||||||||||||||||||||||||||||||||||

THE RIGHT KIND OF MIXED-USE ENVIRONMENT GOES BEYOND A COMBINATION OF VARIOUS FUNCTIONS

||||||||||||||||||||||||||||||||||||||||||||||

Need for Interaction

It is clear that retail does not function in isolation. Retail is deeply embedded in its cultural, economic and geographical environment. Socially, the customer has to be open to this environment. If a purchase is to take place, it is essential that the customer becomes acquainted with an attractive retail context. This context includes everything: the buyer's in-store experience, the retailer who needs a catchment area, the practical yet crucial world of logistics and distribution, and so forth. Of vital importance to the retail atmosphere, therefore, is interaction between parties such as customer and brand or client and shopkeeper. These types of social interaction stimulate the very process of buying and selling. For this reason, retail design must analyse the specific habits and preferences of a client group; on the basis of such analysis, a retail environment can be designed that corresponds to the desires of the contemporary shopper.

However, the way in which this - necessary - interaction is translated into a retail environment varies. The shopping mall, for example, is a 20th-century Western invention that spread vigorously around the globe without taking into account whether it was applicable or considering its usefulness and effect at the local level. Some cultures, for example, put a high value on family ties, and shoppers in these areas may prefer an intimate place - where they can get together with relatives or friends - over a mall.

Mixed-Use Environments

Many parts of the world are seeing a strong movement towards so-called mixed-use environments: spaces that combine retail, residential, office and other functions. There are different reasons for this development, yet the impetus is invariably commercial. Cities around the world can learn from one another and can implement the best global examples. Retailers and shopping destinations play an important role in this mixed-use trend. They cater to large numbers of people and are service-orientated, consumer-minded and experienced in creating a welcoming environment. Although the service level and quality of shops differ considerably among diverse cultures and regions, the general know-how needed to deal with customers can be used to create the urban, retail and mixed-use destinations of the future.

Outlined below are proposals for mixed-use retail space, resulting from cross-cultural research. Certain guidelines may vary from culture to culture, but there are six basic principles that govern the design proposal for any mixed-use retail environment.

1. MIXED FUNCTIONALITY

The concept behind any mixed-use environment has to start with the mix itself, which can include a wide range of functions, including offices, hotels, apartments, public spaces and government facilities. The right mix creates synergies. In a premium area, a mixed-use environment makes things economically viable, whereas in shrinking or declining cities, the clusters formed often serve to keep economic and social activities together. It is better to concentrate such a project within a smaller area than to allow it to sprawl. The US housing crisis has taught us that sprawling cities - parts of Los Angeles and cities in the Midwest, for instance - lack the density to support a viable commercial environment following a financial crisis. The right kind of mixed-use environment goes beyond a combination of various functions.

2. MIXED AUDIENCE: GENERATIONS AND GENDER

It is important to create places that are attractive to a wide audience. While it is good to target a specific group, one has to consider how to create a space that can cater to several generations simultaneously. It should be cool for kids and teenagers, but also safe and accessible for the elderly. And don't forget the aspect of gender. Even today, real estate seems to be a male-dominated industry with too little affinity for a female approach. Asia offers two inspiring examples of places created for mixed audiences. Marunouchi, Tokyo, used to be a boring business district disliked by working women because of the area's lack of retail and service facilities. Tokyo officials offered developers incentives to add more mixed-use projects to Marunouchi. The result is a very attractive part of the city. The Xintiandi complex in Shanghai is another fine example. The original houses there had to be preserved for historical reasons, as this was the place where Mao started the Cultural Revolution. The developer came up with Xintiandi, a mixed-use area that is used day and night by many different people: it's classic enough for the older generation, cool and attractive enough for the younger generation, Chinese enough for the West and Western enough for a Chinese audience.

3. MIXED ACCESS

Mixed access refers to the technological and human aspects of mixed-use, which are interrelated. Many shopping centres were created with private motorists in mind. Nowadays, retail has come to embrace public-transport modes in Europe as well as in Japan and North America. In the US, the concept of development around transit nodes is called 'transit-oriented development'. In the last few years it has become a trend that has resulted in more efficient and cheaper ways to travel between work, retail areas and home. Thus these places have become accessible to users both rich and poor. The original design and layout of New York City's Central Park was aimed at mixed-use; the park was to be a meeting place for all inhabitants of the city. It still fulfils its goal 150 years on. Mixed-use development should strive to take an inclusive approach. Focusing on the means to access a site is the first important step towards achieving this objective.

4. MIXED-USE IN SPACE AND TIME

Mixed-use developments should deal not only with a mix in terms of space, but also with the right mix in terms of time. Dealing with the time factor requires an awareness of the way in which activities can and do evolve. I once heard about a square in South Africa that functioned as a church on Sundays and was used as a second-hand car market during the rest of the week. In Seoul, there is a specific type of establishment that operates as a carwash by day and becomes a big, tented restaurant after dark. Flexible infrastructure - of the type used for pop concerts, festivals, outdoor markets and similar events - facilitates this kind of temporary use. Certain functions and events trigger synergy

|||||||||||||||||||||||||||||||||||||||||||||||||

ONE HAS TO CONSIDER HOW TO CREATE A SPACE THAT CAN CATER TO SEVERAL GENERATIONS SIMULTANEOUSLY

|||||||||||||||||||||||||||||||||||||||||||||||||

and can be clustered, therefore with little regard to time and space, while those that react negatively to one another require more thought in these areas. A disco and church, for example, can thrive in the same space as long as these functions don't run in parallel.

Another way of dealing with time is to look at the opportunities that seasonal change offers. In spring and summer, the Rockefeller Center ice rink is turned into a big outdoor café. If global warming continues, we can expect certain cities to become more focused on outdoor activities, while it might be too hot for outdoor events in other places. The developing world is overly represented in the latter category. High temperatures require places, including retail spaces, that offer users adequate shade.

5. MIXED-USE: FORMAL VERSUS INFORMAL

The principle of 'formal versus informal' is also relevant. If we want to create spaces that adapt well to change, we have to be flexible. Although an example of mixed-use, the Time Warner Center in New York is unable to adapt to a variety of functional needs. The building is luxurious and combines different shops and activities, but everything is geared to the high-end appeal of the complex. In the same city, however, Union Square is flexible enough to host many different events, one of which is a Saturday-morning market where regional farmers sell their products. Squares and other such flexible places are examples of a more informal approach to mixed-use. The world of luxury retail can learn from the ingenuity with which space is used in informal settings, from favelas in Brazil to train stations in Lagos and the slums of Mumbai.

6. MIXED USE: THE PHYSICAL WORLD EMBRACES THE DIGITAL WORLD

In the design and management of urban environments, we are seeing a growing awareness of the public's digital requirements among retailers and real-estate professionals. Bryant Park in New York, for example, has become one big Wi-Fi hotspot thanks to its sponsor, Google. The public library next door has since created an outdoor zone in the park, making Bryant Park a popular source of both knowledge found in 'real' books and information acquired on the digital highway. As our experience of space becomes digitally enhanced, it also becomes more personalized. When content in a store or shopping centre can also be viewed online, it's easy to choose exactly what we want to see. New technology is making it possible to personalize physical advertisements in the same way that those online can be customized. While one person looks at an ad for a car, someone else sees a shoe advertisement. Messages will be geared to viewers' preferences. The implementation of games and other methods of interaction is making physical-virtual space a potential playground for digital-physical interaction of all kinds. This can lead to new ways of using and interacting with the built environment. The field looks promising. British artists' collective Blast Theory created a GPS-based game in which players can interact simultaneously in both physical and virtual worlds via the omnipresence of cellular and GPS devices. It is a new form of multiplayer game that takes place in the real world. Such experiences can be used to enable people to discover as-yet-unknown areas of a city.

THE POWER OF SEDUCTION

MELLE PAMA

SHOPPING IS TIMELESS. IT IS PART OF OUR EVERYDAY LIFE, A NECESSITY AND SOMETHING THAT CAN BRING JOY AND PLEASURE. WHATEVER THE GLOBAL ECONOMIC SENTIMENT MAY BE, PEOPLE WILL ALWAYS GO SHOPPING. IT IS A BASIC AND FUN THING TO DO. CONSUMER SPENDING REACHED AN ESTIMATED STAGGERING US$77.3 TRILLION IN 2007.[1] BEHIND SHOPPING AND THE ENJOYMENT AND ENTERTAINMENT IT BRINGS LIES ANOTHER WORLD, NOT VERY OBVIOUS AT FIRST GLANCE, THAT INVOLVES A MACHINERY WHOSE EXISTENCE IS JUSTIFIED THROUGH THE CONTROL OF CONSUMER BEHAVIOUR AND PURCHASING PATTERNS. THIS IS WHAT STEERS THE RETAIL WORLD, DETERMINING HOW BRANDS, PRODUCTS AND SHOPS SHOULD LOOK, FEEL OR TASTE. HUGE PILES OF BOOKS EXIST THAT COVER A WIDE SCOPE OF APPROACHES TO AND EXPLANATIONS OF THIS VERY SUBJECT.

< Photography: Mitch Tobias
Kara's Cupcakes in San Francisco
was designed by Montalba
Architects. In front of the showcase,
a small boy gazes at the yummy-
looking cupcakes on the other
side of the glass.

Behind the Scenes

This behind-the-scenes world has grown more and more complex in recent decades, in stride with the growing scale and complexity of the marketplace itself. It tries frantically to keep up with the consumer or, even better, to remain one step ahead. Consultants, advisers and other specialists spend a lot of time trying to understand retail, to figure out the wishes, ideas, dreams, habits and desires of the consumer. It's necessary to be well-informed to keep coming up with effective new retail concepts. Sources range from periodic consumer-spending analyses to trend-watchers, such as Lidewij Edelkoort, who give us a heads-up on what the future holds.

There is so much theory on retail that the beauty and strength of simplicity can get lost in the shuffle. The world of retail is simply too complex for us to know and understand everything about it. Key to understanding retail is the realization that consumers are very different from one another and, consequently, that retail designers should create strategies that take account of that basic truth. This means it's time for a reset, a moment of reflection for everyone involved in retail. We need to be reminded of what retail basically is: an exchange of desire and need based on seduction.

THERE IS SO MUCH THEORY ON RETAIL THAT THE BEAUTY AND STRENGTH OF SIMPLICITY CAN GET LOST IN THE SHUFFLE

Taking It to Another Level

Even before people started recording the years, a man saw his fellow Neanderthal with something he felt he desperately needed. He poked the guy in the side, grunted and offered his neighbour something of his own while pointing at the other's possession. Technical innovation and good ideas fed and facilitated the development of retail. A small but basic example can be found in 2000 BC, when carrying commodities around to trade was becoming too much of a drag. At that time the early Egyptians had a brilliant idea: why not store the grain and use silver ingots to represent the stored value? Small chunks of metal were much easier

to carry and trade, of course, and one thing led to another. Coins were first used in ancient Lydia, now part of Turkey, in 700 BC. Now take a giant step forward in time. In 1901, one year after the escalator was introduced at the Paris World Exposition, the first commercial model of this invention was installed at Gimbels department store in Philadelphia. The escalator created an easy flow of people through a huge building full of products, facilitating shopping on a much larger scale than before. From that moment on, the development of retail accelerated. Basically, the introduction of escalators into stores helped shopping to become not simply one of life's activities but a way of defining life. Some years passed and retail gradually became the mother of all businesses, which led to a litany of problems. As development fostered growth, scale became an issue. With scale came risk, and with risk came uncertainty. Retailers began wondering about what was going on in the market, about how well they really knew their customers and about how they could be sure of all this information. Questions and issues such as these meant that everyone involved had to be educated and informed. The retail branch evolved. It entered a stage of transition, grew and changed. But more than that, a new industry grew alongside it: the industry of retailing. Far more than the physical sale of products and services, the industry that developed - as an autonomous entity - became the knowledge base of retailing. The development led to an understanding of retail.

A Personal Approach

Entering a retail-related term such as 'retail books' into the Google search engine results in millions of hits. Part of the endless list are books describing theoretical models, including how to dissect and standardize such models using graphs and diagrams. The relevant issue is not how to get rid of all this but simply how to have a little more faith in a personal approach. Great retail concepts have often been born out of an entrepreneurial gut feeling and out-of-the-box thinking. The starting point is quite basic: seduction! The product should promise to fulfil the consumer's need, the story should be convincing and the offer should be desirable. But it's important to keep in mind that there is so much going on in the customer's perception that many things will not even be noticed. Equally vital, therefore, is to take a step back and keep things simple. It's also good to realize that 'seduction sells' is not limited to retail. Especially these days, when times are tough.

[1] Visa Inc., Commercial Consumption Expenditure (CCE) index, 1 August 2008. See http://www.visa-asia.com/ap/au/mediacenter/pressrelease/NR_Au_010808_Beijing_ATMs.shtml (accessed on 2 July 2009).

RETAIL: A REFLECTION OF SOCIETY

JOHN MAATMAN

A CONTINUAL EVOLUTION IS TAKING PLACE WITHIN THE RETAIL INDUSTRY. IT IS A RESTLESS SEARCH FOR SOMETHING NEW, SOMETHING BETTER OR SOMETHING DIFFERENT. NEVER HAVE SO MANY BRANDS BEEN INVENTED, ESTABLISHED, REDISCOVERED, REMARKETED, COMBINED OR SPUN OUT THAN IN RECENT YEARS. RETAIL IS THE DRIVING FORCE OF THE ECONOMY AND ENORMOUSLY DIVERSE. THE BAKER ALONE HAS DOZENS OF MANIFESTATIONS (ORGANIC BAKER, CATERER, SUPERMARKET BAKER, COUNTRY BAKER - UP TO AND INCLUDING THE BAKER ON THE CORNER), AND ALL FOR THE SAKE OF SELLING A LOAF OF BREAD, A PRODUCT THAT IS, IN TURN, AVAILABLE IN AN ENDLESS RANGE OF MANIFESTATIONS. FOR EVERY PRODUCT YOU HAVE AT HOME AND EVERY SERVICE YOU USE, THERE'S A STORE WHERE IT CAN BE BOUGHT. THE EMERGENCE OF THE INTERNET, TOO, HAS CAUSED AN EXPLOSIVE INCREASE IN THE SUPPLY AND DIVERSITY OF PRODUCTS AND SERVICES.

^ Photography: Bearandbunny
The interior design of the
Iittala store in Amsterdam tells
the brand's story. Many aspects
of the space refer to either the
brand itself or its country of
origin, Finland.

˅ Photography: Bearandbunny
The compartmentalized wall at
the back of the store holds up
to 1500 objects; each season
a fresh display of products,
featuring the latest colours of
Iittala glass, tells a new story.

ᵛ Photography: Bearandbunny
Although each store has an individual look, the brand identity is clearly recognizable at all Man at Work locations.

Translating Trends

As a part and reflection of society, retail is important. Social trends surface quickly in the retail industry because a good retailer keeps pace with his customers. The current penchant for healthy and 'real', for example, was determined by the consumer but subsequently converted by the retailer into 'real' products and services. The rapid translation of major social happenings occurs as well. Thanks to the credit crisis, it's likely that banks will change promptly. Whereas a proportionate relation between the reliability of a bank and its size (the bigger, the safer) existed before the credit crisis, at the moment we note a change in consumer perception. Qualities such as 'conservative' and 'local' have gained in importance. If they want to survive, banks will have to change the way they approach consumers, both internally and externally.

Retail Mix

Retail today is all about 'retail mix': Retail = Remix. The coherence of various activities and ingredients determines the overall quality. Everything is interrelated. The point of departure should be a good product, of course. The product assortment should be well put together. It's necessary to make clear choices about what to purchase. The supply should be geared to the store, and the store should be flexible enough to present a continuously changing assortment to good advantage. Service before, during and after the sale is of the essence. Reliable service lays a foundation for trust, which gives customers a reason to return. The result can be a relationship that reinforces continuity. In the best-case scenario, customers become the ambassadors of

a brand. Mouth-to-mouth advertising - integration into the everyday experiences of consumers - is the best thing that can happen to a brand. In addition, the universal appeal of a store - shop windows, interior design, web design and all forms of communication - should correspond to the values and mission of the brand.

IT IS A RESTLESS SEARCH FOR SOMETHING NEW, SOMETHING BETTER OR SOMETHING DIFFERENT

As a retail designer, you're involved with this retail mix. A nice interior concept is simply not sufficient. The interior reveals the personality of the organization in no uncertain terms. It shows how mature, immature, rebellious, ambitious, weak, strong, fake or authentic the brand is. It's a determining factor in showing whether or not a brand lives up to its claims. The interior defines the brand perception of the consumer. At RunnersWorld, you're surrounded by runners. The salespeople are runners; some even train others to run. After running on a treadmill wearing the shoes you've selected, an exercise to measure your foot mechanics, you're invited to leave the store and test the shoes on an outdoor surface. Just being in the store makes you feel like running, and this is because the interior radiates the running experience and not because it has such an aesthetically fantastic atmosphere. Retail design goes much further than a trendy or attractive interior. It should keep its appeal even after repeated visits. It should absolutely not be a one-night stand.

||||||||||||||||||||||||||||||||||||||||||||||||

IN THE BEST-CASE SCENARIO, CUSTOMERS BECOME THE AMBASSADORS OF A BRAND

||||||||||||||||||||||||||||||||||||||||||||||||

Single-Brand Stores

In my opinion, stores fall into one of two categories: single-brand and multi-brand. A single-brand store sells one brand. Such establishments are often owned by the brand in question. This has its advantages, as the brand can present itself exactly as desired and has no in-store competition with other brands. The brand has complete control over the entire situation. Often the store stocks every product in the current collection, giving the customer a crystal-clear picture of what's available. Single-brands are eager to present themselves in the best possible light, and that includes a consummate venue: the flagship store (preferably in each of the world's main shopping cities). In most cases, quality trumps quantity. Products are displayed in a sea of space, and visual merchandising is powerful. The biggest danger facing single-brand stores is the predictable product supply, which requires a careful effort to avoid the perils of boredom. Change is not easy to illustrate, especially when the turnover rate is low. The single-brand Iittala store in Amsterdam is visually well organized and features many references not only to the brand but also to Finland, where its origins lie. One example is the crosscut parquet floor, the same surface used in the company's old glass factory. The door has a handle based on a cross section of Iittala's Alvar Aalto vase. At the rear of the store, built to display the latest colours of glass, is a compartmentalized wall designed to hold 1500 objects. Together they create an image that is changed each season to tell yet another new story.

∧ Photography: Bearandbunny
Each area of the Man at Work shop is marked by a bright, distinctive colour. Pictured is the yellow zone.

∨ Photography: Bearandbunny
A greenhouse in the Man at Work store holds both the men's and the women's fashion collection.

Multi-Brand Stores

A multi-brand store sells a variety of brands. The correlated composition of these brands determines the store's image. Since all brands are selected and purchased individually, the product assortment is easy to gear to the whims and wishes of the consumer. Consequently, multi-brand stores can take advantage of social developments much more quickly than single-brand stores. When good choices are made, multi-brand stores are the curators of the world. But making choices is the hardest task for a multi-brand store. Is it better to buy a bit of this brand and that or to jump in the deep end and go for a broader selection of fewer brands? A great diversity of products tends to make the assortment uninteresting - it's neither fish nor fowl - whereas a speciality shop is forced to aim its wares at a smaller target group.

I rate Corso Como in Milan as one of the best multi-brand stores. The store is explicit in its choices, and everything is in compliance with everything else. The total store proclaims the style and taste preferred by its owners through its personal signature and product assortment. Then, too, Corso Como's various areas exhibit the interests involved: fashion, design, books, music, art (gallery), food and gardening. The building and its interior reflect all these things

> Photography: Vanni Burkhart
Corso Como consists of a network
of spaces. With a gallery, a book-
shop, a fashion and design shop,
a café and a restaurant, it offers
a complete lifestyle and shopping
experience for like-minded people
----

exceptionally well: avant-garde yet timeless. Corso Como
appears to have grown in a natural way. Another example
is Men at Work, a multi-brand formula with 50 stores that
targets youngsters for the most part. In recent years, the
brand's interiors have been the work of design studio
Bearandbunny. Although each store has a distinctive retail
design, the brand remains recognizable at all times.

||||||||||||||||||||||||||||||||||||||||||||||||||

WHEN GOOD CHOICES ARE MADE, MULTI-BRAND STORES ARE THE CURATORS OF THE WORLD

||||||||||||||||||||||||||||||||||||||||||||||||||

Deliberately imperfect, these interiors illustrate a brand in
evolution, a definition that also applies to the target group.
The Maastricht store, for example, features a wall with 600
recycled speakers, as well as elements made from recycled
timber and a ceiling filled with hanging plants. The various
areas of the Antwerp outlet are highlighted by elementary
colours, and shoppers are surprised to find equipment of
the type used in the Dutch gymnastic game of apenkooi.
The character of a store should be recognizable and should
linger in the mind of the consumer.

Mirror of a Brand
The consumer should grant the retailer permission, as it
were, to sell his products. Required of the retailer are clear
choices in both product assortment and story. The binding
factor here is the interior, where all parts of the equation
come together: product, service, brand vision, brand experience and people. The interior is the mirror and should
reflect the story attached to the brand. The designer is the
translator.

ABOUT THE AUTHORS

Erica Bol p. 10
Erica Bol (1976) works as a consumer-insights researcher and freelances for Bolding. She analyses international markets, trends, cultures and (academic) literature to form or further develop a brand's creative strategy in the current market. Bol, who has lived and worked in the USA and China, is presently based in the Netherlands. She holds a bachelor's degree in communication and design management and a master's degree in retail design.
www.bolding.eu

Martijn Frank Dirks p. 14
Martijn Frank Dirks (1975) has a bachelor's degree in industrial design and a master's degree in retail design. He works part time as a design tutor and is the founder of the Amsterdam-based multidisciplinary design company MFD. As a designer, his aim is to express a client's soul and inspirational values through explicit brand environments, strategic graphics, products and interiors. www.studiomfd.nl

Katelijn Quartier p. 18
Katelijn Quartier works as a retail-design researcher and lecturer at the PHL University College in Hasselt, Belgium. After earning a degree in interior architecture, she studied retail design at the Piet Zwart Academy in Rotterdam (in association with Plymouth University) to obtain the Master of Arts degree. Currently working on her PhD dissertation in architecture, Quartier has published in several Belgian journals and participated in a number of international symposiums. www.retailology.be

Jonah Gamblin p. 22
Jonah Gamblin is an architect with the Office for Metropolitan Architecture (OMA) in Rotterdam, the Netherlands. Gamblin is a founding partner of the UNAME design collective and has written widely on architecture, economics and real estate. A recent book that includes his work is Poetry, Property and Place, which was published by W.W. Norton in 2007.

Maaike van Leeuwen p. 26
Maaike van Leeuwen (1975) works for the Rabobank in Almere, the Netherlands, as a cooperative and community banking adviser. After studying sociology and education, she worked as a consultant for starting entrepreneurs in various types of businesses. Today she combines her passion for developments in society, education and entrepreneurship in her professional as well as her private life.

Kai van Hasselt p. 30
Crossing art with urbanism and economics, Kai van Hasselt (1981) is the founder and director of Amsterdam-based Shinsekai Analysis, a firm that advises companies all over the globe in need of well-developed urban strategies based on local cultures, global trends and comparative city analysis. He started his career in the retail sector as a trend watcher for Signs of Time and, since 2007, he has been a member of the jury for the annual shopping center awards of the NRW (Dutch Council of Shopping Centers).
www.shinsekai.nl

Melle Pama p. 34
Managing partner of design firm Totems, Melle Pama holds a Bachelor of Science in architectural design and a postgraduate degree in retail and communication design. With over ten years of experience in 3D communication and architecture, including more than a year in Beijing as creative director of a retail design and building firm, Pama has an in-depth understanding of Chinese culture. His goal is to create a bridge between Western exhibition excellence and the Chinese market. www.totems.nl

John Maatman p. 36
John Maatman graduated from the Design Academy Eindhoven, the Netherlands, in 1996. He worked as a coordinator for the Piet Zwart Academy (Rotterdam, the Netherlands) for two years (2006-2008) and is the director of the Amsterdam-based design company bearandbunny, which he co-founded in 2001. Bearandbunny focuses on product design and retail interiors but is also involved in the creation of office and residential environments.
www.bearandbunny.com

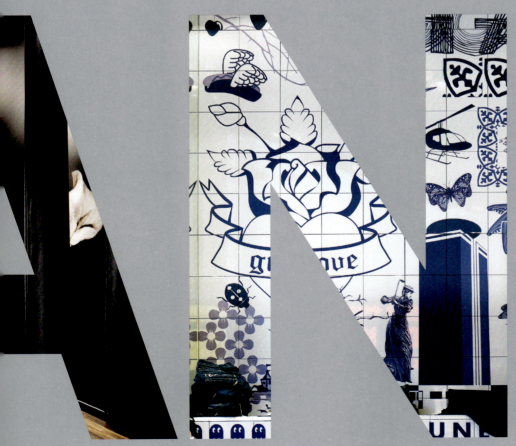

2.mood
VLS Interior Architecture

WHERE:
WHEN:
CLIENT:
SHOP CONSTRUCTOR:
ARCHITECT:
TOTAL FLOOR AREA (M²):

TALLINN, ESTONIA
NOVEMBER 2007
KORMEK TRADING
KMG EHITUS
ARHITEKTUURIBÜROO KOSMOS
110

VLS INTERIOR ARCHITECTURE WAS FOUNDED IN 2007. THE FIRM SPECIALIZES IN INTERIOR ARCHITECTURE AND DESIGN AT BOTH LOCAL AND INTERNATIONAL LEVELS. VLS'S PORTFOLIO INCLUDES PROJECTS RANGING FROM WORK ON THE ART MUSEUM OF ESTONIA AND TALLINN CITY THEATRE TO CRUISE SHIPS, LUXURY-CAR DEALERSHIPS AND SMALL PRIVATE HOMES.

When VLS Interior Architecture (VLS) agreed to refurbish Estonian fashion shop 2.mood, the designers were asked to realize an interior that would communicate with the building and not with the merchandise for sale. An unusual request within a retail industry so focused on branding, but the reason was simple: the selection of multiple brands available at the store changes from time to time. The designers developed the entire concept before learning the names of specific brands.

The highlight of the sculptural interior is an illuminated plastic volume that starts behind the cash desk before moving up the wall and crossing part of the ceiling. Two sculptural pieces of furniture at the middle of the shop rest on panels of clear glass, which create an illusion of levitation. The designers also rethought the existing system of hanging clothes. Gently curving rails, suspended from the ceiling or rising from the concrete floor, are open at the back to accommodate hangers.

VLS Interior Architecture
Gonsiori 5A–13
10117 Tallinn
Estonia

T +372 (0)5078 409
E info@vls.ee
W www.vls.ee

Photography: Ville Lausmäe and Martin Siplane

01   Centrally positioned pieces of freestanding furniture rest on glass panels, creating the illusion of levitation.

02   Buildings in Tallinn's Rotermanni Quarter can be distinguished by their colours. The 2.mood boutique is in the White Building.

03   The cash desk is the starting point for the focal point of the interior: a large sculptural volume featuring Makrolon® multi panels.

04   View of the interior of the shop.

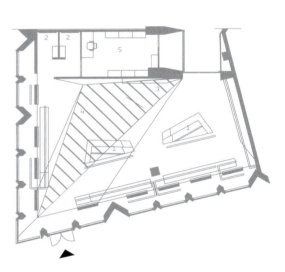

1 Display element
2 Fitting room
3 Cash desk
4 Illuminated sculpture
5 Staff room

Al Sawani Grand
Schwitzke & Partner

WHERE: JEDDAH, SAUDI ARABIA
WHEN: OCTOBER 2008
CLIENT: AL SAWANI GROUP
SHOP CONSTRUCTORS: HAFIZ CONTRACTING
AND WOOD & STEEL

TOTAL FLOOR AREA (M²):   7,000

|||||||||||||||||||||||||||||||||||||||||||||||||

FOUNDED IN 1989, DESIGN FIRM SCHWITZKE & PARTNER ROSE EARLY ON TO ENJOY NATIONAL AND INTERNATIONAL RENOWN IN THE FIELD OF BRAND RETAIL. THE DÜSSELDORF–BASED SCHWITZKE GROUP, WHICH INCLUDES SUBSIDIARIES AND BRANCHES WITHIN GERMANY AND ABROAD, OFFERS A VARIETY OF SERVICES, FROM DESIGN DEVELOPMENT AND PROJECT MANAGEMENT TO PRODUCT RANGE CONSULTING.

|||||||||||||||||||||||||||||||||||||||||||||||||

Based in Jeddah, Saudi Arabia, Al Sawani Group a retailer in the Gulf Region, with over 100,000 m² of sales space. Schwitzke & Partner was asked to create a unique department store composed of distinctive product areas within an interior crafted to reflect the corporate design of Al Sawani Grand and to demonstrate respect for the client's Arabian roots. The store offers a wide range of brands, each of which occupies a different department. Open–structured partitions made of various materials separate these areas, allowing each brand to express its unique character, as the client requested. At the same time, the store remains a coherent whole. As the flagship of eight Al Sawani Department Stores, Al Sawani Grand has a surprising mix of materials, patterns and colours; boulevard–like aisles featuring indoor shop windows; and exclusive 'luxury' areas. Especially challenging was the development of simple detailing solutions in cooperation with local contractors and shop–fitters unfamiliar with European design standards.

Schwitzke & Partner
Tußmannstrasse 70
40477 Düsseldorf
Germany

T +49 (0)211 440 350
E info@schwitzke.com
W www.schwitzke.com

Photography: Oliver Tjaden

01

01 Like every section of the store, the shoe department has a distinctive style created with the use of unique display tables and lighting.

02 Each department is separated from adjacent areas by transparent partitions designed to harmonize with their immediate surroundings.

03 Schwitzke & Partner clad fitting rooms in an exclusive wallpaper, further enhancing the look and feel of luxury that permeates the entire store.

01

Arcade
Montalba Architects

WHERE:	WEST HOLLYWOOD, CA, USA
WHEN:	SEPTEMBER 2008
CLIENT:	ROCHELLE GORES
SHOP CONSTRUCTOR:	SARLAN BUILDERS
TOTAL FLOOR AREA (M²):	145
BUDGET (€):	300,000

MONTALBA ARCHITECTS IS AN AWARD-WINNING PRACTICE WITH A DIVERSITY OF PROJECTS RANGING IN SCALE FROM COMMERCIAL OFFICE INTERIORS TO PRIVATE RESIDENCES, AND FROM RETAIL SPACES AND MIXED-USE BUILDINGS TO MASTER PLANNING IN THE USA AND EUROPE. THE DEPTH OF THE WORK, ALONG WITH THE FIRM'S INNOVATIVE APPROACH AND COLLABORATIVE EFFORTS, HIGHLIGHTS MONTALBA ARCHITECTS' EMPHASIS ON DESIGN-ORIENTED ARCHITECTURE.

Located in West Hollywood, California, amid the growing stretch of Melrose Avenue's trendy retail outlets, the high-end Arcade fashion boutique redefines the shopping experience. The linear space is punctuated by three triangulated displays. These extrusions from floor and ceiling are carved out in the middle of the space, exposing sculpted walnut surfaces and creating distinctive merchandise vignettes. Lit from within, the arrangement is such that the vitrines rhythmically disperse light and produce an 'arcaded' space. Walnut and custom-finished brass elements warm the lighter hues of concrete and acrylic resin. Mirrored surfaces visually expand the space and further reflect and filter the light. The centrality of the vignettes and their visual impact compel the customer to interact with the displays and merchandise rather than requiring her to absorb everything at once. The interior design creates a lasting impression directly related to the experience of shopping at Arcade.

Montalba Architects
2525 Michigan Avenue, Building T4
Santa Monica, CA 90404
USA

T +1 310 828 1100
E info@montalbaarchitects.com
W www.montalbaarchitects.com

Photography: John Linden

03

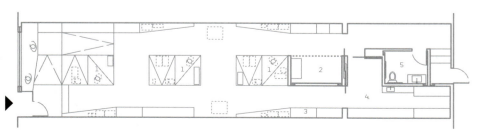

1 Display table / vitrine
2 Fitting room
3 Cash desk
4 Back office
5 Lavatory

0M   5M

01   The logo on the façade is made from brass, a material that reappears in the interior.

02   The use of warm brown and beige tones creates a serene atmosphere.

03   Installed below the ceiling and above the hanging racks and shelves, wall-mounted mirrors visually expand the space.

02

01

BasicBasic
Manifold.
ArchitectureStudio

WHERE:	NEW YORK, NY, USA
WHEN:	JANUARY 2007
CLIENT:	BASICBASIC
SHOP CONSTRUCTOR:	FAIRWAY INTERIOR WORKS
TOTAL FLOOR AREA (M²):	100
BUDGET (€):	190,000

||||||||||||||||||||||||||||||||||||||||

JOINING FORCES IN 2002, ARCHITECTS KIT AND PHILIPP VON DALWIG FOUNDED MANIFOLD. ARCHITECTURESTUDIO, NOW A BROAD-BASED MULTIDISCIPLINARY TEAM OF DESIGNERS. THE NEW YORK-BASED PRACTICE FOCUSES ON BOTH COMMERCIAL AND RESIDENTIAL ARCHITECTURAL AND ENVIRONMENTAL PROJECTS, GIVING SPECIAL ATTENTION TO THE MULTIPLE JUNCTURES OF SOCIAL AND CULTURAL ISSUES THAT INFLUENCE ARCHITECTURE AND DESIGN.

||||||||||||||||||||||||||||||||||||||||

Aiming for a refreshing retail design that would re-establish its name, Manhattan store BasicBasic brought Manifold.ArchitectureStudio (MAS) on board. Known for selling basic women's fashions by top brands, the existing store had a cramped and cluttered air, a mix of fixtures, unclear product displays and a strangely configured layout. MAS's streamlined strategy enhances the store's shopping and spatial integrity. To rescale the high, narrow space, the architects introduced a horizontal datum plane: a zone of polycarbonate wall panels that, together with metal shelving along the walls, generates a horizontal orientation, defines a new volume for merchandising and simplifies circulation. A major goal was to achieve varying tactile experiences with the use of hard and soft materials. One example is the contrast between the powder-coated metal shelving and the industrial 'floating foam' elements at the middle of the store, both purpose-designed for BasicBasic. Another is the opposition of lush, red-felt curtains in the fitting rooms and gleaming, glass-tiled white flooring in the sales area.

Manifold.ArchitectureStudio
10 Jay Street #309B
Brooklyn, NY 11201
USA

T +1 347 223 5975
E contact@mani-fold.com
W www.mani-fold.com

Photography: archphoto (Eduard Hueber)

02

01   Custom-made elements of coated industrial foam, fabricated by Quinze & Milan, provide seating for customers, function as display units and form the cash desk.

02   The fitting rooms - called 'soft areas by the designers - are furnished with curved red felt curtains and Pouf stools by Quinze & Milan.

03   To rescale the high, narrow space, the designers introduced a horizontal zone of powder-coated shelf systems and polycarbonate wall panels.

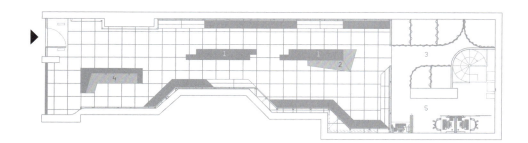

1 Display element
2 Seating element
3 Fitting rooms
4 Cash desk
5 Staff area

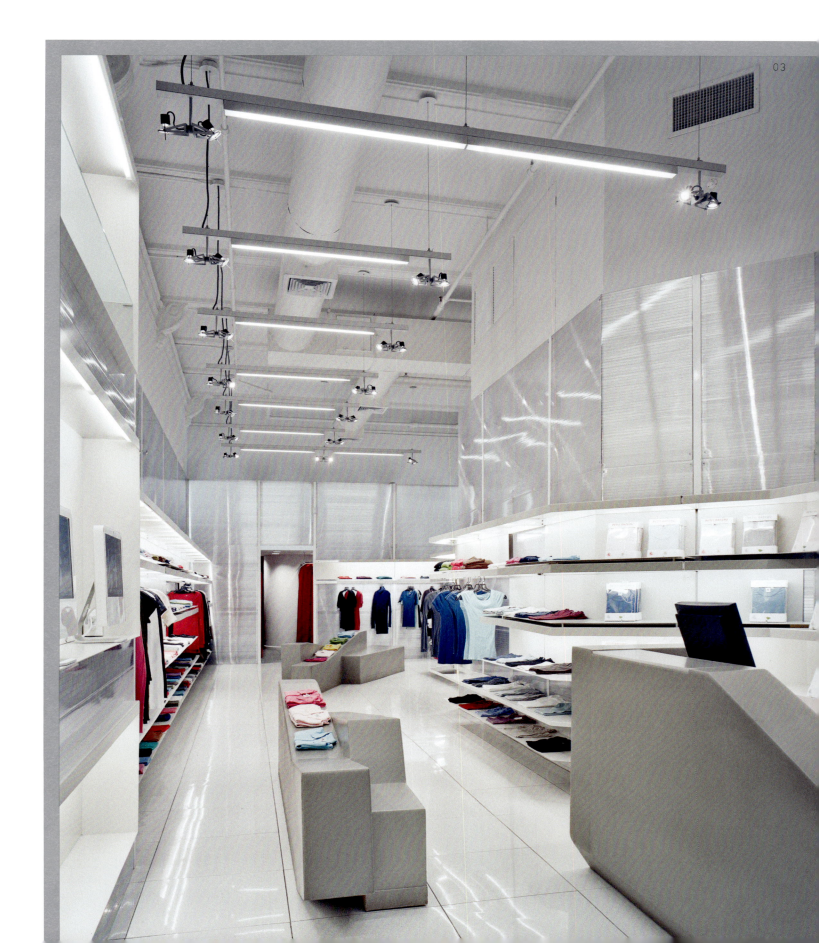

Berliner– klamotten
rmxinteriors

WHERE:	BERLIN, GERMANY
WHEN:	APRIL 2007
CLIENT:	BERLINERKLAMOTTEN
SHOP CONSTRUCTORS:	BERLINERKLAMOTTEN, OBJEKTBAU KLUNDER AND FANDRICH
TOTAL FLOOR AREA (M²):	350
BUDGET (€):	65,000

BERLIN–BASED RMXINTERIORS DEVELOPS PRODUCTS AND INTERIORS FOR PRIVATE AND COMMERCIAL CUSTOMERS. THE MULTIDISCIPLI–NARY TEAM AROUND FOUNDER AND DESIGNER MARK BENDOW OFFERS SOLUTIONS FOR RESIDENTIAL ARCHITECTURE AS WELL AS FOR HIGH–TARGET ENVIRONMENTS SUCH AS TRADE SHOWS, CORPORATE INTERIORS AND RETAIL ARCHITECTURE. THE PRIMARY OBJECTIVE OF THE STUDIO IS A SIMPLE, EFFECTIVE AND SUSTAINABLE DESIGN FOR EACH OF ITS CLIENTS.

01

After two years of planning and implementing several pop–up stores for Berlinerklamotten, a platform for young Berlin fashion designers, rmxinterior's new challenge was to develop a permanent flagship store for the brand - a retail space that would also function as a meeting place.

Since 2004, Berlinerklamotten has represented over 100 labels, from streetwear to high fashion. The new retail area occupies two floors that allow up to 40 designers to present their latest fashion and accessory collections. The ground–floor entrance level is a reception area designed to welcome shoppers to the store. This area features a DJ station, coffee bar and displays for accessories and specialty collections. The basement - furnished with large black tables, display cubes and clothing rails along the walls - is spacious enough to accommodate a diversity of fashion ranges. Both floors, linked by a spiral steel–and–wood staircase, have completely different looks, which underline their distinctive functions. The entrance level features smooth plastered and primed flooring, walls and ceiling. The space is very light, thanks to large windows that cover almost one whole wall. The basement has brownstone walls and a vaulted ceiling. Pipes running along ceiling and walls are exposed, giving the space an industrial look. A permanent video installation, purpose–designed graphic elements, periodic DJ gigs and presen–tations of clothing by featured fashion design–ers create an exceptional and variable shopping experience.

02

rmxinteriors
Schlesische Strasse 27
Haus 2 - 3, Aufgang C
10997 Berlin
Germany

E design@rmxinteriors.com
W www.rmxinteriors.com

Photography: Martin W. Maier

01, 02 & 04   At Berlinerklamotten, the ground floor accommodates a DJ station, a coffee
bar and displays for accessories
and special fashion collections

03   The basement features
brownstone walls.

1 Welcoming area
2 Coffee bar
3 DJ station
4 Accessories
5 Specialty fashion collection
6 Retail area
7 Fitting rooms
8 Cash desk

Basement

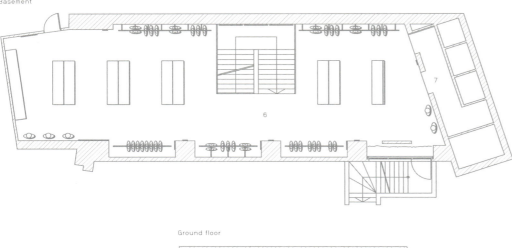

Ground floor

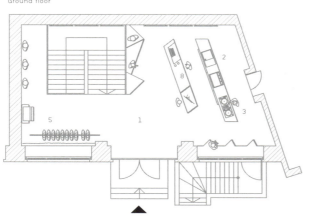

05–07 In the basement, shoppers find the collections of as many as 40 young fashion designers.

Bosco Pi
Karim Rashid

WHERE:	MOSCOW, RUSSIA
WHEN:	APRIL 2008
CLIENT:	BOSCO DI CILIEGI
TOTAL FLOOR AREA (M²):	1300
BUDGET (€):	2.5 MILLION

|||||||||||||||||||||||||||||||||||||||||||||

KARIM RASHID IS A LEADING FIGURE IN THE FIELDS OF PRODUCT, INTERIOR, FASHION, FURNITURE AND LIGHTING DESIGN - AND MUCH OF HIS WORK FALLS UNDER THE CATEGORY OF ART. BORN IN CAIRO AND REARED IN CANADA, THE HALF-EGYPTIAN, HALF-ENGLISH CREATIVE IS CURRENTLY BASED IN NEW YORK CITY. KARIM IS BEST KNOWN FOR TAKING HIS DEMOCRATIC DESIGN SENSIBILITY TO THE MASSES. HE WORKS FOR AN IMPRESSIVE ARRAY OF CLIENTS FROM ALESSI TO DIRT DEVIL, UMBRA TO PRADA, AND MIYAKE TO METHOD.

|||||||||||||||||||||||||||||||||||||||||||||

The world is becoming increasingly visually savvy and info-savvy. The energy and the era are hypertrophic. Consumers demand constant stimulation and super-exciting physical environments. Call it 'the residue of the digital age'. With all this in mind, Karim Rashid imbued Bosco Pi with a *technorganic* seamless fluid ambience conducive to pleasurable and experiential shopping and socializing. Defining the retail space is a large digital pattern, reminiscent of a traditional Russian embroidery motif based on cross-stitch, which surrounds visitors and makes them feel as though they're part of a graphic-art installation. Mimicking the shape of the ever-undulating wall, the pattern evokes images of sound waves, data and information as it envelops the shopper. The space is filled with brightly coloured blobjects - ultramodern expressions of dynamics, depth, motion and emotion made possible by the tools provided by digital technology. Sensually shaped display elements, designed around an extensive grid of columns, assume functions that define specific shopping experiences. The combination of form and orientation eliminates any references to the grid-like structure of the Cartesian world. Customers feel as if they're strolling through an urban organic forest which radiates a memorable multi-sensorial experience unrivalled by any other shopping environment in the world. All their senses are roused within a space where urban youth culture meets local Russian values in a synthesis of global omnipresence and fresh sensation around every corner. The interior creates the desire to return that is so crucial in retail today. Bosco Pi is an experiential event space in every sense of the word.

01   Customers moving among the sculptural display elements feel as though they are walking through a forest.

02   Custom printed wallpaper designed by Karim Rashid provides ornamentation and dimension to the undulating walls

Karim Rashid
357 West 17th Street
New York, NY 10011
USA

T +1 212 929 8657
E office@karimrashid.com
W www.karimrashid.com

Photography: Courtesy of Karim Rashid

01

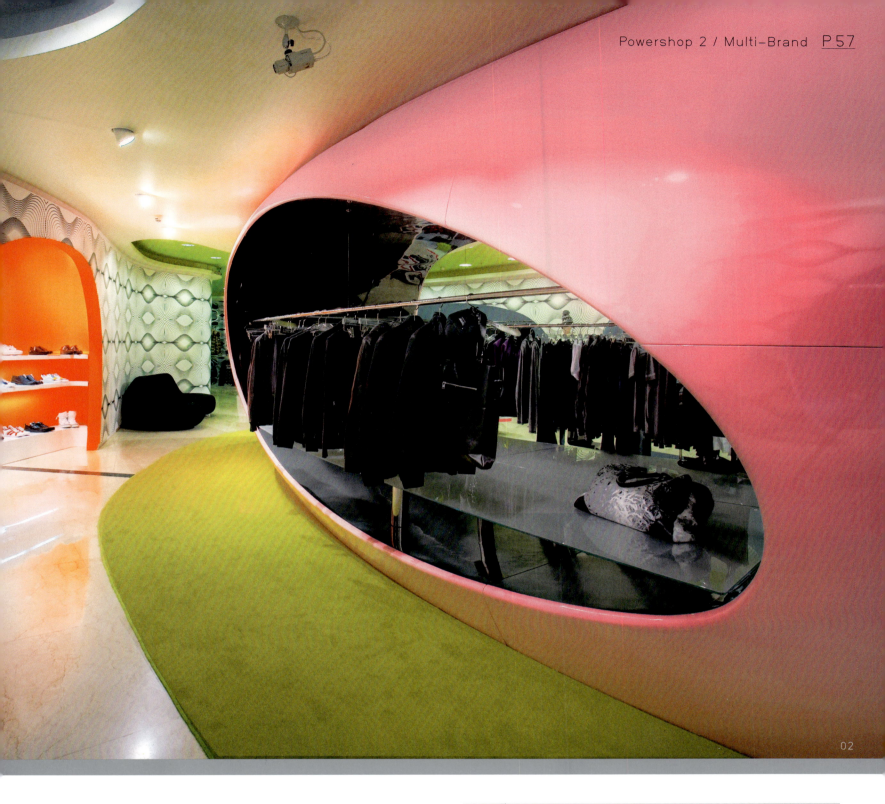

02

1 Womenswear
2 Menswear
3 Lifestyle and gadget area
4 Fitting rooms
5 DJ booth
6 Lounge area
7 Cash desk

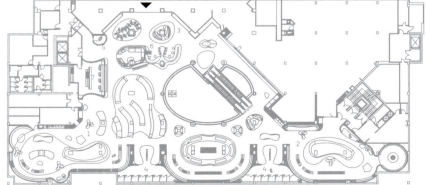

03   Brightly coloured niches
in the walls, that change colour
seasonally, provide hanging racks
and, in some cases, a low shelf.

04   The high-gloss fibreglass
finish used to make the display
units reflects the surroundings.

03

04

Bredl
MAI

WHERE: RAVENSBURG, GERMANY
WHEN: AUGUST 2008
CLIENTS: KARL OTTO GIESEKE, KLAUS
    DIETER GIESEKE AND GERHARD GIESEKE
TOTAL FLOOR AREA (M²):   5000

|||||||||||||||||||||||||||||||||||||||||||

ARCHITECT JOCHEN MESSERSCHMID FOUNDED
MESSERSCHMID ARCHITECTS AND INTERIOR
DESIGNERS, BETTER KNOWN AS MAI. BASED
IN STUTTGART, GERMANY, MESSERSCHMID AND
HIS TEAM HAVE DESIGNED AND REALIZED
A BROAD RANGE OF LOCAL AND INTERNATIONAL
PROJECTS. MAI'S WORK INCLUDES RESIDENTIAL
BUILDINGS, HOTELS, OFFICES, SHOPPING
MALLS, DEPARTMENT STORES AND SHOWROOM
INTERIORS.

|||||||||||||||||||||||||||||||||||||||||||

The five-storey Bredl department store in
Ravensburg, Germany, was due for a complete
update. Step by step, each floor was to be
transformed into a themed world based on
product assortment and target group. MAI was
called on to create these new interiors, each of
which was to have a strong visual impact without
overpowering the merchandise on display.
Highlighting the project was the redesign of the
third floor. Formerly the children's department,
this floor now accommodates designer fashions
for women in a space that breathes an air of
exclusivity. Messerschmid used large beige
ceramic tiles for the flooring. Papered walls
feature rails and shelving mounted on white
Visplay Invisible display panels, which hold part
of the fashion collection. On two distinctively
designed walls in this part of the store, curtains
made from thousands of small metal rings linked
together form a backdrop for displays suspended
from the ceiling. Another eye-catching element
is the cash desk, a volume that combines beige
leather and gloss-painted wood. In a lounge
area next to the fitting rooms, comfy sofas invite
shoppers to relax. Clad in the same beige leather
as the cash desk, the curved wall that marks
this space contains a gloss-painted niche
that is used to showcase special products.
All furniture at Bredl was purpose-designed to
enhance specific areas of the interior. Display
tables in different sizes - some gloss-painted
and others made from mirror glass - appear
throughout the store; they can be combined
in countless configurations to form attractive
display islands.

MAI | Messerschmid
Architects and Interior Designers
Königstrasse 50-52
70173 Stuttgart
Germany

T +49 (0)711 2229 680
E mail@messerschmid.de
W www.messerschmid.de

Photography: panoramapictures (Peter Reichert)

01

01   Next to the fitting rooms,
a gloss-painted display niche in
the curving, leather-covered wall
is used to highlight special items
of merchandise.

02

02 Various pieces of custom‑designed display furniture - some gloss‑painted, some featuring mirror glass - can be used separately or combined to create countless configurations.

03 The cash desk is clad in the same beige leather as the curved wall next to the fitting rooms.

04 A lounge area offers the customer a place to rest before continuing her shopping trip.

03

Breuninger
Exquisite
Blocher Blocher
Partners

WHERE: STUTTGART, GERMANY
WHEN: DECEMBER 2008
CLIENT: BREUNINGER
SHOP CONSTRUCTOR: SCHLEGEL
TOTAL FLOOR AREA (M²):   45,000

FOUNDED IN 1989, BLOCHER BLOCHER PARTNERS IS A MARKET LEADER IN A HIGHLY SPECIALIZED SECTOR: RETAIL DESIGN AND ARCHITECTURE. CURRENTLY WITH A STAFF OF 120, THE COMPANY REALIZES ITS INNOVATIVE RETAIL CONCEPTS FOR A WIDE RANGE OF CLIENTS. BY COMBINING ARCHITECTURE AND INTERIOR DESIGN, BLOCHER BLOCHER PARTNERS HAS BUILT AN IMPRESSIVE INTERNATIONAL REPUTATION.

German-based fashion and lifestyle company Breuninger, with ten locations and over 4000 employees, stands for premium brands displayed and sold in an exclusive retail environment. This is reflected in the 'Exquisite' department of the brand's flagship store in Stuttgart, where top designer labels are sensitively illuminated in a space crafted from quality materials, while playful graphics appeal to Breuninger's female target group. Complementing a much-needed restructuring of the sales area, a pale-grey concrete volume and a black-painted, perforated wooden cube with built-in lighting - both with integrated fitting rooms - are the store's new reference points. Spacious, clearly defined presentation areas make an attractive contrast to a vibrant walkway made from fine natural stone. Inclined smoked-glass panels introduce distinctively designed brand worlds. Glass cabinets, leather elements, high-gloss walls and gold-powdered displays correspond to the quality of the premium brands. Whimsically arranged lounge furniture marks a soft change in style in an area where charming provocation meets discreet luxury.

Blocher Blocher Partners
Lessingstraße 13
70174 Stuttgart
Germany

T +49 (0)711 224 820
E partners@blocherblocher.com
W www.blocherblocher.com

Photography: Nikolaus Koliusis

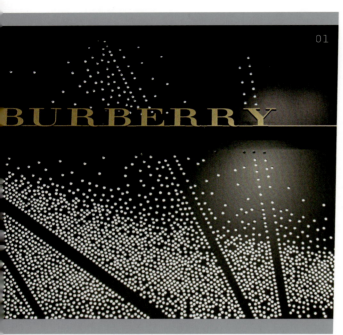

01

01   A black perforated wooden cube with built-in lighting and integrated fitting rooms acts as a landmark within the vast retail interior.

02   Glass cabinets, leather elements and gold-powdered fixtures are used to display the exclusive fashions.

03   Throughout the sales area, each brand is indicated by whimsical graphics that appeal to the store's female target group.

04   Smoked-glass panels separate the various designer labels from one another.

Cenerino
Andrea Tognon Architecture

WHERE:	BASSANO DEL GRAPPA, ITALY
WHEN:	APRIL 2007
CLIENT:	VITTORIO CENERE
SHOP CONSTRUCTOR:	STUDIO TRE CONTRACT
TOTAL FLOOR AREA (M²):	120
BUDGET (€):	200,000

02

ANDREA TOGNON FOUNDED HIS RESEARCH LABORATORY FOR ARCHITECTURE AND COMMUNICATION DESIGN IN 2002. THE OFFICE COMBINES PRACTICE WITH RESEARCH, USING A MULTIDISCIPLINARY APPROACH AND DRAWING UPON A NETWORK OF CREATIVE, TECHNICAL AND ENGINEERING FIRMS FOR THE EXECUTION OF DIFFERENT ASPECTS OF THE DESIGN AND REALIZATION PROCESSES. CLIENTS INCLUDE BOTTEGA VENETA, KRIZIA, TOD'S, LAMARTHE, STILETTO NYC AND TOGNON ARREDAMENTI.

Impressed at the sight of a high-end, multi-brand boutique designed by Andrea Tognon Architecture, Vittorio Cenere contacted the design firm on his own behalf. He asked Tognon and his team to develop a concept for Cenerino, a children's fashion shop.
Having decided to approach the project from an adult perspective, the designers rejected the standard 'retail playground' with toys and games for kids in favour of a child's world interpreted as a sophisticated, design-filled realm that appeals to grown-ups as well. The interior is an installation of components that recall individual childhood sensations. Tognon raised the level of the pavement and used a shallow-stepped ramp at the entrance to lend importance to small objects and to draw attention to the aspect of growing. Out-of-proportion pieces of furniture and folding screens hint at the game of hide-and-seek. The combination of light shining through rose-shaded windows and walls in a pale-blue hue creates a fantastical atmosphere.

Andrea Tognon Architecture
Via Dario Papa 19
20125 Milan
Italy

T +39 0348 580 9677
E studio@atognon.com
W www.atognon.com

Photography: Cristian Guizzo

1 Display counter
2 Fitting room
3 Cash desk
4 Storage
5 Lavatory

01

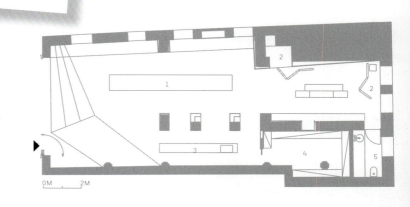

0M   2M

01   A large shop window
occupies the entire façade,
smoothing the transition
between inside and out.

02   Playful display elements
are made of wood and glass in
contrasting colours.

03   Shallow steps at the
entrance draw attention to the
aspect of growing.

04   Pale-blue walls and
rose-shaded windows make the
space suitable for the display
of toys and clothing for both
boys and girls.

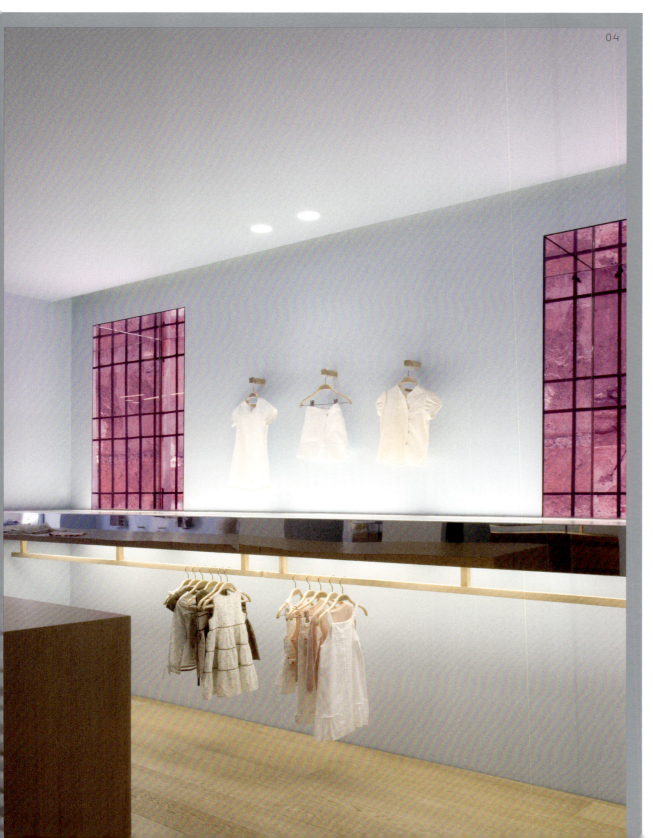

Chocolate & Pickles
HMKM

WHERE: DUBAI, UNITED ARAB EMIRATES
WHEN: OCTOBER 2007
CLIENT: RANDA ABU-ISSA
TOTAL FLOOR AREA (M²):   125

||||||||||||||||||||||||||||||||||||||||||||||

FOUNDED IN 1990 AND BASED IN LONDON'S
SOHO DISTRICT, DESIGN CONSULTANCY HMKM
CONSISTS OF SPECIALISTS IN THE FIELDS
OF BRANDING, ARCHITECTURE, INTERIOR DESIGN,
GRAPHIC DESIGN AND ART DIRECTION.
TAILOR-MADE PROJECT TEAMS HELP CLIENTS
TO REALISE THEIR BRAND VISION, NO MATTER
WHAT THE SCALE OF THE PROJECT. THEIR
INTERNATIONAL CLIENT LIST INCLUDES
HARRODS, SELFRIDGES, SPORTSGIRL,
HYUNDAI, SALAM, NIKE AND LULU GUINNESS.

||||||||||||||||||||||||||||||||||||||||||||||

Targeting the stylish and fashionable soon-to-
be mothers of Dubai, Chocolate & Pickles is a
tongue-in-'chic' boutique in a market sector that
generally focuses on the practical needs of the
baby rather than pampering expectant mums.
The philosophy behind the boutique is 'tickle
that crazy craving'.
Design consultancy HMKM developed the
Chocolate & Pickles brand to fulfil the vision
of Randa Abu-Issa, who founded the label.
The brand name, identity, packaging and retail-
design solution have been developed with a
potential expansion in mind: among the key
locations under consideration are Los Angeles,
New York and London. Dominating the store's
palette is feminine fuchsia, a shade used for
everything from clothes hangers and high-gloss
lacquered display tables to purpose-designed
floral wallpaper and lighting which features a
colour gel that spreads a warm pink glow. Even
part of the shop window is covered in pink film.
The apple-green cash desk clearly stands out
in this interior.

HMKM
14-16 Great Pulteney Street
London W1F 9ND
United Kingdom

T +44 (0)20 7494 4949
E info@hmkm.com
W www.hmkm.com

Photography: Bassam Abu-Issa

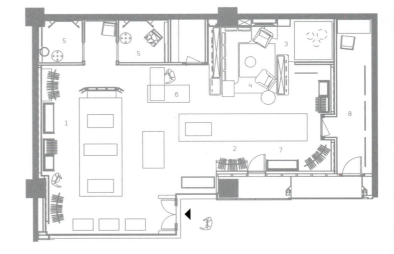

1 Baby clothing
2 Maternity clothing
3 Play zone
4 Seating
5 Fitting room
6 Cash desk
7 Accessories and gifts
8 Storage / office

01

02

01   View of the baby clothing and accessories area.

02   The Chocolate & Pickles shop fascia at the Wafi Mall in Dubai.

03   Details such as the decorative frieze, wallpaper, rugs and the furniture were designed by HMKM and bespoke to Chocolate & Pickles.

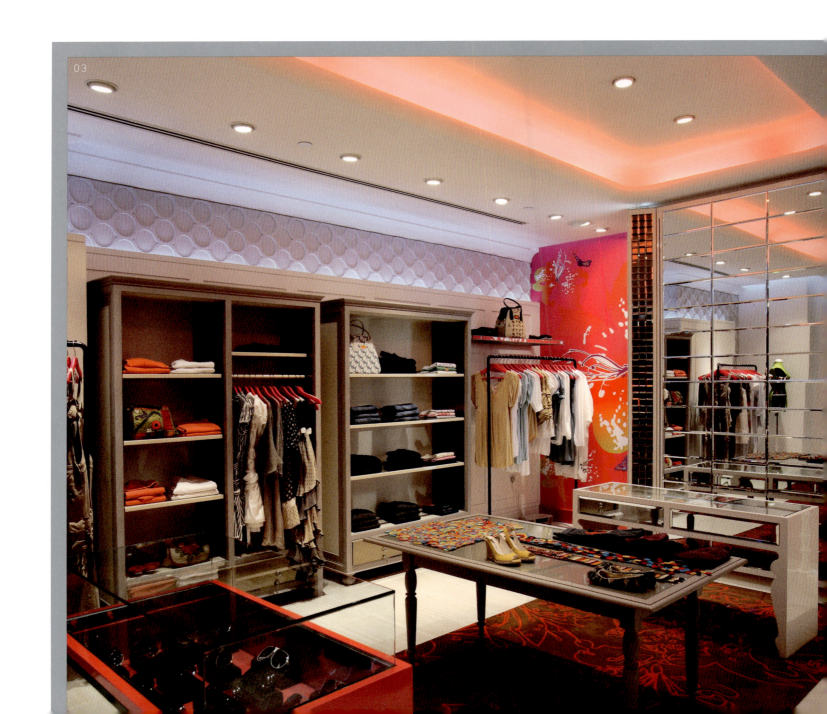

03

Colette
Wonderwall

WHERE: PARIS, FRANCE
WHEN: AUGUST 2008
CLIENT: COLETTE
TOTAL FLOOR AREA (M²):   672

|||||||||||||||||||||||||||||||||||||||||||||||

MASAMICHI KATAYAMA, WHO FOUNDED INTERIOR-DESIGN FIRM WONDERWALL IN 2000, DEMONSTRATES AN UNINHIBITED SENSE OF ENERGY IN HIS ATTITUDE TOWARDS DESIGN. KATAYAMA HAS ALWAYS HAD A BROAD INTEREST IN DESIGN: HE RESPECTS THE CONVENTIONAL AND TRADITIONAL ASPECTS OF ARCHITECTURE BUT ALSO BELIEVES IN BREAKING BOUNDARIES. AS A 'TOTAL CONCEPT' DESIGNER, KATAYAMA'S FOCUS IS ON THE CREATION OF ENVIRONMENTS THAT TOUCH THE SUBCONSCIOUS OF THE CONSUMER AND OCCUPANT. HIS SECOND MONOGRAPH, WONDERWALL MASAMICHI KATAYAMA PROJECTS NO. 2, WAS PUBLISHED IN 2008 BY FRAME PUBLISHERS.

|||||||||||||||||||||||||||||||||||||||||||||||

Wonderwall's redesign project for Colette, one of Paris's major sources of information on the latest trends, included the Water Bar, which is located in the basement of the boutique. The hurdle that faced the designer was the continued development of the charm and strength that had permeated Colette even before the renovation. Katayama designed 'orderly disorder' by incorporating both vertical and horizontal display units. Thanks to the extensive use of steel and glass, the store is ultra-sleek and modern. Visitors are met by a large stainless-steel counter that runs along most of one wall. In the accessories area on the same side of the shop, a wall of alcoves features merchandise in freely hanging boxes equipped with light. Fronting this wall, a large display table holds the latest gadgets. Also on the ground floor, a massive glass wall display presents a selection of brightly coloured sneakers and a large glass-and-steel 'House of T-shirts' containing Colette's entire collection of T-shirts. On the first floor, visitors find a gallery, as well as luxury designer brands and a beauty area. As they walk up the stairs, freestanding mannequins wearing luxury fashions welcome them. The beauty area at one end of the first floor consists of one wall and a range of beauty products displayed attractively next to one another. Stainless-steel tables give customers the opportunity to try each product, while evoking the look and feel of a high-tech pharmacy. The overall result is a visually powerful retail space that conveys an overwhelming amount of information.

Wonderwall
3-4-10 Sendagaya Shibuya-ku
151-0051 Tokyo
Japan

T +81 (0)3 643 817 17
E contact@wonder-wall.com
W www.wonder-wall.com

Photography: Kozo Takayama

02

01   Gadgets are displayed in a custom-made glass case, and CDs from the latest music collection line the walls.

02   Tables surfaced in black leather carry the latest books.

03   A stainless-steel stairway next to the floor-to-ceiling, glass-enclosed sneaker display leads up to the fashion area on the first floor.

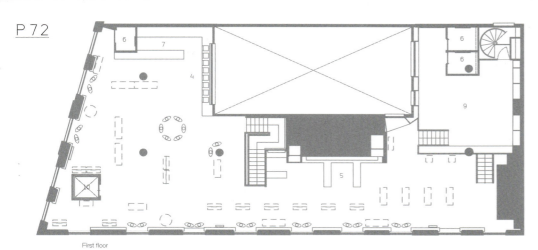

First floor

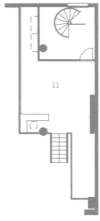

1 House of T–shirts
2 Sneaker display
3 Accessory area
4 Jewellery area
5 Beauty area
6 Fitting room
7 Cash desk
8 Water Bar
9 Temporary space
10 Lift
11 Gallery

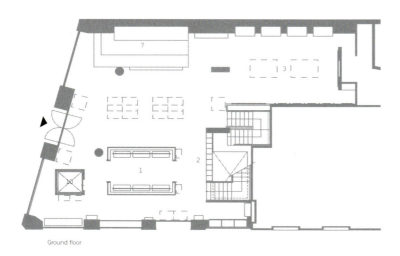

Ground floor

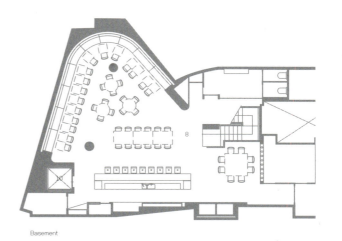

Basement

04

05

04   Upstairs shoppers find
a selection of designer clothes,
as well as skincare and cosmetic
products.

05   In the basement Water Bar,
customers sit on chairs designed
by Robert Mallet—Stevens.

De Rode Winkel
OPERA Amsterdam

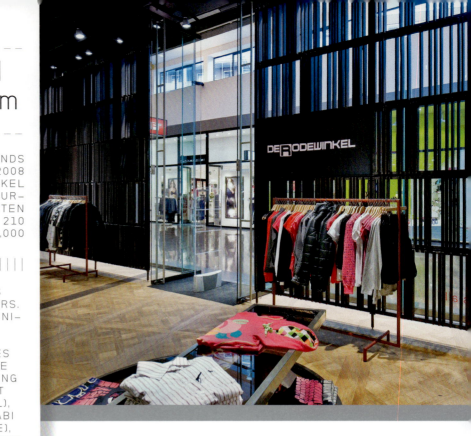

WHERE:	HOUTEN, THE NETHERLANDS
WHEN:	AUGUST 2008
CLIENT:	DE RODE WINKEL
SHOP CONSTRUCTOR:	KEIJSERS INTERIEUR-PROJECTEN
TOTAL FLOOR AREA (M²):	210
BUDGET (€):	300,000

|||||||||||||||||||||||||||||||||||||||||

FOUNDED IN 1981, OPERA AMSTERDAM IS HEADED BY FRANS BEVERS AND LIES WILLERS. THE FIRM SPECIALIZES IN CREATING COMMUNICATIVE SPACES WITHIN ALMOST EVERY CULTURAL OR COMMERCIAL CONTEXT IMAGINABLE. OPERA'S PORTFOLIO INCLUDES LARGE-SCALE MUSEUM INTERIORS, OFFICE PROJECTS AND RETAIL ENVIRONMENTS. AMONG THE CLIENTS ARE THE VICTORIA & ALBERT MUSEUM (UK), MUSEUM VOLKENKUNDE (NL), TEMPO TEAM (NL), SETPOINT (NL), ABU DHABI AUTHORITY FOR CULTURE & HERITAGE (UAE), THE NATIONAL MUSEUM OF DENMARK (DK), THE NATURAL HISTORY MUSEUM (UK) AND EMMA CHILDREN'S HOSPITAL (NL).

|||||||||||||||||||||||||||||||||||||||||

De Rode Winkel, a popular Dutch retailer of jeans, recently opened its third flagship store in Houten. Once again OPERA Amsterdam, which had designed the brand's flagship stores in 's Hertogenbosch and Utrecht, received carte blanche. The client asked for only one thing: a space that would clearly showcase jeans. Each shop has a completely distinctive character based on its particular locality.
One of many shops in a covered arcade in Houten, above all else the latest store had to distinguished itself from its surroundings while treating visitors to a calm, pleasant shopping experience. Determining the image of the interior concept is a purpose-designed wall system that reaches the full height of 5 m and is used throughout the shop. Passing the store's glazed façade, curious shoppers see rows of randomly positioned wooden slats that offer a mere glimpse of what's inside. Unlike a conventional display window, the façade gives the shop a remarkably introverted and mysterious air. The slats filter daylight and generate a warm, intimate interior accentuated by dramatic lighting and fine finishes: rich woods in various patterns for the parquet floor and leather upholstery for the furniture. The large white counter at the centre of the space doubles as a display surface and creates a natural route through the store. Casually arranged ensembles of furniture surrounding the counter include display tables, cabinets and eye-catching floor-to-ceiling fitting rooms. In addition to the slatted wall, the system also accommodates visuals, mirrors and an absolutely amazing array of jeans.

OPERA Amsterdam
Rapenburgerstraat 109
1011 VL Amsterdam
the Netherlands

T +31 (0)20 344 5350
E studio@opera-amsterdam.nl
W www.opera-amsterdam.nl

Photography: Pieter Kers

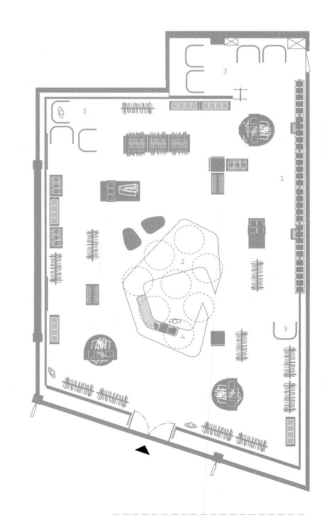

1 Jeans wall
2 Shoe display
3 Fitting rooms
4 Cash desk

01

01   At De Rode Winkel, part of
the display furniture is made of
powder-coated steel and smoked
glass.

02   Hovering above a central
counter of white leather, purpose-
designed by OPERA Amsterdam,
are Kayradome 135 lamps by
Rove Design.

02

03   Steel–framed fitting rooms paired with fabric by Kvadrat were custom–designed by OPERA Amsterdam.

04   Wooden slats in the shop window not only make a display unnecessary but also add a sense of mystery to the store, as passers–by catch only a glimpse of the interior.

05   Thanks to a 5–m–high jeans wall, the store's main product can't be missed.

Distante
Lucijana Radivovic

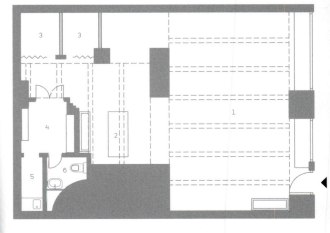

WHERE:	BELGRADE, SERBIA
WHEN:	APRIL 2008
CLIENT:	A-LIST D.O.O.
TOTAL FLOOR AREA (M²):	110

IN 1997 LUCIJANA RADIVOVIC OPENED FASHION STORE DISTANTE, WHICH OFFERS THE PEOPLE OF BELGRADE THE LATEST DESIGNER LABELS. CURRENTLY, DISTANTE HAS A TOTAL OF FIVE STORES, ALL OF WHICH ARE OPERATED BY RADIVOVIC. DISTANTE, WHICH ENJOYS A CULT STATUS IN BELGRADE, IS WELL KNOWN FOR ITS NUMEROUS FASHION SHOWS AND HAPPENINGS.

1 Display area
2 Cash desk
3 Fitting room
4 Storage
5 Kitchen
6 Lavatory

During a period in which concept stores were gaining in popularity worldwide, Distante opened its doors in the Serbian city of Belgrade. Since its introduction in 1997, Distante has evolved into an important hub for collections by the world's most famous fashion designers. In April 2008 Distante opened its fourth Belgrade boutique, a shop with a largely white interior, including white walls and a white resin floor. A red-and-white sofa and bright designer clothes provide the only dashes of colour. One side wall is equipped with T-shaped racks for displaying garments. In the spotlight on the opposite wall are three dresses hanging from a simple hook. In the rear, behind the cash desk, two fitting rooms feature white-brick walls. Satisfied shoppers at Distante take pleasure in beautiful clothes, discuss the latest trends in fashion, and enjoy the atmosphere conjured by a variety of styles within a perfectly balanced interior design.

01

Lucijana Radivovic
T. Koščvška 16
11000 Belgrade
Serbia

T +381 (0)63 213 641
E distante@eunet.rs
W www.distante.rs

Photography: Orange Studio

01   View inside the spacious fitting room.

02   Betty Boop invites passers-by to come in and take a look at Distante's designer collections.

03   The red sofa is the work of Serbian designer Draga Obradovic, who lives and works in Italy.

Geometry
plajer & franz studio

WHERE: BERLIN, GERMANY
WHEN: MARCH 2008
CLIENT: CARMEN SANTOS AND RAPHAEL MEYER
TOTAL FLOOR AREA (M²): 100

FOUNDED IN 1996 BY ALEXANDER PLAJER AND WERNER FRANZ, BERLIN-BASED PLAJER & FRANZ STUDIO IS AN INTERNATIONAL, INTERDISCIPLINARY TEAM OF 45 ARCHITECTS, INTERIOR ARCHITECTS AND GRAPHIC DESIGNERS. ALL PHASES OF A PROJECT - FROM CONCEPT TO DESIGN TO ROLL-OUT SUPERVISION - ARE CARRIED OUT IN-HOUSE. FROM PRIVATE YACHTS AND TRADE STANDS TO BARS AND APARTMENTS, PLAJER & FRANZ STUDIO EXPLORES AND FUSES DISCIPLINES AND NEW AREAS OF EXPERIENCE. THE STUDIO HAS A STERLING REPUTATION IN EUROPE AND ASIA IN THE LUXURY RESIDENTIAL AND HOTEL SECTORS. CLIENTS INCLUDE GALERIES LAFAYETTE, S.OLIVER, BMW, TIMBERLAND AND OTHERS.

Geometry - a name referring to the client's study of mathematics - formed the only guideline for plajer & franz studio, the team responsible for the design of this small concept store, where customers find menswear collections by designers such as Gaspard Yurkievich and Irie Wash, along with labels like Y-3 and Won Hundred.
Not just another shabby-chic store of the genre found all over Berlin, this retail interior reflects the apartment of a weird math professor with clearly excellent taste. The professor is not only a bit of a recluse, but also a man with a cultivated sense of proportions and moods. He's collected an array of strange items for experimentation, calculation and in-depth analysis: take, for example, photographs of skeletons purpose-made by diephotodesigner.de, or Mikado lamps designed by Miguel Herranz, who drew inspiration from the game of jackstraws. Everything in the store tells a tale of symmetry and asymmetry, cleverly underpinned with the most stylish of footnotes: mud-coloured walls, dark oak flooring, blanched-oak furniture by carpenter Dirk Rothe, brown glass by First Glas Vertrieb and bronze mirrors. Carefully chosen elements that work well in a men's concept store. The homey atmosphere is further enhanced by waiting areas with rugs and Hopf & Wortmann's modular DNA lamps.
The main objective of the interior design for Geometry was to generate a sense of surprise. The team at plajer & franz studio wanted visitors to find - and remember - something fresh, positive and new: a retail ambience previously unseen in blasé Berlin.

plajer & franz studio
Erkelenzdamm 59-61
10999 Berlin
Germany

T +49 (0)30 616 558 0
E studio@plajer-franz.de
W www.plajer-franz.de

Photography: diephotodesigner.de

03

01 Because the store is meant to evoke a domestic interior occupied by a weird math professor, plajer & franz studio selected Jacob Wagner's Ray lounge chair and Pirate Black carpeting by Studio NYC to enhance the homey atmosphere.

02 The Geometry concept store is located in central Berlin.

03 Purpose-made photographs of skeletons – shot at the Veterinary Institute of the University of Berlin – are the work of diephotodesigner.de.

04 Carpenter Dirk Rothe is responsible for all woodwork featured in the shop.

05 Mikado lamps by Miguel Herranz represent the strange collection of paraphernalia be–longing to the math professor who supposedly inhabits this store.

06 Even the fitting rooms are decorated with diephotodesigner. de's images of animal skeletons.

1 Display island
2 Seating area
3 Fitting room
4 Cash desk

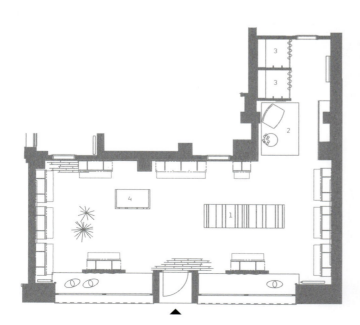

Gigalove
Antonio Gardoni

WHERE:	BRESCIA, ITALY
WHEN:	APRIL 2008
CLIENT:	EUROSPORT SNC
SHOP CONSTRUCTOR:	CHERUBINI CONTRACT
TOTAL FLOOR AREA (M²):	130
BUDGET (€):	250,000

ANTONIO GARDONI, WHO SPENT YEARS IN
LONDON WORKING WITH RON ARAD AND
COFOUNDING JUMP STUDIOS, CURRENTLY
OPERATES A DESIGN STUDIO IN BRESCIA, ITALY,
AND A BRANCH IN BEIJING. GARDONI AND
PARTNERS GIOVANNI PAZZAGLIA AND JULIE
DU BELIEVE IN THE POWER OF COMBINING
MARKETING AND DESIGN TOOLS, AND OF USING
SPACES AND OBJECTS TO COMMUNICATE.

Antonio Gardoni was asked to develop a
design language for Gigalove, a new clothing
brand for teenagers. The commission included
communication branding and the interior design
of Gigalove's first store, located in the Italian
shopping mall 'Freccia Rossa'.
Gardoni divided the space into two areas. Highlighting the front zone is a large hexagonal cash
desk covered in mirrored panels that produce a
kaleidoscopic effect. The cash desk also features
a glass case, used to display the fashion accessories. The 8–m long wall behind it is clad in
'Delft blue' tiles featuring symbols that refer to
the shop's location. At one end of the wall, nonfunctional stairs ascend to a door that doesn't
open.
A mirror-lined passage leads shoppers to
another retail area at the rear of the store.
This second zone also includes the fitting
rooms - each of them clad in a different
tartan fabric. Metal hooks hanging from the
ceiling serve as clothe hangers. Green metal
display units punctured with laser-cut
perforations and equipped with shelves and
hooks can be wheeled from place to place.
A honeycomb structure of acrylic tubes
sandwiched between two layers of glass
reveals the interior of the second zone only
to passers–by who approach the store from
a right angle. The shops front area is visible
to passers–by through a large black-framed
shop window.

Antonio Gardoni
Via Ferramola 14
25121 Brescia
Italy

T +39 034 8259 1730
E info@antoniogardoni.com
W www.antoniogardoni.com

Photography: Antonio Gardoni

01

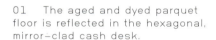

01 The aged and dyed parquet
floor is reflected in the hexagonal,
mirror-clad cash desk.

02 One shop window features
a honeycomb structure of acrylic
tubes sandwiched between two
layers of glass.

03 Antonio Gardoni designed the
green, laser-cut, metal displays
especially for this interior. They
can be stacked to form a shelving
system or simply be used as trolleys.

04 Six large speakers integrated
into the upper part of the cash
desk are invisible to shoppers.

04

1 Nonfunctional stairs
2 Tiled wall
3 Fitting room
4 Cash desk
5 Storage
6 Lavatory

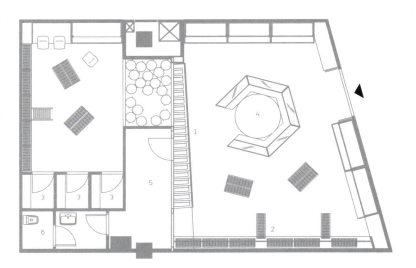

1M   10M

05   Motifs on wall tiles refer to
the shop's location. One image,
for example, is that of Brescia's
historic Loggia Building, currently
the city's town hall.

06   The mirror—clad walls that
surround the fitting rooms give
the space a somewhat chaotic
appearance.

Heikorn
atelier522

WHERE:	SINGEN, GERMANY
WHEN:	SEPTEMBER 2007
CLIENT:	HEIKORN
SHOP CONSTRUCTOR:	SCHLEGEL
TOTAL FLOOR AREA (M²):	800
BUDGET (€):	500,000

ATELIER522 IS A CREATIVE AGENCY WITH A FOCUS ON ARCHITECTURE, INTERIOR DESIGN, PRODUCT DESIGN, VISUAL COMMUNICATION AND PHOTOGRAPHY. THE MULTIDISCIPLINARY TEAM IS BUILDING A COLLECTIVE PORTFOLIO OF INNOVATIVE DESIGN, WHICH REPRESENTS AN ADVENTURE THAT COVERS EVERY DETAIL OF A PROJECT, FROM CONCEPT TO REALIZATION. THE FIRM'S EXPERIENCED SPECIALISTS, FROM VARIOUS PROFESSIONAL AREAS, TRANSFORM IDEAS AND A PASSION FOR DESIGN INTO CLEAR PROJECTS THAT MAKE A LASTING IMPRESSION. AMONG ATELIER522'S MAJOR CLIENTS ARE SERAFINI, HEIKORN, ROSENTHAL, VIZONA AND SEEBERGER/STETSON.

At the Heikorn clothing store in Singen, Germany, the basement level is reserved for fashion brands such as Diesel, Miss Sixty, Tommy Hilfiger, Pepe and G-Star. Responsible for the design of this department, which targets younger customers, is German firm atelier522.
The retail design of the 800-m² shopping area is as original and creative as its name: translated into English, this floor is called '5 Rooms Kitchen, Bath'. In its plans for the basement interior, atelier522 played with fantasy and dreams. The idea was to turn shopping into a live event by stirring up a melting pot of innovation and dura-bility. The starting point was a question: Doesn't everyone miss the good old days? The result is a mix of classic elements and contemporary fashions. The designers gave a new twist to things old and familiar by placing a rusty Fiat 500 at the centre of the retail area. Clothing racks are bordered by traditional wood fences: through the gaps between pickets, shoppers can see photographic wallpaper featuring a garden in the autumn. Huge graphics of Michelin men cover one wall, while an array of graphics also adorn parts of the floor - images of tools applied to the floor around the vintage Fiat are a good example. 'It's important to be different' is the designers' slogan, and Heikorn is clearly no exception to the rule.

atelier522
Fitzenweilerstraße 1c
88677 Markdorf
Germany

T +49 (0)700 522 522 522
E atelier@atelier522.com
W www.atelier522.com

Photography: atelier522

01

01   The creative name given to this floor of the Heikorn fashion shop is '5 Rooms Kitchen Bath'.

02&03   Atelier522 imbued the retail space with an outdoorsy atmosphere. Traditional wooden garden fences and branches decorate the interior.

02

03

04

04   Although a rusty Fiat 500 may look a bit out of place in the middle of a store, it's part of the designers' wish to create an original, sustainable space for their client.

05   Like playground swings, shelves hanging from ropes attached to the ceiling evoke memories of childhood while serving as functional display

05

Icon
Studio Duo

WHERE:	BRUSSELS, BELGIUM
WHEN:	SEPTEMBER 2007
CLIENT:	ICON
SHOP CONSTRUCTOR:	ACCORD 81
TOTAL FLOOR AREA (M²):	170
BUDGET (€):	180,000

CECILE DELCOURT, OWNER OF STUDIO DUO, BELIEVES IN MAINTAINING GOOD RELATIONS WITH CLIENTS. THE BEST APPROACH TO A PERFECT CONCEPT STARTS WITH COLLABORATION BETWEEN THE INTERIOR DESIGNER AND THE CLIENT. WHAT FOLLOWS IS A MATTER OF RESEARCH AND WORK. REFRESHING, CALM AND AUSTERE, STUDIO DUO'S INTERIORS ARE BASED ON HUMAN DESIRE AND MATHEMATICS.

In early 2007 Icon discovered a great location in the Antoine Dansaert section of Brussels, an area prized by fashion designers. Without hesitation, Icon launched a renovation project with the help of Studio Duo. The aim was a shop with an open feeling. The original ceiling was to be restored by the owner and a parquet floor installed to accentuate the overhead surface. The shop comprises a series of four rooms and features an elongated tubular-steel clothes rail. Mannequins welcome shoppers into the entrance area, while in the following room a white cash desk balances precariously on its yellow base. The third space is used for display, and the final room boasts an enormous mirror and three spacious fitting rooms. Studio Duo chose white to create a fresh, feminine atmosphere and yellow as a contrasting colour. Track lighting illuminates the front half of the shop, and moulding with built-in lighting brightens the third area.

Studio Duo
5, avenue du Cor de Chasse
1170 Brussels
Belgium

T +32 (0)473 400 713
E cecile.delcourt@studioduo.be

Photography: Chantal Breuer

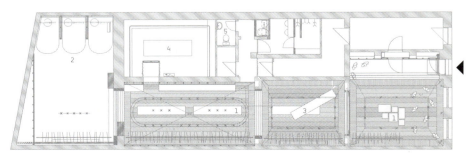

1 Display area
2 Fitting room
3 Cash desk
4 Storage
5 Lavatory

01   Three spacious fitting rooms at the back of the shop are finished in white for a fresh, feminine look.

02   White and yellow enamelled-steel sheet and an elongated tubular-steel rail are the materials used for display.

03   Colourful forms on the wall behind the cash desk attract the attention of customers.

Intersport Bründl
Blocher Blocher Partners

WHERE:	KAPRUN, AUSTRIA
WHEN:	OCTOBER 2008
CLIENT:	SPORT BRÜNDL
SHOP CONSTRUCTORS:	GANTER AND UMDASCH SHOP-CONCEPT
ARCHITECT:	BLOCHER BLOCHER PARTNERS
TOTAL FLOOR AREA (M²):	3200

FOUNDED IN 1989, BLOCHER BLOCHER PARTNERS IS A MARKET LEADER IN A HIGHLY SPECIALIZED SECTOR: RETAIL DESIGN AND ARCHITECTURE. CURRENTLY WITH A STAFF OF 120, THE COMPANY REALIZES ITS INNOVATIVE RETAIL CONCEPTS FOR A WIDE RANGE OF CLIENTS. BY COMBINING ARCHITECTURE AND INTERIOR DESIGN, BLOCHER BLOCHER PARTNERS HAS BUILT AN IMPRESSIVE INTERNATIONAL REPUTATION.

01

Bründl's flagship store in Kaprun is a leading Alpine sport shop. The retail interior refers to the mountainous surroundings in a playful way. An instant eye-catcher is a sculptural metal installation that rises to the sky through a glazed atrium, accentuating the separation of the two sides of the concrete-framed building. The artificially created landscape inside the shop - with its glass roof and windows offering panoramic views - literally merges with the great outdoors. Located throughout the store, huge photos showing scenes of sports and natural themes give customers a sense of being outside. A granite core and the repeated use of materials - concrete, brick, oak and steel - link all shopping floors. The openness of the interior is an invitation to meet and greet. Even at night, lighting inside the store animates the building and draws the attention of passers-by. The building's bold, urban, polarizing architecture provokes its traditional lederhosen setting.

Blocher Blocher Partners
Lessingstraße 13
70174 Stuttgart
Germany

T +49 (0)711 224 820
E partners@blocherblocher.com
W www.blocherblocher.com

Photography: Johannes Vogt

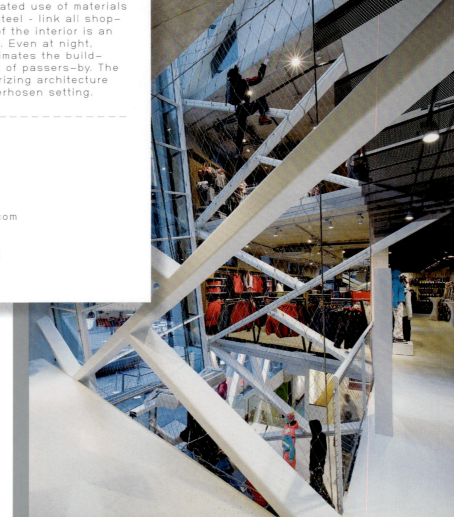

02

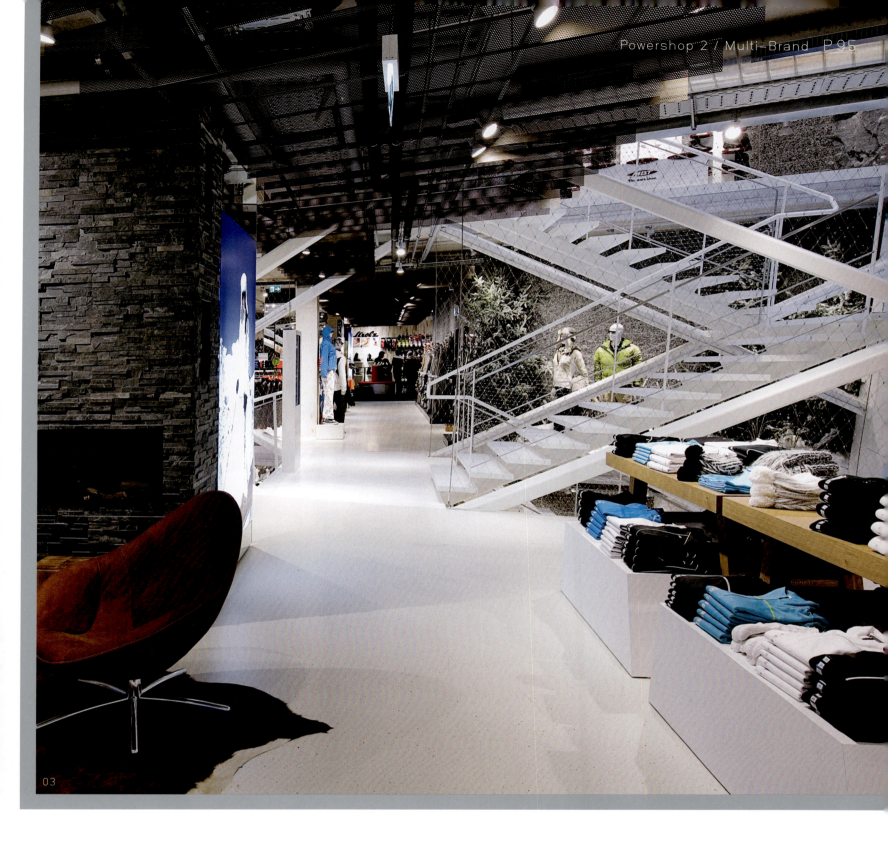

03

01   A glazed atrium cuts through the building's concrete frame like a glacial crevasse.

02   The interior design repeats this methodology and interprets the geometry of the facade.

03   Alternating lounge and display areas create a relaxing shopping environment.

JeansLab
Yalın Tan & Jeyan Ülkü

WHERE:	ISTANBUL, TURKEY
WHEN:	AUGUST 2007
CLIENT:	ÖZLENIR GIYIM
TOTAL FLOOR AREA (M²):	120
BUDGET (US$):	150,000

||||||||||||||||||||||||||||||||||||||||||

IN JUNE 2000, YALIN TAN AND JEYAN ÜLKÜ ESTABLISHED THE TURKISH INTERIOR-DESIGN PRACTICE THAT BEARS THEIR NAMES. THE FIRM FOCUSES ON THE INTERIOR DESIGN OF SHOPS, OFFICES, RESIDENTIAL PROJECTS AND HOTELS; AND ON THE DESIGN OF TRADE-FAIR STANDS. BESIDES CREATING, BUDGETING AND IMPLEMENTING PROJECTS FOR ITS CLIENTELE, THE PRACTICE ALSO FUNCTIONS AS A CONSULTANCY FOR A RANGE OF DESIGN-RELATED ACTIVITIES.

||||||||||||||||||||||||||||||||||||||||||

Fashion brand distributor Özlenir Giyim operates JeansLab, which he refers to as a Turkish 'future shopping experiment'. JeansLab boasts several great labels - including Diesel, Replay, Wrangler, Lee and 55DSL - all under one roof. Facing design firm Yalin Tan & Jeyan Ülkü was the task of finding a common design language for individual brands while coming up with a shop concept that was suitable for the outlets of a chain store. In setting the scene for JeansLab shoppers, Yalin Tan and Jeyan Ülkü aimed for a clear distinction between men's and women's wear. A centrally positioned display unit acts as a natural partition that also creates corridors along its sides. A recessed Barrisol ceiling above this unit accentuates the division and acts as a focal point. White-painted wall panels support shelves and rails, which display fashion items for sale. A contrast is formed by the ceiling and the rest of the walls, all painted dark grey. The designers chose a neutral, nearly monochrome setting to draw the customer's eye to the products within a retail space free of distractions. Once you pass the merchandise and reach the back of the shop, however - an area reserved for the cash desk and fitting rooms - it's one big colour explosion. Here floor and walls are covered in carpet tiles that range from reds, pinks and purples on the women's side to blues and greens on the men's side, separated in the middle by a bright touch of yellow.

Yalin Tan & Jeyan Ülkü
Abdi Ipekci cad. Arman Palas No.7/14
34376 Istanbul
Turkey

T +90 212 2316 968
E info@yalintan-jeyanulku.com.tr
W www.yalintan-jeyanulku.com.tr

Photography: Ali Bekman

1 Sales area
2 Fitting room
3 Cash desk
4 Storage

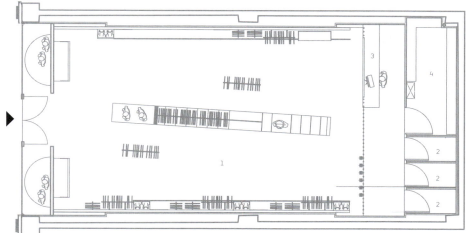

02   Hidden within a wall of mirrors are doors to the fitting rooms.

03   A centrally positioned display
unit serves as a natural divider
between the men's and women's
sections.

04   Merchandise is displayed
in a more neutral setting, which
allows shoppers to focus on the
products.

Labels
Maurice Mentjens

WHERE: SITTARD, THE NETHERLANDS
WHEN: DECEMBER 2008
CLIENT: LABELS FASHION
SHOP CONSTRUCTOR: BOUWSERVICE PHILIPPEN
ARCHITECT: HAN WIJNEN
TOTAL FLOOR AREA (M²):   124

MAURICE MENTJENS DESIGNS INTERIORS, INTERIOR OBJECTS, FURNITURE AND EXHIBITION CONCEPTS. NEARLY ALL THE FIRM'S REALIZED PROJECTS ARE IN THE RETAIL, HOSPITALITY AND OFFICE SECTORS. YEARS OF EXPERIENCE HAVE NOT DIMINISHED A PREFERENCE FOR SMALL-SCALE PROJECTS WITH A FOCUS ON QUALITY AND CREATIVITY. THE FIRM HAS WON THREE DUTCH DESIGN AWARDS (INTERIOR DESIGN) AND, IN 2007, THE DESIGN AWARD OF THE FEDERAL REPUBLIC OF GERMANY. CLIENTS INCLUDE THE BONNEFANTENMUSEUM (MAASTRICHT), FRANS HALS MUSEUM (HAARLEM), DSM AND SOLLAND SOLAR (HEERLEN) AND POST PANIC (AMSTERDAM).

A subtle feel for mythology and the mystical appears in all work by interior designer Maurice Mentjens, including fashion shop Labels, designed in 2008. The shop consists of three small spaces, the middle of which has a glass roof. Mentjens created a division between the women's and men's sections precisely at the midpoint of this central space, where half the floor is white and half is black, colours representing yin and yang, feminine and masculine, elegant and rugged, like the intangible, graceful realm of Venus and the earthy, black smithy of Vulcan, her husband, in Roman mythology. Connections between spaces are formed by two sales counters, half protruding into the glass-roofed space and half into the white or black areas. Highlights include steel espaliers in the glass-roofed space. Handy clothes racks, they refer primarily to the Garden of Eden. Venus occupies a virginal white fairy-tale domain marked by vertical tubes at a slight slant like swaying reeds. They support stainless-steel racks and Plexiglas tableaux. Halogen lamps built into the ceiling in circles alternate with round fluorescent lamps. The circular forms are repeated in eye-catching wall niches of various diameters, which are used to display bags and shoes. The men's section is a rugged, strong, linear space capped by a ceiling of heavy wooden beams. Here wooden elements of various sizes are arranged in a neat lattice. Clothes racks are tucked beneath horizontal beams along one wall. On the other side of the room, thick wooden planks display sweaters, shoes and accessories. Dim lighting creates a mysterious atmosphere.

Maurice Mentjens
Martinusstraat 20
6123 BS Holtum
the Netherlands

T +31 (0)46 4811 405
E info@mauricementjens.com
W www.mauricementjens.com

Photography: Leon Abraas

01

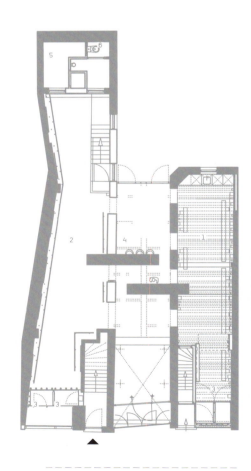

1 Menswear
2 Womenswear
3 Fitting room
4 Cash desk
5 Storage
6 Lavatory

01   A wooden counter in the
central space appears to have
broken through the wall and
entered the men's section.

02   Forming a transition between
the women's section, done in
white, and the men's section, done
in black, is a wall of brown bricks.

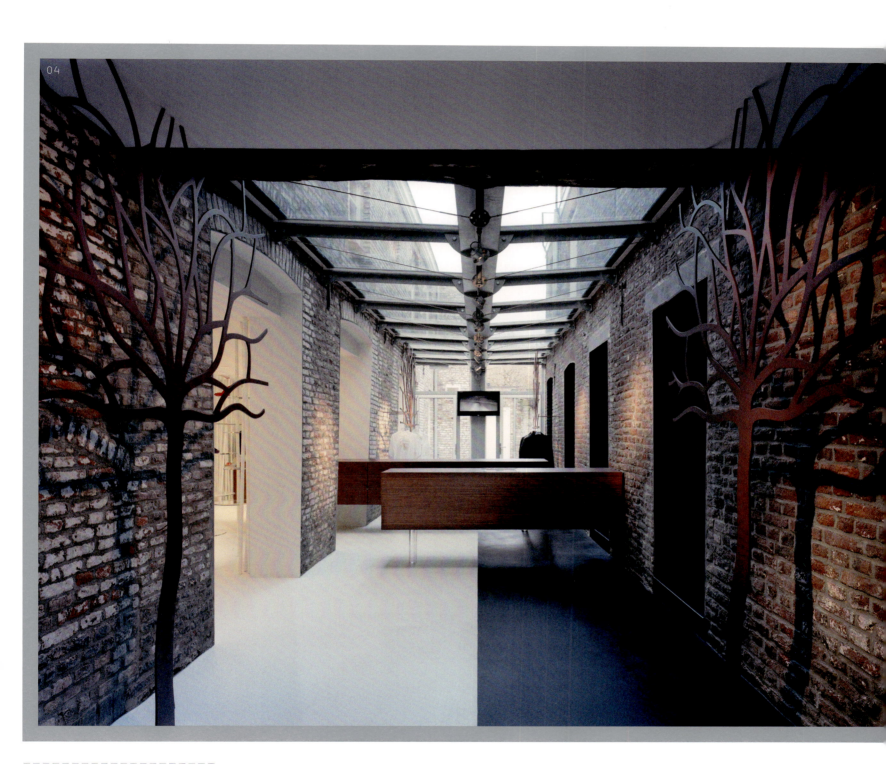

04

03   A wall of white powder–
coated steel with circular display
niches highlights the women's
section.

04   Mentjens transformed an
existing garden into the centrally
located area of the shop, where
two sales counters seem to float
in space.

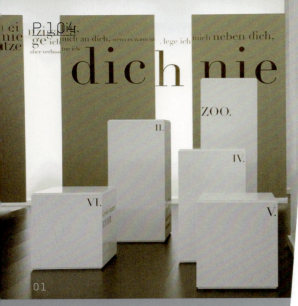

dich nie

ZOO.

01

01 Display units in the menswear department are marked by clear, angular forms.

02 The use of white, beige and brown creates a natural background for the leather goods.

03 In the women's department, circular display units made from pipes are evidence of the tight budget.

Laura Zanello
VON M

WHERE: METZINGEN, GERMANY
WHEN: OCTOBER 2006
CLIENT: LAURA ZANELLO
SHOP CONSTRUCTOR: SCHÜTTLER
INNENAUSBAU
TOTAL FLOOR AREA (M²): 160
BUDGET (€): 40,000

ESTABLISHED BY MATTHIAS SIEGERT IN 2004, VON M - CURRENTLY RUN BY THREE ASSOCIATE PARTNERS - SPECIALIZES IN ARCHITECTURE, MEDIA DESIGN AND THE CROSS-DISCIPLINARY FUSION OF THE TWO. THE FIRM'S PORTFOLIO INCLUDES BOTH RETAIL PROJECTS AND VIDEO AND SPATIAL INSTALLATIONS. WITH ITS OPEN-MINDED, UNBIASED APPROACH, VON M CONCENTRATES ON THE ESSENTIALS TO ACHIEVE CLEAR, SIMPLE AND EFFECTIVE SOLUTIONS.

Visiting Laura Zanello is like entering a fairy tale. The architects were inspired by works of German literature featuring leather. Quotations used as subtle graphic-design elements create an enchanting connection between the interior and the exclusive merchandise. The balanced use of natural brown and beige for furniture, walls and floors - combined with generous white surfaces and striking indirect lighting - forms a background for the leather goods. Contrasting with the clear angular forms of the menswear section are the softly curving contours found in womenswear. Illustrating a close attention to detail are the various display ensembles. A limited budget demanded unconventional solutions, such as piping used to make round, perfectly painted displays, each fitted with a picture and a mirror; and fringed curtains skilfully draped to conceal mechanical systems. If the Brothers Grimm had shod 'Puss in Boots' in footwear made of anything other than fine leather, who knows how the story would have ended?

VON M
Rosenbergstraße 93
70193 Stuttgart
Germany

T +49 (0)711 6276 9750
E info@vonm.de
W www.vonm.de

Photography: Boris Wiechulla

02

03

Eleganz und kleidet sie.

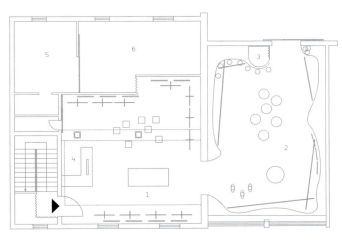

1 Menswear
2 Womenswear
3 Fitting room
4 Cash desk
5 Back office
6 Storage

Magazin Zing
AdaDesign

WHERE: ST PETERSBURG, RUSSIA
WHEN: MARCH 2008
CLIENT: UK STYLE
SHOP CONSTRUCTOR: SEVZAPSTROY
TOTAL FLOOR AREA (M²): 125
BUDGET (€): 130,000

IN 1995 ARIADNA SHMANDUROVA COMPLETED HER INTERIOR ARCHITECTURE AT A DUTCH ART ACADEMY. AFTER WORKING FIVE YEARS FOR A DUTCH DESIGN STUDIO, IN 2000 SHMANDUROVA FOUNDED HER OWN FIRM, ADADESIGN. WORKING FROM OFFICES IN BOTH AMSTERDAM AND MOSCOW, SHE DESIGNS AND REALIZES PROJECTS THAT VARY FROM RETAIL AND HOSPITALITY INTERIORS TO PRODUCT DESIGN.

Magazin Zing is a multi-brand fashion boutique that carries a wide range of apparel by Scandinavian and British fashion designers. The interior of the St Petersburg store is the work of AdaDesign.
The tunnel-like form of the space hints at its previous use: this was once a passage that provided access to an inner courtyard from the street. AdaDesign left the vaulted ceiling and most of the original masonry work intact. Several walls are clad in Flavor Paper, a customized wallpaper that enhances the shop's rather monastic atmosphere, with its wood beams and archways. Part of the floor is covered in oak boards and part in grey Mosa tiles. Ariadna Shmandurova selected vintage furniture which harmonizes perfectly with the authentic ambience. In striking contrast is the contemporarily crafted shape of her purpose-designed clothes racks. Laser cut from stainless steel and painted black, the racks are attached to cables that hang from the ceiling. The lighting scheme is also a mix of old and new; Shmandurova combined atmospheric vintage lights with functional modern luminaires by Belgian manufacturer Modular.

AdaDesign
Westerstraat 13-D
1015 LT Amsterdam
the Netherlands

T +31 (0)6 1709 0924
E info@adadesign.nl
W www.adadesign.nl

Photography: G. Kronberg

01

02

01   Ariadna Shmandurova
left the original masonry intact.

02   Clothing racks were
laser-cut from stainless steel
and painted black.

03   The lighting is a mix
of old and new.

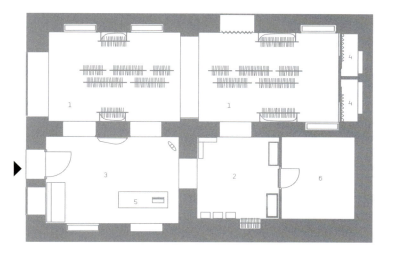

1 Clothing
2 Shirts and shoes
3 Accessories
4 Fitting room
5 Cash desk
6 Storage

03

Mode d'Emploi
Zoom Industries

WHERE: THE HAGUE, THE NETHERLANDS
WHEN: JULY 2007
CLIENT: MODE D'EMPLOI
SHOP CONSTRUCTOR: GELENS BOUWBEDRIJF
TOTAL FLOOR AREA (M²):   280

||||||||||||||||||||||||||||||||||||||||||||

FOUNDED IN 2000 BY RENE THIJSSEN AND
OEP SCHILLING, ZOOM INDUSTRIES DESIGNS
AND DEVELOPS BRAND IDENTITIES, RETAIL
CONCEPTS, TRADE-FAIR STANDS AND CORPORATE
ARCHITECTURE. WITH OFFICES IN MAASTRICHT
AND AMSTERDAM, AND AN INTERNATIONAL TEAM
COMMITTED TO PROVIDING CLIENTS WORLDWIDE
WITH INNOVATIVE SOLUTIONS, ZOOM CREATES
COHERENT, UNCONVENTIONAL CONCEPTS IN
WHICH ATTITUDE AND VISION ARE AS IMPORTANT
AS FUNCTIONALITY.

||||||||||||||||||||||||||||||||||||||||||||

A quintessentially contemporary air fills Mode
d'Emploi, a boutique in The Hague that Zoom
Industries designed for Gerard Backx. Highlighting the façade is a combination of translucent
glass panels etched with the Mode d' Emploi logo
and clear-glass panes that offer passers-by a
glimpse of the retail interior. Inside the 280-m²
store, a neutral grey concrete floor and a large
steel counter give the store a robust look and
feel. Steel columns along inner walls form display
niches; their straight lines are reflected in
a false ceiling of slatted steel. Austerely
designed rectangular display units on casters
present merchandise in a modest way. Together,
the various subdued design elements form a
perfect backdrop for the textures and colours
of Mode d'Emploi's denim fashions. Claiming
centre stage, however, is a red-glass display wall
lit by a string of lamps, which adds a splash of
colour to an otherwise neutral space.

Zoom Industries
Brusselsestraat 55
6211 PB Maastricht
the Netherlands

T +31 (0)43 3260 078
E info@zoom-industries.nl
W www.zoom-industries.nl

Photography: Kim Zwarts and Henny van Belkom

01   Sneakers move on a small,
glass-covered conveyor belt.

02   Jeans attached to carbine
hooks hang from an aluminium
frame.

03   Jeans are presented as
luxury products against two walls
whose gleaming surfaces look as
though they may have been finished in the traditional Japanese
lacquer known as urushi.

04   A Zen garden, complete with
bamboo, has been created next to
the long steel cash desk.

Mode Weber
MAI

WHERE: ST MARGRETHEN, SWITZERLAND
WHEN: APRIL 2008
CLIENT: FAM. WEBER
TOTAL FLOOR AREA (M²):   1600

|||||||||||||||||||||||||||||||||||||||||||||

ARCHITECT JOCHEN MESSERSCHMID FOUNDED
MESSERSCHMID ARCHITECTS AND INTERIOR
DESIGNERS, BETTER KNOWN AS MAI. BASED
IN STUTTGART, GERMANY, MESSERSCHMID AND
HIS TEAM HAVE DESIGNED AND REALIZED
A BROAD RANGE OF LOCAL AND INTERNATIONAL
PROJECTS. MAI'S WORK INCLUDES RESIDENTIAL
BUILDINGS, HOTELS, OFFICES, SHOPPING
MALLS, DEPARTMENT STORES AND SHOWROOM
INTERIORS.

|||||||||||||||||||||||||||||||||||||||||||||||

Erected in the 1970s, Rheinpark was one of
Switzerland's first shopping centres. Recently
the complex underwent a complete renovation.
Among other Rheinpark retail establishments was
Mode Weber, a three-storey department store that
was to be converted into a single-level, 1600-m²
store with fashions for men and women, as well
as a more youthful target group. MAI assumed
responsibility for the interior design.
To organize a space as vast as this one, the
designers began by focusing on the development
of a good circulation plan: clear customer routing
throughout the store was a basic necessity. They
opted for dark industrial flooring in retail areas
and grey-oiled beech parquet for walking routes.
The women's department features meandering
routes, while those in the men's department are
more linear. Suspended plastered ceilings above
retail areas are combined with open ceilings
above walking routes. Partitioning the available
space in the most optimal way, MAI positioned
a 6-m-long cash desk at the centre of the store.
Covered in concrete and wood, the desk has a
simple but elegant design and appears to float
in midair. Behind the cash desk, two large cubes
clad in leather provide storage space. The same
material covers a wall used to display shirts in
the men's area. The designers opted for panels
from the Visplay Invisible system for many of the
wall displays, most of which are finished in high-
gloss white paint. Other walls feature a
combination of wood and bright-coloured
panels. All remaining display furniture was
purpose-designed for the store.

MAI I Messerschmid
Architects and Interior Designers
Königstrasse 50–52
70173 Stuttgart
Germany

T +49 (0)711 2229 680
E mail@messerschmid.de
W www.messerschmid.de

Photography: panoramapictures (Peter Reichert)

01   Dark industrial flooring in the retail area contrasts with the beech parquet used for circulation routes.

02

02&03 A cash desk clad in concrete and wood takes centre stage at Mode Weber in Rheinpark.

04 Walls clad in leather mark the area where men's shirts are sold.

Mode Weber
MAI

WHERE:	ST GALLEN, SWITZERLAND
WHEN:	APRIL 2008
CLIENT:	FAM. WEBER
TOTAL FLOOR AREA (M²):	900

ARCHITECT JOCHEN MESSERSCHMID FOUNDED MESSERSCHMID ARCHITECTS AND INTERIOR DESIGNERS, BETTER KNOWN AS MAI. BASED IN STUTTGART, GERMANY, MESSERSCHMID AND HIS TEAM HAVE DESIGNED AND REALIZED A BROAD RANGE OF LOCAL AND INTERNATIONAL PROJECTS. MAI'S WORK INCLUDES RESIDENTIAL BUILDINGS, HOTELS, OFFICES, SHOPPING MALLS, DEPARTMENT STORES AND SHOWROOM INTERIORS.

As part of the Weber Group's expansion strategy, the corporation opened a new Mode Weber store in the AFG Arena shopping centre in St Gallen, Switzerland. This store offers women's and young fashion only, unlike Mode Weber's other outlets, which also carry menswear. Fam. Weber asked design firm MAI - also in charge of the retail design of other Mode Weber shop locations - to create the interior of the AFG Arena store. The new interior is ultra-dynamic. Connecting the store's two entrances is a parquet 'walking path'. The ceiling - partly suspended and partly open - has a maximum height of 5 m at certain places. Simple display walls with gloss-painted surfaces feature the Visplay Invisible system. Chromed display elements hang from the ceiling in the Young Fashion area, where shop windows are not used for display but offer passers-by a clear view of the retail interior. MAI selected a lighting system by Ansorg.

MAI | Messerschmid
Architects and Interior Designers
Königstrasse 50–52
0173 Stuttgart
Germany

T +49 (0)711 2229 680
E mail@messerschmid.de
W www.messerschmid.d

Photography: panoramapictures (Peter Reichert)

02

01   Mode Weber is located in the AFG Arena shopping centre in St Gallen, Switzerland.

02   A parquet walkway runs along the merchandise and connects the two entrances to the store.

03   Purpose-designed for this particular shop - and not for the fashion chain's overall retail concept - is a unique display element that was built around one of the concrete columns supporting the roof.

01

03

Paper Chest
Line—Inc

WHERE:	OSAKA, JAPAN
WHEN:	AUGUST 2007
CLIENT:	MELROSE
SHOP CONSTRUCTOR:	ALEN'S CRAFT
TOTAL FLOOR AREA (M²):	232

TAKAO KATSUTA (1972) IS A JAPANESE DESIGNER AND A FORMER PARTNER OF EXIT METAL WORK SUPPLY. IN 2002 HE SET UP AN INDEPENDENT COMPANY, LINE—INC, WHICH SPECIALIZES IN THE DESIGN OF RETAIL INTERIORS BOTH AT HOME AND ABROAD. IN 2004 TAKAO KATSUTA ESTABLISHED ANOTHER CREATIVE ORGANIZATION, LINE—PRODUCTS.

Paper Chest is a Japanese shop that sells imported and domestic clothing brands. Melrose, the concern responsible for Paper Chest, commissioned Line—Inc to design the retail interior of its Paper Chest boutique in Osaka. The client wanted a shop with various unique areas that would meld seamlessly within one coherent space.
Line—Inc mixed Oriental and European styles. To achieve the desired atmosphere, the designers introduced diversely patterned vintage partitions - sourced both in Asia and Europe - made from a number of materials. Combining elements from both sides of the world, they created entirely new boundaries, which separate one retail area from another. This symbolic gesture appears conspicuously both inside the shop and at the entrance, where it provides the shop with an eye-catching feature. Merchandise is attractively displayed on antique tables and in antique showcases. Thanks to rounded shop windows and soaring arches, the shop has a friendly, welcoming ambience.

Line—Inc
Kazami Bldg 2F+3F
1-1-6 Higashiyama Meguro-ku
153-0043 Tokyo
Japan

T +81 (0)3 5773 3536
E line@line-inc.co.jp
W www.line-inc.co.jp

Photography: Kozo Takayama

01   A large cash desk at the back of the shop has been painted in contrasting colours: black and white.

02   Birdcages given a new purpose serve as pendant lamps.

03   Room dividers made of various types of vintage fencing add the look and feel of mixed cultures to the retail space.

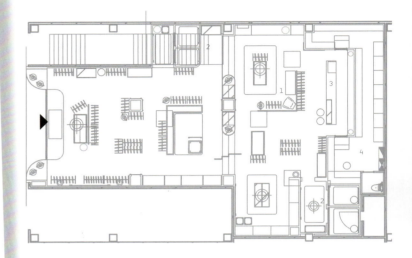

1 Seating area
2 Fitting room
3 Cash desk
4 Storage

Project No. 8
RSVP Architecture Studio with Various Projects

WHERE: NEW YORK, NY, USA
WHEN: JANUARY 2007
CLIENT: VARIOUS PROJECTS
SHOP CONSTRUCTOR: ACME BYPRODUCTS
TOTAL FLOOR AREA (M²):   51

||||||||||||||||||||||||||||||||||||||||||||||||||||

FOUNDED IN 2004, BY BRIAN RIPEL, BROOKLYN–BASED RSVP ARCHITECTURE STUDIO EMPLOYS A COLLABORATIVE DESIGN PROCESS THAT EXPLORES THE BOUNDARIES BETWEEN ARCHITECTURE, ART AND ENVIRON- MENT, WHILE EXPLOITING THE QUALITIES OF MATERIALS AND SPACE. CLIENTS INCLUDE VARIOUS PROJECTS, A MULTIDISCIPLINARY DESIGN COLLABORATION FORMED IN 2005 BY BRIAN JANUSIAK AND ELIZABETH BEER. VARIOUS PROJECTS HAVE COMPLETED 8 PROJECTS TOGETHER.

||||||||||||||||||||||||||||||||||||||||||||||||||||

Project No. 8 is a flexible gallery space for fashion, art and design. With a floor area of 51 m², the site revealed a high degree of complexity marked by the absence of parallel walls. The architects used sustainable building products and technologies to create a series of layers that mediate between the front and rear geometries of the space. Dominant among these is a single angled wall that delineates a show- room clad in concrete panels and provides a neutral canvas for merchandise display. Tucked behind the wall is a service zone comprised of a small office, storage space, lavatory and fitting room. Constructed entirely in engineered woods, these intimate spaces contrast sharply with the display area. A spacious shop window gently pulls away from the street line to define a point of entry. A triangular planting bed between pavement and window adds a touch of colour to the neutral palette, while alluding to the 'green' intentions of the design.

RSVP Architecture Studio
25 Washington St. Suite 655
Brooklyn, NY 11201
USA

T +1 (0)718 625 1948
E info@rsvp-studio.com
W www.rsvp-studio.com

Photography: Seong Kwon

01   Most of the display units in this open–plan shop are mobile to accommodate changing needs and special events.

02   The storefront forms the final layer within the plan, gently pulling away from the street line to define a point of entry.

03   The middle wall, made of concrete panels, provides merchandise with a neutral canvas for optimum display.

04   The office, constructed entirely in engineered woods, is in sharp contrast to the front of the shop.

01

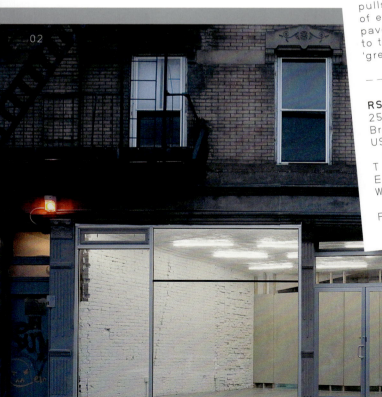

02

03

04

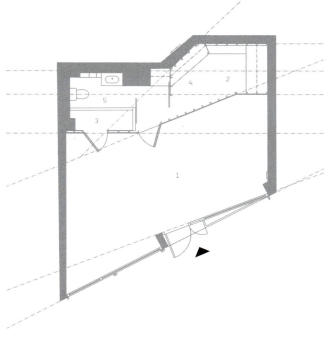

1 Showroom
2 Office
3 Fitting room
4 Storage
5 Lavatory

Riki Niki
Architetto Baciocchi & Associati

01   Pieces of clothing are folded neatly and displayed on wooded shelves.

02&03   Shoes presented in illuminated boxes cover the wall from floor to ceiling.

04   Drawing of the cash desk.

WHERE:	BUSTO ARSIZIO, ITALY
WHEN:	MAY 2008
CLIENT:	MR RICCARDO RIZZOTTI
TOTAL FLOOR AREA (M²):	80

|||||||||||||||||||||||||||||||||||||||||

ARCHITECT ROBERTO BACIOCCHI FOUNDED BACIOCCHI & ASSOCIATI IN 1974, THE YEAR IN WHICH HE GRADUATED FROM THE UNIVERSITY OF FLORENCE. TODAY BACIOCCHI, SIX ASSOCIATE PARTNERS AND 40 TECHNICIANS AND DESIGNERS ARE INVOLVED IN RESIDENTIAL, INDUSTRIAL AND COMMERCIAL PROJECTS. A LIFELONG INTEREST IN ART AND FASHION HELPS BACIOCCHI TRANSLATE BRAND PHILOSOPHIES INTO A CONTEMPORARY ARCHITECTURAL LANGUAGE.

|||||||||||||||||||||||||||||||||||||||||

Riki Niki is a 'total look', multi-brand shop for women. The owner, Mr Riccardo Rizzotti, asked Studio Baciocchi to create an interior for this retail location with a warm, cosy, feminine atmosphere. The designers were to approach the space as though it were a private residence. The one-level store has a floor area of 80 m² and a 4-m-high ceiling. Merchandise is displayed in countless wooden boxes attached to the wall: a solution that takes full advantage of the high ceiling. The designers aimed for a welcoming, living-room ambience - a touch of domesticity reflected in the use of classic materials such as wood, fabric, canvas and leather. Comfortable armchairs contribute to the homey atmosphere. A focal point of the store is the cash desk, a wooden volume that is suspended from the ceiling; its upper section can be utilized as a display.

Architetto Baciocchi & Associati
Strada B, 24 Loc. San Zeno
52100 Arezzo
Italy

T +39 0575 94901
E studio.baciocchi@baciocchi.it
W www.baciocchi.it

Photography: Andrea Ferrari

01

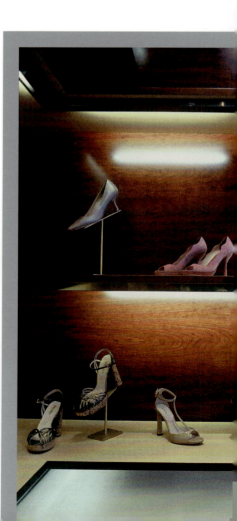

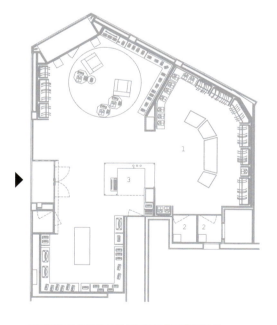

1 Retail area
2 Fitting room
3 Cash desk

Röling Import
Osiris Hertman

WHERE: AMSTERDAM, THE NETHERLANDS
WHEN: MAY 2008
CLIENT: RÖLING IMPORT
SHOP CONSTRUCTORS: MOOIWERK INTERIEUR
AND URSEMBOUW
CO-OPERATING DESIGNER: SJOUCKE
HOOGHIEM
TOTAL FLOOR AREA (M²): 400

OSIRIS HERTMAN STUDIED AT THE DESIGN ACAD-
EMY EINDHOVEN UNDER LIDEWIJ EDELKOORT
BEFORE GOING TO WORK FOR ULF MORITZ AND,
LATER, MARCEL WANDERS. IN 1997 HERTMAN
ESTABLISHED HIS AMSTERDAM-BASED STUDIO.
HE CREATED A TEAM OF ARCHITECTS, INTERIOR
DESIGNERS, AND BRAND CONSULTANTS AND
IS KNOWN FOR HIS BACKGROUND IN PRODUCT
DESIGN AND HIS LOVE FOR CRAFTSMANSHIP.
PROCESSING BASE MATERIALS TO CREATE SUB-
TLE DETAILS RECURS IN HIS WORK. THE STU-
DIO HAS PROVED TO BE A TRUSTED PARTNER IN
HANDLING DESIGN PROJECTS FROM CONCEPT TO
COMPLETION IN THE WORLDS OF FASHION, LIFE-
STYLE, HOSPITALITY AND PRIVATE DOMAIN. CLI-
ENTS INCLUDE MAJOR NAMES SUCH AS BACARDI,
DOLCE & GABBANA, HILTON HOTEL GROUP, MARC
AUREL, MARCEL WANDERS AND PACO RABANNE.

Marc Cain, Cambio, Backstage, Marc Aurel and
React are the five brands that required individual
faces and spaces at Röling Import's high-end
showroom. Entrepreneur Marc van Hilst and his
team requested that each brand be given a clear
identity within a seamlessly integrated interior.
The overall objective was a coherently designed
layout.
The showroom was created to provide a space in
which a network of 700 important Dutch fashion
stores and warehouses could be invited to
do their in-store buying. Transparency,
accessibility and the privacy needed for sales
negotiations prompted Osiris Hertman to base
his design on 'a scenario'. For the floor,
Hertman's unique solution enhances the high
quality and eye for detail of the clothing on
display; he opted for a grid of stainless-steel
strips that form 140-x-140-cm floor tiles. The
unifying floor pattern interconnects the various
showrooms. The laborious method, by which tiles
are epoxy-poured one at a time, leaves the floor
irregular and creates an organic and lively effect.
To create partitions that would separate one
workstation from another, Hertman selected
solid oak and smoked glass, in some instances
creating a 'bus stop for mannequins' and in
others glass walls marked with diagonal wooden
strips that make mannequins appear to be floating in midair.

01

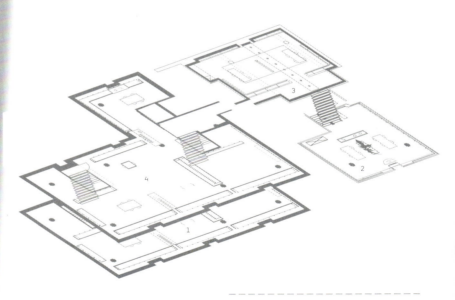

1 Showroom 0
2 Showroom 1
3 Showroom 2
4 Showroom 3

02

01   Eames Plastic Armchairs
paired with Hertmans' custom—
designed tables made of wood and
stainless steel provide staff and
visitors with a suitable place for
sales negotiations.

02   A Moaré lamp - designed by
Antoni Arola for Santa & Cole -
hangs from the ceiling above each
workstation. The irregular floor
of epoxy—poured tiles creates an
organic and lively effect.

Neutral black and white dominates the space.
To further fuse the separate area's, hassocks,
covered in gold fabric by Imperial Collection,
are placed on the intermediate staircase
platforms against a backdrop of soft purple
walls. By working with an expansive surface
of continuous flooring and, for the most part,
movable furniture, Osiris Hertman created a
flexible space in which the diverse fashion labels
all have individual areas and, at the same time,
other brands accommodated in the showroom
remain invitingly transparent. All pieces of
furniture throughout the interior were purpose-
designed by Osiris Hertman, from door handles
and extra long work surfaces to clothing racks
and movable shelving. Each of Hertman's
designs bears the unique signature of one
of the exclusive and predominantly German
brands featured here.

Osiris Hertman
Nieuwendammerkade 28—A9
1022 AB Amsterdam
the Netherlands

T +31 (0)20 6701 357
E info@osirishertman.com
W www.osirishertman.com

Photography: Kasia Gatkowska

03

04

05

03   Osiris Hertman designed the furniture of stainless steel and smoked glass mirrors.

04   View of a multi-functional presentation room. Spotlights and a catwalk-like floor lead visitors towards the smoked-glass mirror at the back wall.

05   Wood and stainless steel dominated the design team's palette of materials.

06   Mannequins show off the latest fashions in oak and glass 'bus stops' that also serve as partitions between workstations.

07   Osiris Hertman's custom-designed furniture was made by Mooiwerk Interieur.

08   Osiris Hertman made subtle adjustments to massive display units - such as notches in the woodwork - to give them a less static appearance.

She & He
Architetto Baciocchi & Associati

WHERE: DONETSK, UKRAINE
WHEN: SEPTEMBER 2008
CLIENT: MR AND MRS KLYMENKO
TOTAL FLOOR AREA (M²):   1000

ROBERTO BACIOCCHI FOUNDED BACIOCCHI & ASSOCIATI IN 1974, THE YEAR IN WHICH HE RECEIVED HIS DEGREE IN ARCHITECTURE FROM THE UNIVERSITY OF FLORENCE. TODAY, BACIOCCHI AND HIS SIX ASSOCIATE PARTNERS, ALONG WITH A TEAM OF 40 TECHNICIANS AND DESIGNERS, ARE INVOLVED IN RESIDENTIAL, INDUSTRIAL AND COMMERCIAL PROJECTS, ALL DRIVEN BY A PASSION FOR INTERIOR DESIGN. BACIOCCHI RELIES ON HIS LIFELONG INTEREST IN ART AND FASHION TO TRANSLATE BRAND PHILOSOPHIES INTO A CONTEMPORARY ARCHITECTURAL LANGUAGE. MOST NOTABLY, SINCE 1982 THE FIRM HAS BEEN REALIZING COMMERCIAL AND CORPORATE ENVIRONMENTS FOR PRADA GROUP BRANDS SUCH AS PRADA, MIU MIU, CHURCH'S AND CAR SHOE. OTHER SIGNIFICANT PROJECTS INCLUDE PRIVATE RESIDENCES IN SAINT MORITZ, MILAN AND TUSCANY; A LUXURY SPA IN MOSCOW; AND FIVE-STAR HOTELS IN BUCHAREST, FLORENCE AND MILAN.

Located in the heart of the Ukrainian city of Donetsk, this two-level She & He multi-brand store sells women's clothing, handbags, shoes and accessories. The complementary She & He shop next door serves the discriminating male customer. Studio Baciocchi was asked to contribute to both the interior and exterior design of the women's store. The main objective was a plush environment with a pleasing visual impact. Studio Baciocchi used precious materials in its translation of the client's brief: the store features bevelled black glass, marble panelling, polished steel, iridescent velvet, mother-of-pearl and black wood. An array of mirrors emphasizes and optically enlarges the spacious character of the interior, while allowing the customer a quick surreptitious glance to check her appearance. Sparkling reflections of large chandeliers - strategically positioned in front of mirrors - add to the effect of an ever-expanding space, and ornamental plasterwork on the ceiling heightens the lavish atmosphere. At the back of the shop, impressive double stairs of grey stone lead to the first floor for more shopping enjoyment. Covering the walls of the staircase are panels of black glass.

>>

01   Vistosi's Giogali lamps contribute to the plush interior.

02   The VIP area on the first floor includes a bar.

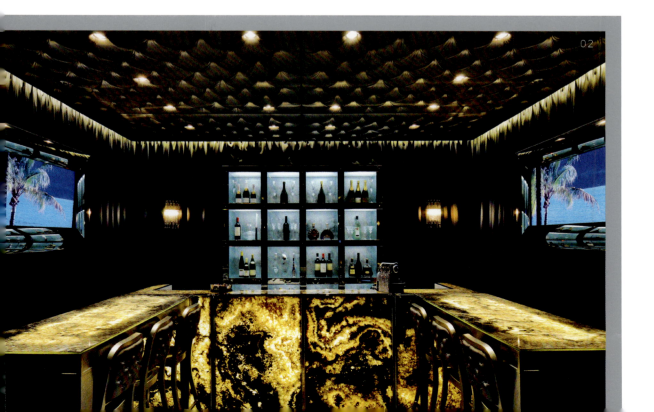

The customer who crosses the sales area on the
first floor ultimately reaches the VIP area, a warm,
cosy space that consists of fitting rooms and
a bar. Fitting rooms are furnished with chic sofas
that boast a mirror finish. Padded pearl-grey
fabric covers the ceiling and part of the walls,
while dark-grey curtains conceal the remaining
walls. The same luxurious ceiling and wall
cladding is found in the bar. Completing the
picture here are bar stools with upholstered,
fabric-covered backrests. Shoppers seated at
the onyx bar, aglow with built-in lighting, choose
their drinks from a polished-steel bottle display
integrated into the wall behind the counter.
LCD screens framed in black glass have been
installed for their viewing pleasure.

Architetto Baciocchi & Associati
Strada B, 24 Loc. San Zeno
52100 Arezzo
Italy

T +39 0575 94901
E studio.baciocchi@baciocchi.it
W www.baciocchi.it

Photography: courtesy of She & He

1 Accessories
2 Women's fashions
3 Fitting room
4 Bar
5 Lavatory

First floor

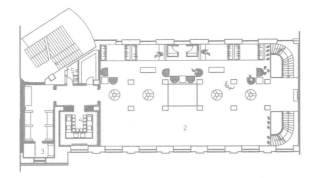

Ground floor

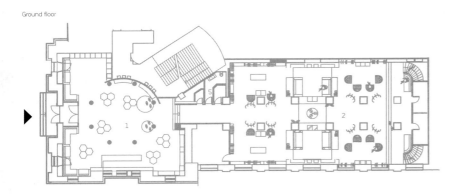

03

03   Niches with padded fabric walls display evening dresses.

04   The luxurious fitting room on the first floor is furnished with comfortable leather sofas.

05   Shoppers entering the store
at ground level find themselves
in the accessories area.

06   An array of mirrors both
emphasizes and optically enlarges
the spacious character of the
interior.

Sid Lee Amsterdam Atelier
Sid Lee with Workshop Architecture + Design

WHERE: AMSTERDAM, THE NETHERLANDS
WHEN: NOVEMBER 2008
CLIENT: SID LEE
TOTAL FLOOR AREA (M²):   550

||||||||||||||||||||||||||||||||||||||||||||||||

SINCE 1993 SID LEE HAS BEEN DEVELOPING
BRAND EXPERIENCES - INVOLVING PRODUCTS,
SERVICES AND SPACES - BASED ON EXCELLENCE
IN ADVERTISING, EXPERIENTIAL MARKETING
AND INTERACTIVE COMMUNICATION.
A MULTIDISCIPLINARY TEAM OF 250
PROFESSIONALS WORKING IN MONTREAL
AND AMSTERDAM APPROACHES EACH PROJECT
FROM THE PERSPECTIVE OF 'COMMERCIAL
CREATIVITY'. CLIENTS INCLUDE CIRQUE DU
SOLEIL, RED BULL AND MGM GRAND.

||||||||||||||||||||||||||||||||||||||||||||||||

Sid Lee opened its Amsterdam Atelier in November
2008. This newly designed space in De Pijp,
the city's creative hub, functions as a full-
service creative agency and includes not only
a café but the first-ever Sid Lee Collective
gallery-cum-store, a boutique-type establishment
that features an exclusive collection of designer
products from Montreal and other parts of
Canada. Above all else, the Sid Lee Amsterdam
Atelier and its complementary facilities form
the agency's 3D European business card.
The space reflects Sid Lee's unique, multidisciplinary, collective approach and serves as
an environment in which new ideas can flourish.
At the centre of the atelier, the rustic plank
floor evolves into a catwalk and a meeting table,
ultimately extending into the in-house art gallery.
Like the façade, walls, ceilings and furnishings
are all in black, allowing products to stand out.
Artists are regularly invited to use Sid Lee's
blackboard walls as temporary 'canvases'.

Sid Lee
75 Queen Street, Suite 1400
Montreal, QC, H3C 2N6
Canada

T +1 (0)514 282 2200
E media@sidlee.comm
W www.sidlee.com

Photography: Jeroen Musch

01

01   The boutique sells a broad selection of Canadian brands as a tribute to Canadian talent and creativity.

02   Like all furniture in the shop, display tables are black.

03   A long table rises from the floor to become a conference table that can even be used as a catwalk.

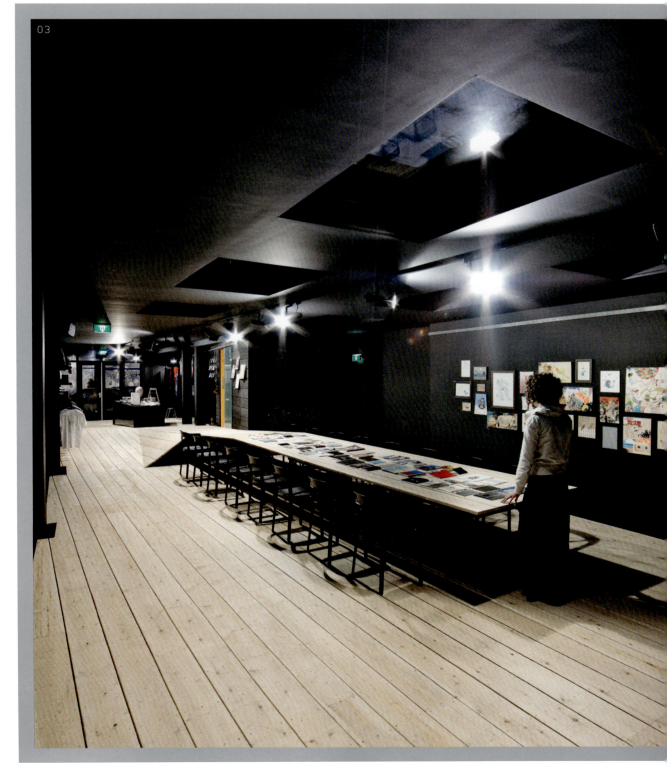

Son's & Daughter's
Breil + Partner

WHERE:	NEUFRA, GERMANY
WHEN:	MARCH 2009
CLIENT:	SON'S & DAUGHER'S COMPANY
SHOP CONSTRUCTOR:	KORDA LADENBAU
TOTAL FLOOR AREA (M²):	1500
BUDGET (€):	1.5 MILLION

||||||||||||||||||||||||||||||

PLANNING AGENCY BREIL + PARTNER WAS FOUNDED IN 2005 BY CLAUDIA BREIL. THE FIRM'S MAIN FOCUS IS OVERALL BRAND COMMUNICATION WITHIN THE TEXTILE INDUSTRY. COMPLETED PROJECTS INCLUDE THE DESIGN AND REALIZATION OF STAND-ALONE STORES, SHOPS-IN-SHOPS AND DEPARTMENT STORES, AS WELL AS GRAPHIC DESIGN AND BRAND DEVELOPMENT.

||||||||||||||||||||||||||||||

Breil + Partner developed the retail concept for Son's & Daughter's, a new children's fashion brand based in Starnberg, Germany. The client asked for a store interior that would be fashionable, stylish and cool - but by no means childish, overly tidy or playful. Besides creating an interior design, Breil + Partner had another extremely important task: to develop a corporate image that would give the new brand an absolutely unmistakable identity. During the design process, the team came up with the idea of having two cartoon figures, Sonny and Daughty, personify the new label. These characters appear on walls and furniture, are printed on bags and are used as giveaways. To differentiate the brand from its competitors, Breil + Partner applied pebble shapes to surfaces - walls and ceiling - throughout the store. All custom-designed furniture features smooth curving forms with rounded edges and the brand's corporate colours, white and orange.

Breil + Partner
Susannenstrasse 1
20357 Hamburg
Germany

T +49 (0)40 4109 5908
E info@breilundpartner.de
W www.breilundpartner.de

Photography: Tjaard M. Spiering

01 Drop 1 Liquid Lights, designed by Hopf & Wortmann for Next, seem to drip from the ceiling onto the cash desk.

02 All furniture in the store was designed by Breil + Partner.

03 Cartoon characters Sonny and Daughty are part of the store's identity; they appear throughout the interior, on bags and as giveaways. In the fitting rooms, images of Daughty and a friend decorate the walls.

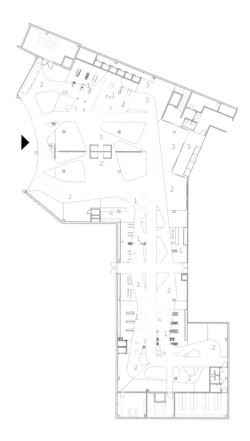

1 Son's and Daughter's label
2 Other labels
3 Fitting rooms
4 Cash desk

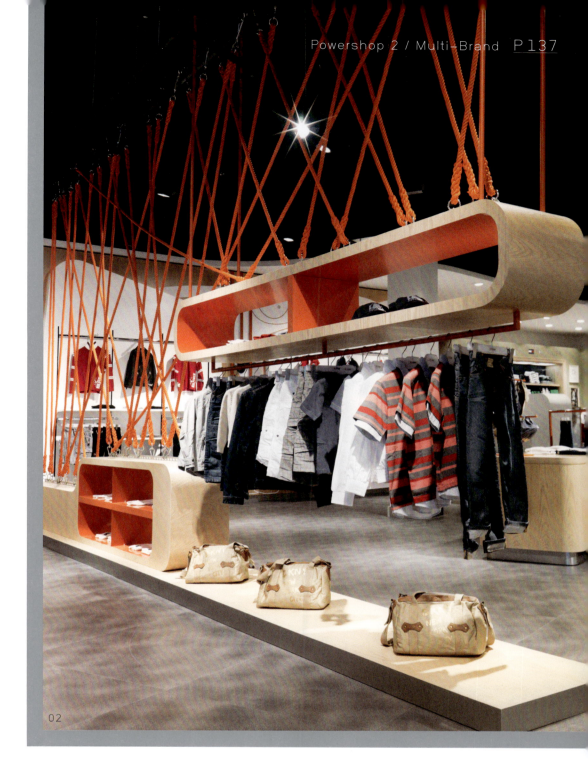

01

02

03

Van Dijk
Osiris Hertman

01

WHERE:	WAALWIJK, THE NETHERLANDS
WHEN:	DECEMBER 2008
CLIENT:	VAN DIJK
SHOP CONSTRUCTORS:	BRANDWACHT EN MEIJER
	AND MOOIWERK INTERIEUR
TOTAL FLOOR AREA (M²):	1700

||||||||||||||||||||||||||||||||||||||||||

OSIRIS HERTMAN STUDIED AT THE DESIGN ACAD–EMY EINDHOVEN BEFORE GOING TO WORK FOR ULF MORITZ AND, LATER, MARCEL WANDERS. IN 1997 HERTMAN ESTABLISHED HIS AMSTERDAM–BASED STUDIO. HE CREATED A TEAM OF AR–CHITECTS, INTERIOR DESIGNERS, AND BRAND CONSULTANTS AND IS KNOWN FOR HIS BACK–GROUND IN PRODUCT DESIGN AND HIS LOVE FOR CRAFTSMANSHIP. HERTMAN HAS PROVEN TO BE A TRUSTED PARTNER IN HANDLING PROJECTS FROM CONCEPT TO COMPLETION IN THE WORLD OF FASHION, HOSPITALITY AND PRIVATE DOMAIN.

||||||||||||||||||||||||||||||||||||||||||

For Van Dijk Waalwijk, vendors of fine fashions for men and women, Osiris Hertman designed a jeans bar, a corridor and various furnishings. The client's 1700–m² store, with its ever-changing collections, was to provide fashion-fanatics with an 'amusement park experience'. Brainstorming sessions involving Hertman and Hans van Dijk led to the 'jeans apothecary' concept: a bar that offers both personal advice on choosing jeans and refreshing mineral water in custom-made bottles. A wall of alcoves painted black and white and embellished with a fleur-de-lys motif in relief leads shoppers from clothing by Marc Cain and Airfield to fashions by Girbaud and Essentiel. Furnishings include a custom-designed work surface made from an antique table with legs that were halved and given a silhouette of glass and black powder-coated steel. The table and other pieces of customized vintage furniture accentu–ate interaction between old and new, hidden and visible. In the men's casual-wear department, Hertman combined a chesterfield sofa with the expressive lines of Paul Smith for Kvadrat.

Osiris Hertman
Nieuwendammerkade 28–A9
1022 AB Amsterdam
the Netherlands

T +31 (0)20 6701 357
E info@osirishertman.com
W www.osirishertman.com

Photography: Kasia Gatkowska

02

01   The whole interior is a sphere of interaction between old and new.

02   Each pile of neatly folded denim pants on the leather-clad shelves is illuminated by a LED light.

03   Antique French metro station benches with brass-milled lettering are placed in the corridor that links two retail areas.

04   The counter of the 'jeans apothecary' is covered with black leather and features built-in showcases.

05   One of the alcove walls boasts a Lincrusta covering embossed with a fleur-de-lys motif.

Villa Moda
Marcel Wanders

WHERE:	MANAMA, BAHREIN
WHEN:	JUNE 2008
CLIENT:	SHEIKH MAJED AL-SABAH
TOTAL FLOOR AREA (M²):	1000

||||||||||||||||||||||||||||||||||||||||||||||||||

MARCEL WANDERS CREATES PRODUCTS FOR INTERNATIONAL COMPANIES FROM HIS STUDIO IN THE CENTRE OF AMSTERDAM. HIS INTERIOR-DESIGN PROJECTS RANGE FROM THE VILLA MODA FLAGSHIP STORE IN BAHRAIN TO THE SLEEPING-BEAUTY MAGIC OF THE MONDRIAN SOUTH BEACH HOTEL IN MIAMI. ALL HIS PRODUCTS AND PROJECTS REFLECT A SENSE OF THE THEATRICAL AND A REMARKABLE USE OF SPACE AND TEXTURES. WANDERS' MISSION STATEMENT IS: 'HERE TO CREATE AN ENVIRONMENT OF LOVE, LIVE WITH PASSION AND MAKE OUR MOST EXCITING DREAMS COME TRUE.'

||||||||||||||||||||||||||||||||||||||||||||||||||

As part of Sheikh Majed Al-Sabah's plans for Villa Moda's seventh luxury multi-brand fashion store, to be located in the new Bahrain World Trade Center, the founder of Villa Moda looked for a designer who hadn't yet created a retail environment. His choice fell on Dutch designer Marcel Wanders, known to the sheikh through his furniture designs. The brief was simple: draw inspiration from the chaos of the souk - a Middle Eastern market place - and use it to craft a luxury fashion context. Al-Sabah and Wanders toured the Middle East, exploring souks and traditional retail concepts. The theme of Wanders' resulting design is the 'International Souk'. He designed the space as if it were a small city where customers can discover something new each time they visit. The store consists of a number of architectural elements and areas, each of which accommodates a specific department, sometimes literally shaped like a miniature house. Local motifs combined with Wanders' fantastical aesthetic form an environment with an 'Alice-in-Wanders-land' appeal. First to catch the visitor's eye are giant pearl-like spheres that cover the façade and refer to Bahrain's heritage. A long, narrow corridor leads customers into the store before opening to reveal an impressive, high-ceiled space with giant patterns in black and white on purpose-designed carpets and wallpaper. Wanders worked with local and international craftsmen who used their expertise, at his request, in quite unusual ways. A good example is the giant sculptural flower pattern carved from wood that covers the wall behind the cash desk.

Marcel Wanders studio
Westerstraat 187
1015 MA Amsterdam
the Netherlands

T +31 (0)20 422 1339
E joy@marcelwanders.com
W www.marcelwanders.com

Photography: Marcel Wanders studio

01

01   The Al Othman shop-in-shop is accessible through large double doors.

02   Custom-designed carpets featuring various patterns have been used throughout the store. Wanders created these motifs for Colorline of the Netherlands.

03   Marcel Wanders' Zeppelin lamps hover above the cash desk, behind which giant hand-carved wooden flowers cover the wall.

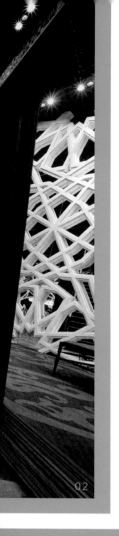

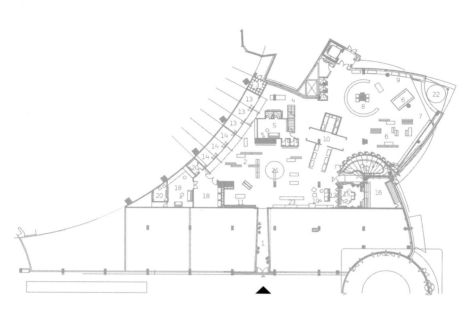

1 Entrance corridor
2 Womenswear
3 Women's bags
4 Women's shoes
5 Women's salon
6 Menswear
7 Men's jeans
8 Men's shoes
9 Men's accessories
10 Jeans house
11 Sunglasses / fragrances
12 Books / magazines
13 Dries Van Noten
14 Marni
15 Manolo Blahnik
16 Anja Hindmarch
17 Gaia&Gino
18 Al Othman
19 Lounge area
20 Fitting room
21 Mannequin display sphere
22 Rotating mannequin display
23 Cash desk

04   A staircase covered in black
and white mosaic tiles based on
a traditional Moroccan pattern
leads to another retail space on
the floor above.

05   Mannequins with mirrors
as heads occupy a large display
unit composed of hexagons.

06   View of the white 'jeans
house' through a tunnel in
menswear made from fibreglass-
reinforced gypsum. Featured here
are Paper Chandeliers by Studio
Job for Moooi.

07   Three chic mannequins strike
a theatrical pose beneath a huge
lacy plaster dome inspired by
traditional Middle Eastern motifs.

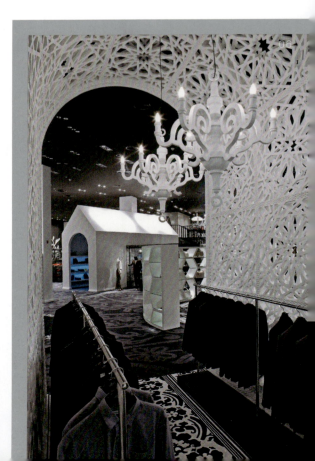

Wertgarner 1820
BEHF Architects

WHERE: VIENNA, AUSTRIA
WHEN: JUNE 2008
CLIENT: WERTGARNER 1820 JAGD UND
SPORTHANDEL
SHOP CONSTRUCTOR: BEHF ARCHITECTS
TOTAL FLOOR AREA (M²):   87

INSPIRED BY A SUCCESSFULLY PLANNED OUTLET IN 1995, SUSI HASENAUER, STEPHAN FERENCZY AND ARMIN EBNER WENT ON TO ESTABLISH BEHF ARCHITECTS, WHICH CURRENTLY HAS A STAFF OF ABOUT 80 ARCHITECTS, AS WELL AS IN-HOUSE PROJECT-MANAGEMENT AND CONSTRUCTION DEPARTMENTS. BEHF ARCHITECTS WORKS WITHIN A BROAD SPECTRUM OF SECTORS, INCLUDING HOUSING, RETAIL, HOSPITALITY-INDUSTRY AND OFFICE DESIGN. THE FIRM HAS COMPLETED INTERIOR-DESIGN AND ARCHITECTURAL PROJECTS IN AUSTRIA, KAZAKHSTAN, POLAND, UKRAINE, SERBIA, CROATIA, MACEDONIA AND THE PHILIPPINES.

BEHF Architects was asked to design the façade and interior of the new Wertgarner 1820 shop in Vienna. The hunting and sports company wanted not only its long-standing tradition to be embraced and included in the design, but also - in terms of architecture - its shop to distinguish itself from similar establishments in the city.
In June 2008 the project was completed. The new retail concept features a spatial colour-coding programme that breaks with conventional systems for directing visitors through a shop interior. Different colours indicating the various zones of the shop guide customers to the desired product area, from the colour-intensive sports department to a section for outdoor clothing done in neutral white. In the green hunting room, shoppers find a selection of more exclusive goods. A heavy curtain of dark-green velvet separates this room from the storage area and a small office, hiding them from the public eye. Although the interior design itself cannot be called traditional, contrasting elements - such as the green room's vintage chandelier, chairs and table - have been included to create a unique atmosphere that brings history and tradition to mind. Lighting busbars equipped with Antares compass spots hang from the light-grey ceiling, illuminating the lacquered built-in furniture that covers all walls. The façade comprises two large neutral windows, a glass entrance door and three showcases, all part of the colour scheme. Passers-by viewing the shop through the door see a seemingly red interior, while those peering through the windows have the impression of a yellow space inside.

BEHF Architects
Kaiserstrasse 41
1070 Vienna
Austria

T +43 (0)1 524 1750 12
E behf@behf.at
W www.behf.at

Photography: Bruno Klomfar

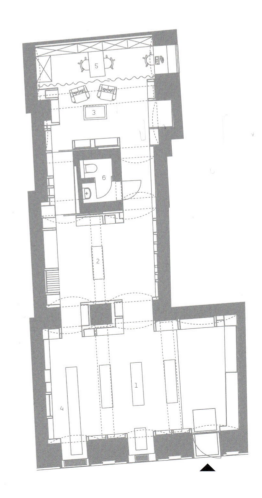

1 Sports area
2 Outdoor-clothing area
3 Hunting room
4 Cash desk
5 Office / storage
6 Lavatory

01

01&03   At the Wertgarner 1820 shop in Vienna, red blends into yellow, marking the sporting-goods area.

02   Passers-by catching sight of the interior through the display window to their right see a red interior, whereas those standing more to the left or at the centre of the façade are rewarded with the view of an interior that appears to be bright yellow.

02

03

04   Exclusive goods are sold
in the green hunting room.

05   A section devoted to
outdoor apparel has been done
in neutral white.

Powershop 2 / Multi—Brand   P 147

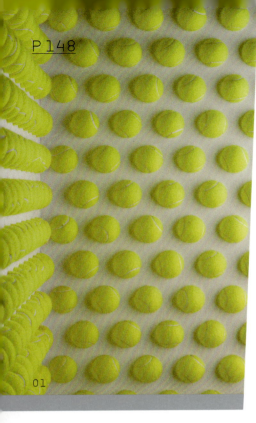

01

Wigmore Sports
Portland Design

WHERE: LONDON, UNITED KINGDOM
WHEN: NOVEMBER 2008
CLIENT: WIGMORE SPORTS
TOTAL FLOOR AREA (M²):   350

|||||||||||||||||||||||||||||||||||||||||||||||||||

PORTLAND DESIGN CREATES BRANDS AND
PLACES FOR PEOPLE. WITH OFFICES IN LONDON
AND DUBAI, THEIR INTERNATIONAL PROJECT LIST
SPANS A BROAD RANGE OF CONSUMER ENVIRON-
MENTS, FROM BRAND EXPERIENCES TO
AIRPORTS AND SHOPPING MALLS. THE FIRM'S
CULTURE IS BASED ON AN INTERDISCIPLINARY
TEAM APPROACH THAT FOCUSES ON UNDER-
STANDING CONSUMERS' RELATIONSHIPS WITH
BRANDS AND INTERACTION WITH ENVIRONMENTS.

|||||||||||||||||||||||||||||||||||||||||||||||||||

Wigmore Sports is an independent racquet-sports
specialist. A high level of personal service is core
to the Wigmore brand; its consultative approach
to sales can take up to 45 minutes per customer.
Portland Design was brought in to create the
design concept for Wigmore's new store in
London's West End, just a few minutes' walk
from the old shop location.
The new store includes a hitting room in the
basement, where customers can put equipment
through its paces in a practice-court environment. Portland used Wigmore's blue and white
corporate colours throughout the interior, along
with acidic 'tennis ball yellow' accents. Other
graphic references to racquet sports are the
tennis-court lining on the Capri Blue Pulastic
2000 floor and inspirational tennis quotations
from past masters on walls throughout the store.
Highlighting the vertical circulation area is a
feature wall decorated with 3000 tennis balls.

Portland Design
63 Gee Street
London EC1V 3RS
United Kingdom

T +44 (0)20 7017 8780
E studio@portland-design.com
W www.portland-design.com

Photography: Francesco Foroni

01   One wall is decorated with
no fewer than 3000 tennis balls.

02   Customers can test the
equipment in the hitting room.

03   The wall behind the cash
desk showcases 500 tennis
rackets.

04   Trying on sneakers couldn't
be more comfortable. A tennis ball-
inspired seat pad complements the
scheme.

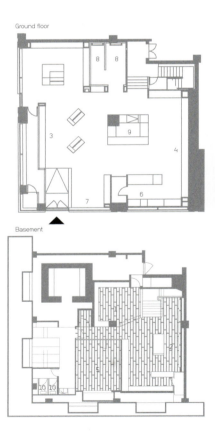

Ground floor

Basement

1 Children's department
2 Shoe wall
3 Apparel wall
4 Racquet wall
5 Hitting room
6 Stringing area
7 Accessories
8 Fitting room
9 Cash desk
10 Lavatory

02

361°
::dan pearlman

WHERE:	GUANGZHOU, CHINA
WHEN:	MARCH 2009
CLIENT:	361°
SHOP CONSTRUCTOR:	VIZONA
TOTAL FLOOR AREA (M²):	604

||||||||||||||||||||||||||||||||||||||

IN 1999 NICOLE SROCK-STANLEY, VOLKER KATSCHINSKI, MARCUS FISCHER AND KIERAN STANLEY FOUNDED ::DAN PEARLMAN, AN AGENCY WITH A FOCUS ON BRAND ARCHITECTURE AND EXPERIENCE ARCHITECTURE. THE BERLIN-BASED FIRM RESPONDS TO THE VARIOUS COMMUNICATION-RELATED OBJECTIVES OF ITS CLIENTS BY MEANS OF FOUR INDEPENDENT SPECIALIST UNITS: STRATEGY, RETAIL, EXHIBITION AND MEDIA.

||||||||||||||||||||||||||||||||||||||

Chinese sporting-goods manufacturer 361° operates more than 6000 stores in China. The name expresses the brand's claim to 'remain one degree ahead of the competition'. In 2009 361° commissioned ::dan pearlman to translate its slogan into a vanguard retail concept.
Giving the tagline a slight twist, the designers focused on 'one degree more': more dynamics, more challenges, more excellence, more passion. The key visual, a circle featuring that crucial extra degree, returns as a strong element inside the store. A white stripe on the floor draws customers deeper into the shop, where it ultimately runs into a turbine-shaped display element. The turbine in combination with the white stripe is a prime example of ::dan pearlman's use of visual highlights. Accents in orange, the brand colour, create the impression of dynamic movement. Repositioning the brand by means of a new retail concept has made 361° markedly different from its competitors.

::dan pearlman
Kiefholzstrasse 1
12435 Berlin
Germany

T +49 (0)30 5300 0560
E office@danpearlman.com
W www.danpearlman.com

Photography: Bettina Matthiessen

01   The walls at 361° are painted grey and equipped with display panels.

02   Chinese sportswear brand 361° offers complete outfits - clothing, shoes and accessories - for a variety of sports.

03   Enlivening the turbine display are orange accents that give the impression of movement.

04   Orange elements on floor, walls and ceiling - all with built-in lighting - lead the customer through the store.

01

03

First floor

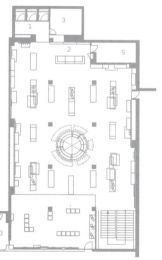

Ground floor

1 Fitting rooms
2 Cash desk
3 Storage
4 Equipment room
5 Lavatory

04

01

adidas Original's Atelier
Sid Lee

WHERE: NEW YORK, NY, USA
WHEN: FEBRUARY 2008
CLIENT: ADIDAS ORIGINALS
CO-OPERATIVE DESIGNER: AEDIFICA
TOTAL FLOOR AREA (M²):   215

|||||||||||||||||||||||||||||||||||||||||||||||||||||||||||||||||

SINCE 1993 SID LEE HAS BEEN DEVELOPING BRAND EXPERIENCES - INVOLVING PRODUCTS, SERVICES AND SPACES - BASED ON EXCELLENCE IN ADVERTISING, EXPERIENTIAL MARKETING AND INTERACTIVE COMMUNICATION. A MULTIDISCIPLINARY TEAM OF 250 PROFESSIONALS WORKING IN MONTREAL AND AMSTERDAM APPROACHES EACH PROJECT FROM THE PERSPECTIVE OF 'COMMERCIAL CREATIVITY'. CLIENTS INCLUDE CIRQUE DU SOLEIL, RED BULL AND MGM GRAND.

|||||||||||||||||||||||||||||||||||||||||||||||||||||||||||||||||

When adidas Originals hired Sid Lee, in partnership with AEdifica, to review the overall concept and setup of its stores worldwide, the design team came up with a plan that invites visitors to interact with the adidas Trefoil brand in an enjoyable and educational way. The Workshop-Atelier project - a tribute to company founder Adi Dassler - allows adidas Originals to share its rich brand history. Featured in the store are all the tools needed to bring Originals' core values to life.
The unique atmosphere forms the ultimate platform for self-expression and authenticity. Located in New York City, the first shop to be adapted has a functional atelier-like interior that includes workbench-inspired tables with cobblers' lasts; footwear walls that reveal the inner workings of the storage system; boxes built into the Brand, Basics and Denim walls; and communication tools like windows, graphics, frames, televisions, books and globes, right through to the creative mi-Originals tooling area and its first-generation blueprints.

Sid Lee
75 Queen Street, Suite 1400
Montreal, QC, H3C 2N6
Canada

T +1 (0)514 282 2200
E media@sidlee.com
W www.sidlee.com

Photography: Sid Lee and AEdifica

02

03

01   White display tables are inspired by workbenches.

02   Customers can design personalized adidas shoes in the mi-Original section of the store.

03   The arm chairs in each adidas Originals store feature the work of a local artist.

adidas signature brand store
JudgeGill

WHERE:	PARIS, FRANCE
WHEN:	MARCH 2008
CLIENT:	ADIDAS
TOTAL FLOOR AREA (M²):	1765

JUDGEGILL DESIGNS ENVIRONMENTS - EFFECTIVE, MULTI-SENSORY SPACES FOR BRANDS THAT LEAVE CUSTOMERS WITH POSITIVE, ENDURING MEMORIES. JUDGEGILL WORKS WITH ADIDAS AND ITS RETAIL TEAM TO ENSURE THAT THE BRAND'S SPORT PERFORMANCE CONCEPT CONSISTENTLY OFFERS AN INNOVATIVE SPORTS RETAIL EXPERIENCE. BESIDES ADIDAS, THE FIRM'S CLIENT LIST INCLUDES NAMES SUCH AS FRED PERRY, HERTZ, VIRGIN AND MTS. THE DESIGN COMPANY HAS BUILT OVER 1000 STORES GLOBALLY. THE LATEST PROJECTS ARE IN RUSSIA, CHINA, NORTH AMERICA AND THE MIDDLE EAST.

Sportswear brand adidas was in need of a new retail concept that would bring the adidas brand promise - 'enabling a better you' - to life in a unique environment that showcases the full breadth of adidas products. The brand and its retail team invited design company JudgeGill to collaborate in the development of this global flagship concept.

The store unites the two divisions of adidas - 'Sports Style', the home of authentic sportswear brand Originals, and 'Sport Performance', a range of functional and innovative sportswear - under one roof. Also highlighted are the brand's collaborative collections, such as adidas by Stella McCartney, Y-3 by Yohji Yamamoto and premium footwear from Porsche Design Sport. Additional brands include Style Essentials, a line of casual sportswear for everyday use, and the latest adidas brand, SLVR. The use of leading-edge technologies injects the whole store with an exciting, sports-inspired atmosphere. The latest touchscreens, featuring miCoach Core Skills, let customers test their athletic prowess in a fun, interactive way using sophisticated technology usually reserved for elite athletes. Foot-scanning analysis provided by mi adidas allows shoppers to customize trainers to their individual needs. Both features reinforce the adidas brand promise by helping customers to understand their own fitness levels and the benefits of sport. Housed in an environment inspired by both the architecture and emotion of sport and dominated by the adidas brand signature - the three adidas stripes wrap the full length of the space - this concept has been rolled out in major cities worldwide.

JudgeGill
3 Cobourg Street
Manchester M1 3GY
United Kingdom

T +44 (0)161 228 3066
E info@judgegill.co.uk
W www.judgegill.co.uk

Photography: Johannes Marburg Photography

01

01   Porsche Design and adidas merged timeless design and the functionality of sports to create the line of products sold at the adidas signature brand store

02   The familiar trademark stripes that characterize adidas extend the full length of the store.

03   Customers can take a 'reflex test' to see how fast they really are.

1 SPC Men collection
2 Footwear
3 SPC Women collection
4 Kids collection
5 Mi adidas
6 Core Skills
7 Originals collection
8 Porsche Design collection
9 Stella McCartney collection
10 SLVR collection
11 Y3 collection

First floor

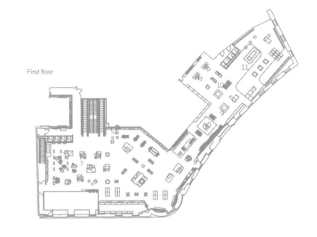

Ground floor

05

04

04   Special seats equipped
with foot-scanning analysis allow
shoppers to customize their trainers to satisfy individual needs.

05   Trainers are categorized
according to type of sport.

06   The Paris store covers two
floors of a building on the famed
Champs-Elysées.

Alexandre Herchcovitch
Studio Arthur Casas

WHERE:	TOKYO, JAPAN
WHEN:	MARCH 2007
CLIENT:	ALEXANDRE HERCHCOVITCH
ARCHITECT:	ARTHUR CASAS
TOTAL FLOOR AREA (M²):	72

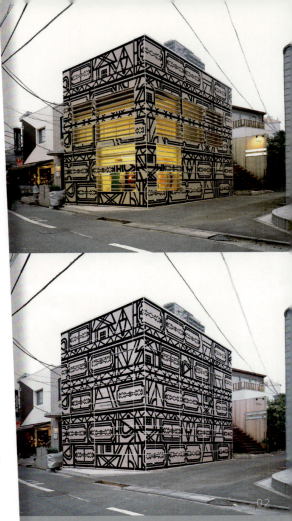

STUDIO ARTHUR CASAS (BASED IN SÃO PAULO, WITH OFFICES IN NEW YORK) HAS BEEN INVOLVED IN ARCHITECTURE AND INTERIOR DESIGN SINCE 1985. RETAIL, RESIDENTIAL AND HOTEL PROJECTS HEADED BY ARTHUR CASAS HAVE A CONTEMPORARY BRAZILIAN FLAIR. RECENT EXAMPLES ARE A CONDOMINIUM IN ANGOLA, A SUSTAINABLE OCEANFRONT CONDOMINIUM IN FLORIANÓPOLIS, AND A ZEFERINO SHOP IN SÃO PAULO.

01 Gleaming wall panels in various sizes fold down to serve as display surfaces.

02 The boldly decorated façade, which sometimes looks like a closed box, takes on a different appearance when the windows are open.

03 Garments and accessories hang on fluorescent light tubes suspended from the ceiling.

The Alexandre Herchcovitch boutique in Tokyo is in the Japanese capital's fashion and architecture enclave: Daikanyama. Brazilian designer Arthur Casas based the exterior of the shop on the concept of a 'box'. When all windows are closed, the façade rouses shoppers' curiosity, but even when they're open, the retail interior remains partially concealed. Outside walls are covered in motifs printed on adhesive acrylic sheets, which are updated seasonally to correspond to the fashion designer's current collection. The interior - with women's apparel on the ground floor and menswear in the basement - is completely white. A system of hanging displays highlights the space. Garments hang on fluorescent tubes suspended from the ceiling, and shiny glazed tiles provide shelving. Tree trunks scattered throughout the shop add a touch of simplicity. Explaining his motives for creating such a surprising shop, Arthur Casas says that Japanese people, being quite curious, 'don't need to see merchandise on display in a window like Brazilians do'.

Studio Arthur Casas
Rua Itapolis 818
01245 000 São Paulo
Brazil

T: +55 (0)11 2182 7500
E: sp@arthurcasas.com
W: www.arthurcasas.com

Photography: Eusike Fukumochi

03

1 Menswear
2 Womenswear
3 Display table
4 Fitting room
5 Bench
6 Cash desk
7 Storage

Ground Floor   Basement

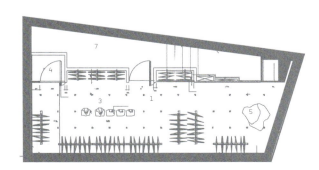

All Saints
Brinkworth

WHERE:	LONDON, UNITED KINGDOM
WHEN:	AUGUST 2008
CLIENT:	ALL SAINTS
SHOP CONSTRUCTOR:	RTS CONTRACTS
TOTAL FLOOR AREA (M²):	370

|||||||||||||||||||||||||||||||||||||||

BRINKWORTH IS AN INDEPENDENT INTERIOR AND BRAND CONSULTANCY, FORMED IN 1990 BY FOUNDER AND COMPANY DIRECTOR ADAM BRINKWORTH, WHO - ALONG WITH DIRECTORS KEVIN BRENNAN AND DAVID HURREN - CURRENTLY HEADS A STAFF OF OVER 35. ACTIVE PROJECTS WORLDWIDE INCLUDE BRAND DESIGN, RETAIL DESIGN, WORKPLACE DESIGN, BAR AND RESTAURANT DESIGN, EXHIBITION DESIGN AND DOMESTIC DESIGN. THE MULTIDISCIPLINARY TEAM OFFERS A TOTAL CREATIVE PROGRAMME INCORPORATING IN-HOUSE SOLUTIONS AT ALL STAGES, FROM INCEPTION TO COMPLETION. CLIENTS OF THE LONDON-BASED COMPANY INCLUDE THE SCIENCE MUSEUM, HEINEKEN, SELFRIDGES, KAREN MILLEN, DINOS CHAPMAN, DIESEL AND CASIO.

|||||||||||||||||||||||||||||||||||||||

Brinkworth and All Saints have collaborated for a number of years, continually redefining and developing the unique store design that has made All Saints a runaway success. Their collaboration recently resulted in a new, exciting flagship store in London's famous Camden Lock. Demonstrating the strength of the All Saints brand, Brinkworth designed an environment that directly reflects the confident personality of the label and intentionally challenges the competition with a bold design statement. The shop front features no window, simply a vast, solid, riveted-steel façade running the full height of the store, reminiscent of Victorian gasometers from the industrial age. A sliding, steel-framed timber door is the only entrance, providing a focused and powerful view of the space within. A trademark All Saints ram-skull logo is etched into the steel, which has been allowed to rust over time, further adding to the overall aesthetic. Inside, the scale of the shop front is emphasized by a double-height void. Here a wall carries a system of chains for hanging and displaying products, while still revealing the I-beam support structure of the shop front behind. To further exaggerate the sense of height, the staircase connecting the three floors resembles a towering lift-shaft cage, clad in polished copper fencing on a steel frame. Complementing this, a carefully designed range of materials and techniques, which have become the All Saints hallmark, includes shot-blasted brickwork, distressed-ceramic tiles and reclaimed-timber floors. All Saints source reclaimed furniture and modify the pieces to create industrial-looking display units, which complete the overall ethos of the brand.

Brinkworth
4–6 Ellsworth Street
London E2 0AX
United Kingdom

T +44 (0)20 7613 5341
E info@brinkworth.co.uk
W www.brinkworth.co.uk

Photography: Alex Franklin

01

01   A windowless façade made
of riveted steel evokes images
of Victorian gasometers in the
industrial age.

02   A trademark All Saints
ram—skull logo is etched into the
steel wall that fronts the shop.

03   A sliding, steel—framed
timber door is the only entrance
to the shop.

04   The staircase, which resembles a towering lift—shaft cage, is clad in polished copper fencing on a steel frame.

05   Chains on one wall - used for hanging and otherwise displaying products - reveal the structure of the shop front behind.

06   A carefully designed range of materials and techniques has become the All Saints hallmark.

Barbie® Shanghai
Slade Architecture

WHERE: SHANGHAI, CHINA
WHEN: MARCH 2009
CLIENT: MATTEL
SHOP CONSTRUCTOR: EDG INTERNATIONAL
ARCHITECT: AD INCORPORATED (CHINA)
TOTAL FLOOR AREA (M²):   3800

JAMES SLADE AND HAYES SLADE FOUNDED SLADE ARCHITECTURE IN 2002. SLADE ARCHITECTURE HAS DESIGNED AND REALIZED A WIDE VARIETY OF PROJECTS, BOTH LARGE AND SMALL, IN THE UNITED STATES, EUROPE, KOREA AND CHINA. THE WORK OF SLADE ARCHITECTURE IS CHARACTERIZED BY INNOVATION, CREATIVITY AND QUALITY. THEIR PROJECTS HAVE BEEN RECOGNIZED INTERNATIONALLY. THEIR WORK HAS BEEN EXHIBITED AT NEW YORK CITY'S MUSEUM OF MODERN ART, THE NATIONAL BUILDING MUSEUM, THE DEUTSCHES ARCHITEKTURMUSEUM, THE SWISS INSTITUTE, THE VENICE BIENNALE AND OTHER NATIONAL AND INTERNATIONAL VENUES.

Mattel wanted a store in which Barbie® would be a heroine: an environment that would present Barbie® as a global lifestyle brand by building on Barbie's® historical link to fashion. Barbie® Shanghai is the first fully realized expression of this broader vision. Slade Architecture was asked to design the complete package: exterior, interior, fixtures and furnishings.
Slade's design is a sleek, fun, unapologetically feminine interpretation of Barbie®: past, present and future. Combining references to product packaging, decorative arts and architectural iconography, Slade created a modern retail identity that reflects Barbie's® cutting-edge fashion sense and history. The entirely new façade is made of two layers. Moulded, translucent polycarbonate interior panels reference decorative architectural and fashion elements. A whimsical lattice frit printed on the exterior glass panels reinforces the shapes of the interior, moulded panels. The two layers interact dynamically through reflection, shadow and distortion. Visitors initially enveloped by the curvaceous, pearlescent surfaces of the lobby step into a pink escalator tube that takes them from the bustle of the street to the double-height main floor. The central element of the store is a three-storey spiral staircase enclosed by 800 Barbie® dolls. The staircase links three retail floors: the women's floor (women's fashions, couture, cosmetics and accessories), the doll floor (dolls, designer doll gallery, doll accessories and books) and the girls' floor (girls' fashions, shoes and accessories).

>>

01

01   The new façade was designed by Slade Architecture for the existing structure. Graphics for the ceramic frit on the outer layer of the façade were designed by BIG, the branding and design division of Ogilvy & Mather, who also worked with Mattel on the overall creative concept for Barbie® Shanghai.

02   Linking the three retail floors is a staircase enclosed by 800 Barbie® dolls.

03   Beauty products or nail art - the Barbie® Beauty Bar has it all.

02

Slade Architecture worked with Chute Gerdeman Retail to develop two in-store activities: at the Barbie® Design Centre, located on the doll floor, a girl can design her personalized Barbie®; and at the Barbie® Fashion Stage, located on the girls' floor, she can take part in a real runway show. The Barbie® café-restaurant and gelato bar is on the sixth floor. Throughout the retail areas, Slade played with differences in scale between dolls, girls and women. The designers reinforced the feeling of youth and the possibilities of an unapologetically girlish outlook (regardless of age) by mixing reality and fantasy and keeping play and fun at the forefront. The result is a space in which optimism and possibility reign supreme as expressions of core Barbie® attributes.

Slade Architecture
150 Broadway, Suite 807
New York, NY 10038
USA

T +1 212 677 6380
E info@sladearch.com
W www.sladearch.com

Photography: Iwan Baan

05

04   View of the Barbie® fashion
collection on the Everything Girl
floor. Visible above is the Collector
Doll area and the Designer Gallery outside of the Barbie® Design
Centre.

05   The Candy Wall and the
Beauty Bar turn into an interactive
play wall in the Collector Doll area
above.

07

06

06   Shown here is a huge selection of Barbie® dolls and related
toy products on the floor that is
completely dedicated to them.

07   Pink mannequins welcome
customers to the Dream Lobby.

08   Shoppers enter a pink
escalator tube to reach the
main retail area.

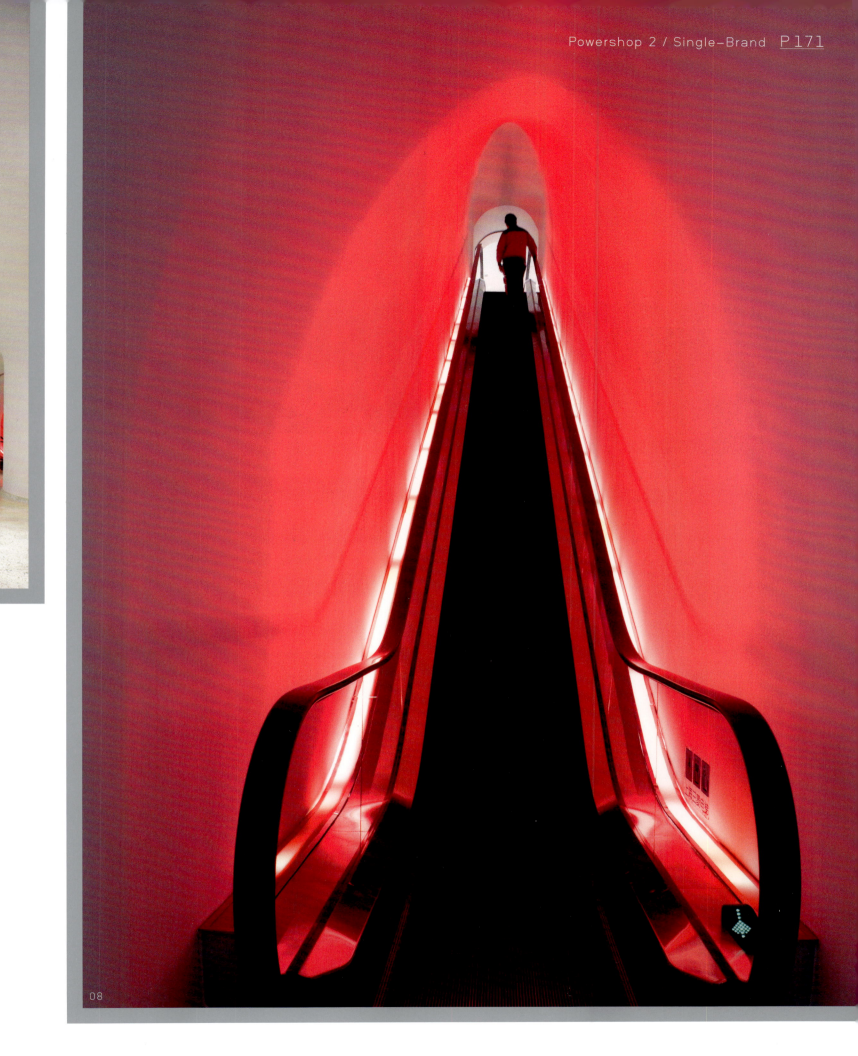

Campus
::dan pearlman

WHERE:	DÜSSELDORF, GERMANY
WHEN:	APRIL 2008
CLIENT:	CAMPUS BY MARC O'POLO
SHOP CONSTRUCTOR:	KNOBLAUCH LADENBAU
TOTAL FLOOR AREA (M²):	220
BUDGET (€):	220,000

IN 1999 NICOLE SROCK-STANLEY, VOLKER KATSCHINSKI, MARCUS FISCHER AND KIERAN STANLEY FOUNDED ::DAN PEARLMAN, AN AGENCY WITH A FOCUS ON BRAND ARCHITEC-TURE AND EXPERIENCE ARCHITECTURE. THE BERLIN-BASED FIRM RESPONDS TO THE VARIOUS COMMUNICATION-RELATED OBJECTIVES OF ITS CLIENTS BY MEANS OF FOUR INDEPENDENT SPECIALIST UNITS: STRATEGY, RETAIL, EXHIBITION AND MEDIA.

Campus is a student-inspired brand belonging to Marc O'Polo, a Swedish manufacturer of casual clothes. Focusing on the youthful, value-conscious, innovative consumer, Campus expresses a sense of freedom and independence. The brand stands for quality fashions that are sexy, authentic and sporty. The collection celebrates the relaxed lifestyle of the affluent student. Creating an image for the Campus brand fell to :: dan pearlman, which aimed for a retail environment with a personal, cosy atmosphere. The designers based the interior-design con-cept on the university lifestyle, using details like bikes, loving cups and typical college accessories as accents to enliven the store. Quality furniture made of dark-stained marsh oak reflects the venerable splendour of traditional educational institutions. Gold and blue, the Campus corporate colours, appear throughout the store. A new shop design and brand-alone stores allow Campus to present itself as an independent casual-lifestyle label rather than Marc O'Polo's tag-along kid brother.

::dan pearlman
Kiefholzstrasse 1
12435 Berlin
Germany

T +49 (0)30 5300 0560
E office@danpearlman.com
W www.danpearlman.com

Photography: Christoph Musiol

First floor

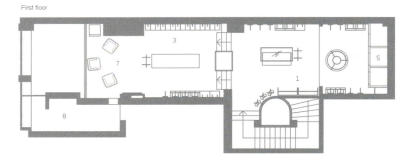

Ground floor

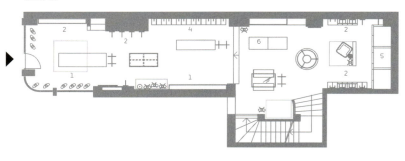

1 Women
2 Men
3 Denim women
4 Denim men
5 Fitting rooms
6 Cash desk
7 Lounge
8 Storage

01

02

01   Customized by an artist, walls surrounding the natural-stone staircase feature statements that reflect the attitudes of the young, stylish 'Campus generation'.

02   The store calls to mind the typically cluttered but cosy look of a student's room.

03   Irregular plaster structures and hand-mounted wall panels add to the collegiate atmosphere.

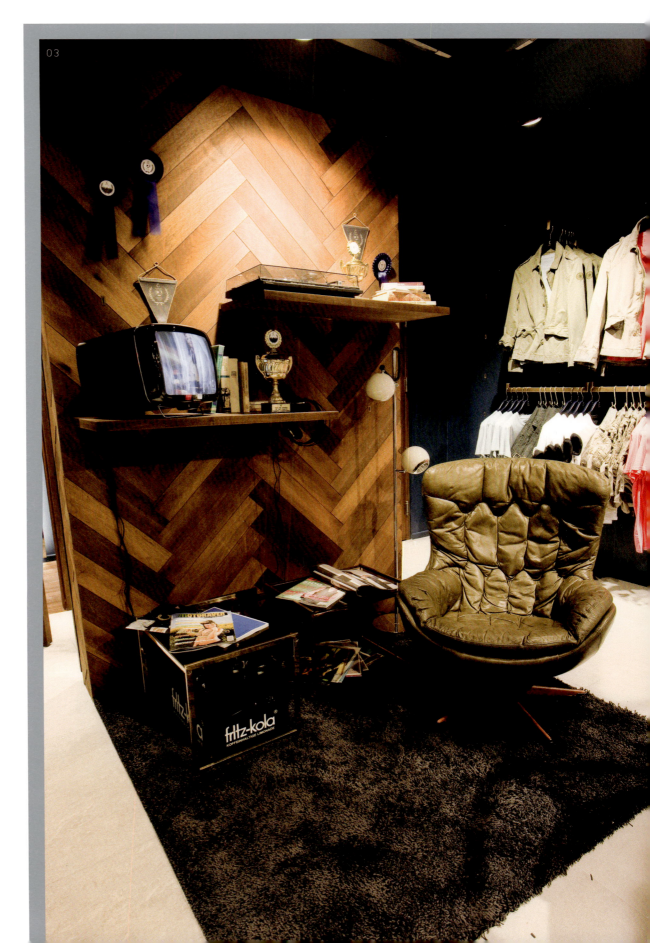

03

Cinque
Pankrath

WHERE: BERLIN, GERMANY
WHEN: JANUARY 2009
CLIENTS: RESPECTMEN AND
                              CINQUE MODA
SHOP CONSTRUCTORS: MINGA NETWORK AND
                   FOLLENIUS UND MARTIN TISCHLEREI
TOTAL FLOOR AREA (M²):   150
BUDGET (€):   100,000

ASTRID PANKRATH FOUNDED PANKRATH ON HER OWN IN 2005. TWO YEARS LATER SHE WENT INTO PARTNERSHIP WITH SEBASTIAN WINDISCH. THE BERLIN-BASED FIRM FOCUSES ON THE DESIGN OF RETAIL, OFFICE AND RESIDENTIAL INTERIORS.

Cinque - 'the embodiment of Italian style' - wants to reflect an image of inner passion and emotion with a smart, cool appearance. The objective of the clothing brand's new partner shop interior, designed by Pankrath, was to put these characteristics 'on stage'. Key words in the brief were 'innovation', 'timelessness', 'originality', 'authenticity', 'independence' and 'pragmatism'. Pankrath used the colours of the logo, red and black, as a starting point. Applying the red underline directly to the interior, the designers had it extend across the entire width of the black-painted oak floor and up the wall to the ceiling, from which hangs a long black-steel catwalk. Garments on a rail fastened to the bottom of the catwalk hover above the floor. The logo itself is clearly present at the very rear of the store, illuminated and mounted above a large wall mirror, which opens up the space and creates an illusion of infinity.

Pankrath
Stargarder Strasse 56 A
10437 Berlin
Germany

T +49 (0)30 4403 3438
E wir@pankrath-plus.de
W www.pankrath-plus.de

Photography: Stefan Maria Rother

1 Suspended catwalk
2 Fitting room
3 Cash desk
4 Staff area
5 Lavatory

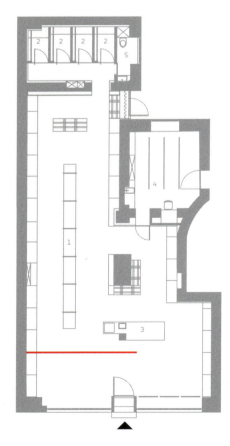

01   The red line featured in the Cinque logo also appears on the oak floor of the shop interior.

02   Indirect lighting is integrated into the wall panels.

03   A black-steel catwalk hangs from the ceiling at the centre of the shop.

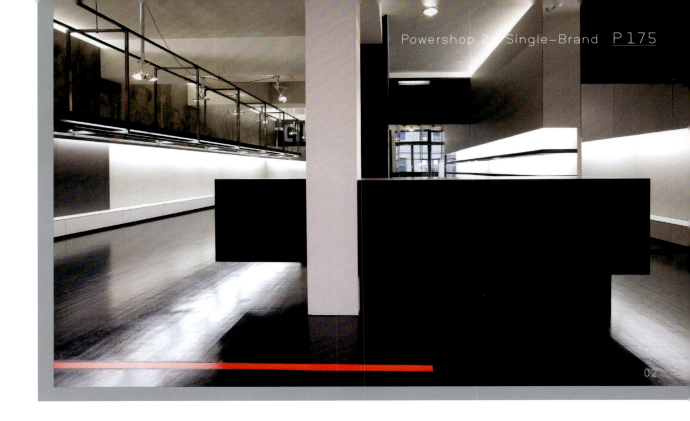

Citrus Notes
Ito Masaru Design Project / SEI

01

WHERE:	TOKYO, JAPAN
WHEN:	FEBRUARY 2006
CLIENT:	NOTES,INC
SHOP CONSTRUCTOR:	D.BRAIN
TOTAL FLOOR AREA (M²):	95

|||||||||||||||||||||||||||||||||||||||||||||||||||

A MAN WITH A SHARP SENSE OF FASHION, MASARU ITO WAS BORN IN OSAKA, JAPAN, IN 1961. AFTER GRADUATING FROM TOKYO ZOKEI UNIVERSITY IN 1987, HE ESTABLISHED ITO MASARU DESIGN PROJECT / SEI, A FIRM WITH A STRONG FOCUS ON RETAIL SPACES. MASARU ITO'S MOTTO IS: 'ALWAYS CONSIDER AN INTERIOR DESIGN FROM THE CONSUMER'S POINT OF VIEW.'

|||||||||||||||||||||||||||||||||||||||||||||||||||

Citrus Notes is a clothing brand known for quality, luxury and sex appeal. The interior of the label's Omotesando (Tokyo) outlet was designed by Ito Masaru Design Project / SEI. Most of Citrus Notes' retail interiors express a regal sense of glamour embodied in a relatively simple plan. In consideration of the creative character of Omotesando, however, Masaru Ito aimed for a space that would stimulate the imagination.Colours, materials and textures correspond to the merchandise: sexy fashions with an air of luxury. A black-tiled façade - the counterpoint of a largely white interior - attracts the attention of passers-by. Inside, black tiles reappear on the cash desk and its backdrop. Organic forms evoking fantasy and creativity include a custom-made carpet featuring a rose motif, and a lowered ceiling that follows the curves of the shop. A chandelier designed by Angelo Mangiarotti enhances the glamorous ambience, as do display tables and a bench, all in white leather.

Ito Masaru Design Project / SEI
#101 Daikanyama Tower
1-35-11, Ebisunishi, Shibuya-ku
150-0021 Tokyo
Japan

T +81 (0)3 5784 3201
E sei@itomasaru.com
W www.itomasaru.com

Photography: Kozo Takayama

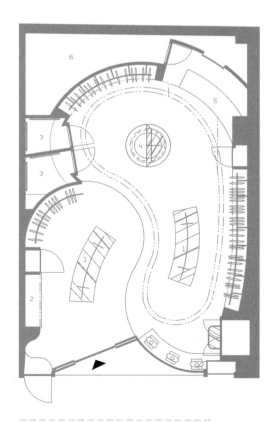

1 Display table
2 Display shelves
3 Fitting room
4 Seating area
5 Cash desk
6 Storage

01   A lowered ceiling follows the flowing lines of the retail space.

02   The black-tiled façade makes a sharp contrast to the predominantly white interior.

03   Display tables feature button-tufted white leather and an elevated glass panel that provides each table with two levels.

01

02

Closed
e15 Design und Distribution

WHERE:	ANTWERP, BELGIUM
WHEN:	AUGUST 2007
CLIENT:	CLOSED
SHOP CONSTRUCTOR:	DS INTERIEURBOUW
TOTAL FLOOR AREA (M²):	86
BUDGET (€):	190,000

INSPIRED BY ART, CULTURE AND FASHION, E15 IS AN INTERNATIONALLY RENOWNED BRAND WHOSE SERVICES INCLUDE ALL PHASES OF ARCHITECTURE AND INTERIOR DESIGN: FROM CONCEPTUAL DESIGN TO CONSTRUCTION-SITE SUPERVISION, AS WELL AS THE DEVELOPMENT AND PRODUCTION OF CUSTOM FURNITURE AND INTERIOR FITTINGS. A KEY AREA IS THE DEVELOPMENT OF CORPORATE ARCHITECTURE FOR SMALL BUSINESSES, MULTINATIONALS AND EVERYTHING IN BETWEEN.

In 2004, Hamburg-based fashion label Closed began its collaboration with e15's architecture and interior-design team, which led to the realization of the first Closed flagship store in central Hamburg. Since then, e15 has furnished Closed stores and showrooms worldwide and has helped shape an unmistakable corporate architecture and establish a distinctive global reputation for the Hamburg label. Closed stores and showrooms designed by e15 include those in Hamburg, Sylt, Düsseldorf, Vienna, Munich, Amsterdam, Milan, Antwerp, Montpellier, Lyon, Paris and Hong Kong. In Antwerp, the main challenges were a façade in need of remodelling and the creation of a smooth transition between exterior and interior. Replacing the original façade are room-high glass panels that stretch the entire width of the premises. The retail concept consists of natural, deliberately un-designed features that are both casual and polished. The space contains purpose-designed furniture, vintage cabinets and farmhouse tables - all part of the brand architecture that e15 has developed for Closed.

e15 Design und Distribution
Hospitalstrasse 4
61440 Oberursel
Germany

T +49 (0)6171 97950
E e15@e15.com
W www.e15.com

Photography: courtesy of Closed

03

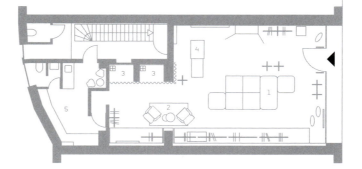

1 Display tables
2 Lounge area
3 Fitting room
4 Cash desk
5 Back office

01   The façade was redesigned
to create a smooth transition from
the outside of the shop to the
retail interior of this Closed store
in Antwerp.

02   A combination of purpose-
designed and vintage furniture
is part of the brand architecture
that distinguishes Closed.

03   One eye-catching black
wall features images in gold
graphic foil.

Double Standard Clothing
Propeller Design

WHERE:	TOKYO, JAPAN
WHEN:	NOVEMBER 2008
CLIENT:	FILM
SHOP CONSTRUCTOR:	NITTEN, SHIFT, N2 AND SOGO FURNITURE
TOTAL FLOOR AREA (M²):	1033

||||||||||||||||||||||||||||||||||||||

YOSHIHIRO KAWASAKI ESTABLISHED PROPELLER INTEGRATERS IN 2000 AND PROPELLER DESIGN IN 2006. HIS COMPANY IS ACTIVE IN THE FIELDS OF INTERIOR DESIGN FOR BOUTIQUES, BEAUTY SALONS, SHOWROOMS, EXHIBITION SPACES AND RESTAURANTS. IT IS ALSO INVOLVED IN GRAPHIC, DISPLAY AND PRODUCT DESIGN.

||||||||||||||||||||||||||||||||||||||||||||

Masahisa Takino, the president of FILM, established the fashion brand Double Standard Clothing. Double Standard Clothing consists of four sub-brands: DSC, a line of medium-priced clothes; Sov., a collection of more exclusive fashions; D/him', a menswear brand; and DSC-accessories. Yoshihiro Kawasaki of Propeller Design was asked to come up with a concept for a flagship store, which would also serve as a pressroom. A large space - more than 1000 m² - was found in the Aoyama district of Tokyo. The diverse styles that make up Double Standard Clothing's multi-brand image demanded a 'double standard' interior concept full of antitheses: an environment both modern and classic, both cool and emotional, both casual and feminine. The shop is divided into four rooms: three for the three clothing labels, including accessories, and one which is used as an office. The black-painted ceiling makes a striking contrast to walls and floor clad in white ceramic tiles. All furniture is based on straight lines, but walls curve gently at the corners. Display units made from metal and glass juxtaposed with furniture featuring wood and leather provide another interesting contrast. Mirrors are arranged to give the interior an abstract air and, at the same time, to enlarge the space optically. Despite the many contrasts, Propeller Design has managed to create a flagship store that feels like a coherent whole.

Propeller Design
5-9 Takezono-cho
659-0055 Ashiya, Hyogo
Japan

T +81 (0)797 255 144
E info@propeller-design.com
W www.propeller-design.com

Photography: Nacása & Partners

01

01   The flagship store also functions as a pressroom.

02   The interior is a combination of modern and classic elements.

03   High-gloss ceramic tiles are used for the floor, while the walls are covered in matt 3D-patterned ceramic tiles.

04   Black epoxy paint is used for the ceiling.

03

02

04

05   The large display and
storage cube immediately attracts
the customers attention.

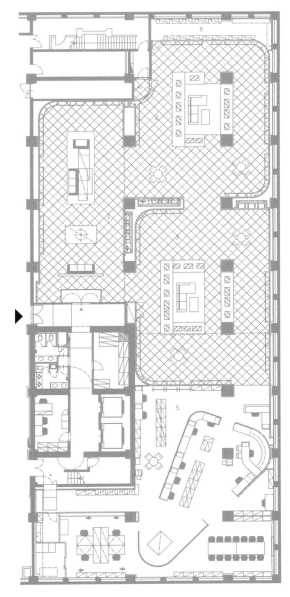

1 D/him area
2 DSC area
3 Sov. area
4 Fitting room
5 Office
6 Storage

06 A black–lacquered Diamond billiard table provides visitors with some entertainment.

EQ:IQ
AlexChoi design & Partners

WHERE:	BEIJING, CHINA
WHEN:	JUNE 2007
CLIENT:	GRI GROUP
SHOP CONSTRUCTOR:	ART-WELL ENGINEERING
TOTAL FLOOR AREA (M²):	390
BUDGET (€):	340,000

|||||||||||||||||||||||||||||||||||||||||||||||

ALEXCHOI DESIGN & PARTNERS WAS FOUNDED BY ALEX CHOI IN 1997. THE HONG KONG-BASED FIRM SPECIALIZES IN COMMERCIAL PROJECTS SUCH AS BRANDING, EXHIBITION DESIGN AND INTERIOR DESIGN FOR RETAIL AND OFFICE ENVIRONMENTS. THE TEAM HAS ALSO DESIGNED AND REALIZED A NUMBER OF HOSPITALITY AND RESIDENTIAL PROJECTS. ALEXCHOI DESIGN & PARTNERS FOCUSES ON ROLL-OUTS IN THE CHINESE MARKET. CLIENTS INCLUDE SUCH NAMES AS AZONA A02, AVEDA, BMW AND QUICKSILVER.

|||||||||||||||||||||||||||||||||||||||||||||||

EQ:IQ is an apparel, accessory and home-decoration brand belonging to the Hong Kong-headquartered GRI Group. Launched in 1999, the brand targets modern, confident, well-travelled women from about 25 to 55 years of age. AlexChoi design & Partners transferred the characteristics of the EQ:IQ brand to the interior of a new shop in Beijing.
The designers aimed for a concept that - much like EQ:IQ fashion collections - is minimalist in style but rich in detail and texture. They divided the U-shaped store into three retail zones. Accessible from the main entrance is an area where the most important pieces of the current collection can be found. A custom-made chandelier, which immediately grabs the customer's attention, consists of a cluster of rods made from solid ash, acrylic resin, brass, and metal painted matte white. Below the chandelier is a rug featuring the EQ:IQ branding icon: a tree. Farther along and to one side, a narrower area contains fashions from the young-women's collection, which are showcased on transparent shelves supported by vertical brass tubing across from - and contrasting with - a horizontal pine structure that screens off the fitting area. Shoes and bags are displayed in the third zone, which has another point of access: the entrance to the store from the shopping mall. A nearby escalator inspired the white staircase in the shop window, a tiered element that serves as a product display. The exterior of the shop is wrapped in a tree pattern that unifies the whole. High-intensity discharge downlights give the store a sparkling appearance after dark.

AlexChoi design & Partners
Unit A1, 2/F, Cheung Kong Factory Building
5 Cheung Shun Street
Lai Chi Kok, Kln, Hong Kong
China

T +852 2893 5907
E pm@alexchoi.com.hk
W www.alexchoi.com.hk

Photography: AlexChoi design & Partners

01   EQ:IQ's branding icon is a tree, which the designers used many times as a reference to both client and merchandise. Here the silhouette of a tree becomes a highly contemporary chandelier.

02   Black rugs adorned with images of white trees are scattered throughout the store.

03   A tree pattern even covers the store's shiny façade.

eq:iq

01

02

03

107B

04   Inside the shop, the white staircase that functions as a wall display matches an escalator outside, on the other side of the wall.

05   White powder-coated steel racks carry the latest fashion collection.

1 Main collection
2 Young-women's collection
3 Shoes and bags
4 Fitting rooms
5 Cash desk

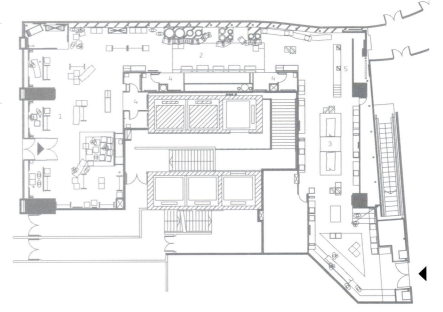

Escada
CAPS Architecture
Interior Design

WHERE: BEVERLY HILLS, CA, USA
WHEN: MAY 2007
CLIENT: ESCADA
SHOP CONSTRUCTORS: PWI CONTRACTORS
                                AND GANTER
TOTAL FLOOR AREA (M²):   580

ZÜRICH-BASED CAPS, FOUNDED IN 1997 BY FRENCH PRINCIPAL CHRISTOPHE CARPENTE, IS A MULTIDISCIPLINARY ARCHITECTURE AND DESIGN COMPANY OPERATING ON THE GLOBAL STAGE. CAPS HAS WORKED ON FOUR CONTINENTS WITH SOME OF THE WORLD'S MOST PRESTIGIOUS BRANDS. KNOWN FOREMOST FOR INNOVATIVE AND AWARD-WINNING RETAIL ARCHITECTURE AND DESIGN, CAPS HAS EVOLVED THROUGH A JOURNEY OF EXPERIENCES. NOW A FULL-SERVICE COMPANY, CAPS IS ALSO RENOWNED FOR RESIDENTIAL WORK, CORPORATE PROJECTS, PRODUCT DESIGN AND MERCHANDISING PROGRAMMES. CAPS SPECIALIZES IN HANDLING THE ENTIRE SERVICE ASPECT OF ANY PROJECT. CAPS' PHILOSOPHY IS A STRONG BELIEF IN PARTNERSHIP, AND ITS FLEXIBLE WORK STYLE IS EXEMPLIFIED BY A WIDE VARIETY OF CLIENTS AND PROJECTS.

The design of a new retail identity for Escada called for a delicate balance, including less emphasis on pure glamour in favour of a more subtle expression of elegance and contemporary luxury.
Responsible for Escada's design is Zürich-based CAPS, whose team converted a 580-m² space in a huge building on ultra-chic Rodeo Drive in Beverly Hills. The retail space is divided into product areas featuring Escada's Mainline, Sport and Event collections, as well as an area for accessories. Black granite flooring boasting tiles in alternating textures (honed and highly polished) was used throughout the store as a unifying element, while each product segment appears in an individualized environment with walls in various gradations of warm grey and recessed fabric panels and furniture finishes in collection-specific colours. The result is a sequence of en suite rooms, each with a distinctive residential atmosphere. The sparkle of the reflecting, platinum-plated ceramic tiles and the brilliance of chandeliers covered in metallic mesh make a striking contrast to the dark elegance of the background. The Mainline Collection is in an area featuring purple silk and brown, shiny fabric-clad panels.

>>

01   The prestigious Wilshire Hotel is a perfect match for a brand that radiates elegance and contemporary luxury.

02   Inspired by the dark paintings of Pierre Soulage, the designers chose textured, black-lacquered wood panels for the wall behind the cash desk.

03   The Escada-branded atrium welcomes the customers. Covered in platinum-plated tiles, the atrium separates the entrance area from the rest of the interior.

098

In the section housing the Sport Collection, shiny, wavy-textured, brown-and-beige fabrics line wall niches, generating a contemporary, high-tech atmosphere. Materials selected for the most exclusive area, where shoppers find the Event Collection, include a silky plissé in anthracite grey, gleaming black leatherette and an undulating fabric in silver metallic: all chosen to enhance the preciousness of Escada's elegant gowns and dresses. Adding a strong rhythmic note to the series of product areas are a number of centrally positioned tables with glossy, black-lacquered, opaque finishes covered by a display in crystal-clear glass with finely engraved patterns, a trademark of the Escada design concept. Each round table sits on a deep-pile woollen rug that matches the fabric wall panels.
In tune with the cool but refined personality of the Escada woman, a visit to the store is like a stroll through the rooms of a luxurious mansion that radiates an air of refined opulence.

CAPS Architecture Interior Design
Stampfenbachstrasse 48
8006 Zürich
Switzerland

T +41 (0)44 3652 365
E info@caps-architects.com
W www.caps-architects.com

Photography: Jean-Philippe Defaut

04

05

04   An en suite view through
the store which radiates refined
elegance.

05   Designed by India Madhavi,
a side table in platinum—plated
ceramic enhances the residential
atmosphere of each room. Around
it are architect Mies van der
Rohe's Barcelona chairs clad in
white leather.

06   All areas of the store feature
a Nero Assoluto granite floor with
a pattern of honed and polished
tiles: an underlying surface that
imbues the interior with a sense
of coherence.

07   Reminiscent of furniture
found in fine libraries is a
built-in-unit used for displaying
accessories.

Fashion Studio Tamara Radivojevic
Dsignedby.

WHERE:	BELGRADE, SERBIA
WHEN:	JANUARY 2007
CLIENT:	PEMIT DOO
TOTAL FLOOR AREA (M²):	56
BUDGET (€):	30,000

||||||||||||||||||||||||||||||||||||||||||||||||

DSIGNEDBY. WAS FOUNDED IN 2008 BY IVA (VISUAL–COMMUNICATION PROFESSIONAL) AND IRENA KILIBARDA (ARCHITECT), WHO HAD PREVIOUSLY DONE FREELANCE WORK IN THE AREAS OF ARCHITECTURE, WEB DESIGN, PACKAGING DESIGN AND INTERIOR DESIGN.

||||||||||||||||||||||||||||||||||||||||||||||||

With a floor area of only 47 m² and the need for a private studio and a retail area, fashion designer Tamara Radivojevic called on the team at Dsignedby.
The designers lowered the floor and simultaneously raised the height of the ceiling to 4.4 m, making it possible to add a mezzanine gallery for Radivojevic's studio, leaving the entrance level free to accommodate the retail area. High windows provide the entire space with plenty of daylight. A tin window bench hides the heating system and serves as a platform for mannequins visible to passers-by. Stainless-steel fixtures above the windows enable frequent display changes. Most of the current fashion collection hangs from a single rail that runs along one concrete wall. The lighting scheme was designed to emphasize this rail. The store opening turned Belgrade's Strahinjica Bana Street - known mostly for its restaurants and bars - into an interesting promenade for up-and-coming fashion designers.

Dsignedby. / Irena Kilibarda
Internacionalnih Brigada 20
11118 Belgrade
Serbia

T +381 (0)11 3089 107
E contact@dsigned-by.com
W www.dsigned-by.com

Photography: Ana Kostic

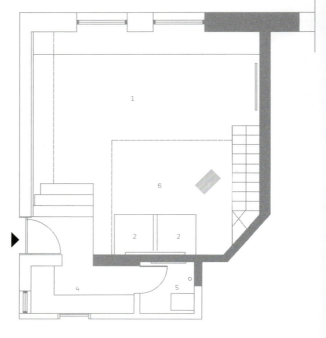

01   A single rail holds most of the current fashion collection.

02   The fashion designer's private studio occupies the mezzanine gallery. The glass is laminated with purple Vanceva interlayers.

1 Retail space
2 Fitting room
3 Cash desk
4 Kitchen
5 Lavatory
6 Gallery

Filippa K
Aaro
Arkitektkontor

WHERE: THE HAGUE, THE NETHERLANDS
WHEN: OCTOBER 2008
CLIENT: FILIPPA K
TOTAL FLOOR AREA (M²): 140

||||||||||||||||||||||||||||||||||||||||||||||||||

AARO ARKITEKTKONTOR OFFERS CLIENTS A RANGE OF CREATIVE EXPERTISE THAT INCLUDES EVERYTHING FROM ARCHITECTURE AND FURNITURE DESIGN TO HISTORIC-PRESERVATION PROJECTS. CURRENT OWNERS, ARCHITECTS MARIANNE BORK-AARO AND BJÖRN AARO - PARTNERS IN PRIVATE LIFE AS WELL - FOUNDED THE COMPANY IN 1997. IN RECENT YEARS THE FIRM HAS SPECIALIZED IN COMMERCIAL INTERIORS.

||||||||||||||||||||||||||||||||||||||||||||||||||

Since 1997 Aaro Arkitektkontor has designed more than 60 shops for fashion label Filippa K in Germany, the Netherlands, Belgium, Switzerland, the Nordic countries and the USA. The distinctive style shared by all the brand's boutiques is constantly adapted, however, to provide each boutique with unique features and a look geared to the location.
The Filippa K shop in The Hague comprises a sequence of rooms done in contrasting materials. Bamboo used in the front section of the shop runs from the high ceiling over walls and floor to form a seamless surface interrupted only by white alcoves with rails for hanging clothes. The narrow entrance area opens into a more abstract world of white, where rather complex forms fully display the brand's Swedish simplicity. Men's and women's departments occupying opposite sides of the space are separated by fitting rooms. Stylishly patterned floor tiles add a touch of ornamental elegance to an otherwise austerely designed interior.

Aaro Arkitektkontor
Drakens Gränd 6
11130 Stockholm
Sweden

T +46 (0)8 4482 270
E aaroarkitektkontor@aaroarkitektkontor.se
W www.aaroarkitektkontor.se

Photography: Marita Janssen

01&02 Flooring for the section of the store at the back of the shop consists of white injection-moulded tiles that contrast nicely with bamboo flooring nearer the entrance.

03 Bamboo used as cladding in the area where fashions are displayed creates a tunnel effect that leads shoppers deeper into the space and ultimately to the far end of the interior.

01

Section

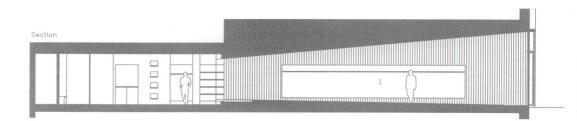

1

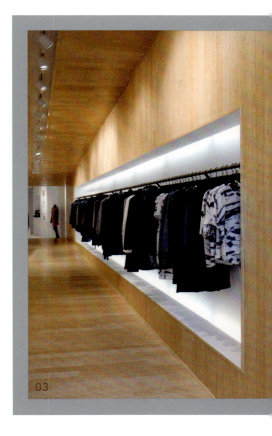

Floor plan

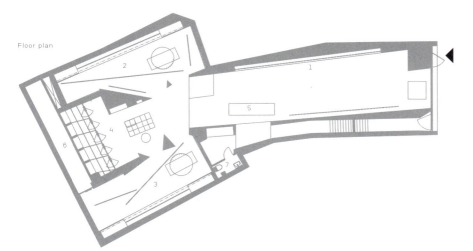

1 Display area
2 Women's clothing
3 Men's clothing
4 Fitting rooms
5 Cash desk
6 Storage
7 Lavatory

Firma
Pankrath

WHERE:	BERLIN, GERMANY
WHEN:	JULY 2008
CLIENT:	FIRMA BERLIN
SHOP CONSTRUCTOR:	INTERZONE
TOTAL FLOOR AREA (M²):	70
BUDGET (€):	70,000

||||||||||||||||||||||||||||||||||||||||||||||||||||

ASTRID PANKRATH FOUNDED PANKRATH ON HER OWN IN 2005. TWO YEARS LATER SHE WENT INTO PARTNERSHIP WITH SEBASTIAN WINDISCH. THE BERLIN-BASED FIRM FOCUSES ON THE DESIGN OF RETAIL, OFFICE AND RESIDENTIAL INTERIORS.

||||||||||||||||||||||||||||||||||||||||||||||||||||

Pankrath designed the Berlin store for German fashion brand Firma, which wanted an interior that would enhance Firma's identity as an elegant, cool, contemporary label. The interior was to be a spatial logo that would guarantee high quality: a three-dimensional business card. Sticking to the corporate colours of the brand, Pankrath used black, ecru and silver throughout the entire shop. The walls are covered partly in linoleum - a horizontal black border beneath an ecru border - and finished at the very top with a thin inlay of polished stainless steel. Displaying the fashion collection are two polished stainless-steel rails that start at the entrance - one on either side - and follow a generous curve along the walls to the back of the shop. In between, a black linoleum counter with polished stainless-steel edges appears to hover above the anthracite tiled floor. A light box placed over the entire length of the store casts a pleasant glow. The graphics were created by graphic designer Jutta Drewes.

Pankrath
Stargarder Strasse 56 A
10437 Berlin
Germany

T +49 (0)30 4403 3438
E wir@pankrath-plus.de
W www.pankrath-plus.de

Photography: Alexander Gnädinger

01

02

01

01   The logo was designed by Jutta Drewes.

02   Chrome light fixtures custom—made for the shop feature headlights taken from rally cars.

03   The cash desk - made from black linoleum and MDF - has a protective edge of polished stainless steel.

1 Retail area
2 Fitting room
3 Cash desk

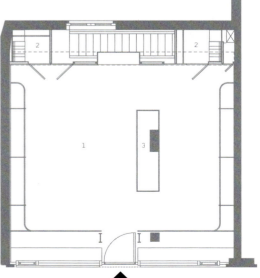

01

Fred Perry
JudgeGill

WHERE: LONDON, UNITED KINGDOM
WHEN: OCTOBER 2008
CLIENT: FRED PERRY
SHOP CONSTRUCTOR: PORTVIEW FIT-OUT
TOTAL FLOOR AREA (M²):   171
BUDGET(£):   270,000

|||||||||||||||||||||||||||||||||||||||||||||||||||

JUDGEGILL DESIGNS ENVIRONMENTS - EFFEC-
TIVE, MULTI-SENSORY SPACES FOR BRANDS
THAT LEAVE CUSTOMERS WITH POSITIVE,
ENDURING MEMORIES. THE FIRM'S CLIENT LIST
INCLUDES NAMES SUCH AS ADIDAS, FRED PERRY,
HERTZ, VIRGIN AND MTS. THE DESIGN COMPANY
HAS BUILT OVER 1000 STORES GLOBALLY. THE
LATEST PROJECTS ARE IN RUSSIA, CHINA, NORTH
AMERICA AND THE MIDDLE EAST.

|||||||||||||||||||||||||||||||||||||||||||||||||||

When sportswear brand Fred Perry wanted a
stronger presence in shopping areas, the company asked the designers at JudgeGill to create
a store concept that would get its customers in
touch with the brand's rich history and its future
as a fashion-savvy brand.
JudgeGill's solution - the 'Fred Perry authenticity concept' - is an evolving blueprint for a store
that brings the brand's past and future to life.
The design combines common elements inspired
by the Fred Perry brand with unique design features, such as vintage shop fittings, that give
each store an individual flavour. Archive photography, the iconic use of the laurel wreath -
Fred Perry's logo - and visual references to the
brand's classic T-shirt subtly endorse the Fred
Perry legacy. The design is flexible, allowing each
store to create a unique 'cultural reference point'
for Fred Perry that reinforces the brand's enduring relationship with the ever-changing worlds of
fashion, sport and youth culture.

JudgeGill
3 Cobourg Street
Manchester M1 3GY
United Kingdom

T +44 (0)161 228 3066
E info@judgegill.co.uk
W www.judgegill.co.u

Photography: Nick Hufton

01&03 Flooring is a combination
of Sondrio porcelain concept tiles
and reclaimed timber panels.

02   Unique vintage shop fittings
are featured in every Fred Perry
store.

04   JudgeGill applied Fred Perry
archive images to glass panels.

02

1 Footwear wall
2 Accessory wall
3 Polo display
4 Glass staircase display
5 Fitting room
6 Cash desk

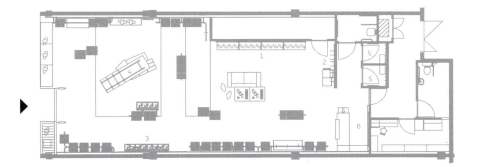

Fullcircle
Brinkworth

WHERE:	LONDON, UNITED KINGDOM
WHEN:	OCTOBER 2008
CLIENT:	FULLCIRCLE
SHOP CONSTRUCTOR:	SYNTEC
TOTAL FLOOR AREA (M²):	163

||||||||||||||||||||||||||||||||||||||||

BRINKWORTH IS AN INDEPENDENT INTERIOR AND BRAND CONSULTANCY, FORMED IN 1990 BY FOUNDER AND COMPANY DIRECTOR ADAM BRINKWORTH, WHO - ALONG WITH DIRECTORS KEVIN BRENNAN AND DAVID HURREN - CURRENTLY HEADS A STAFF OF OVER 35. ACTIVE PROJECTS WORLDWIDE INCLUDE BRAND DESIGN, RETAIL DESIGN, WORKPLACE DESIGN, BAR AND RESTAURANT DESIGN, EXHIBITION DESIGN AND DOMESTIC DESIGN. THE MULTI-DISCIPLINARY TEAM OFFERS A TOTAL CREATIVE PROGRAMME INCORPORATING IN-HOUSE SOLUTIONS AT ALL STAGES, FROM INCEPTION TO COMPLETION. CLIENTS OF THE LONDON-BASED COMPANY INCLUDE THE SCIENCE MUSEUM, HEINEKEN, SELFRIDGES, KAREN MILLEN, ALL SAINTS, DIESEL AND CASIO.

||||||||||||||||||||||||||||||||||||||||

Commissioned to design Fullcircle's new flagship store in Westfield, London - a premium shopping destination - Brinkworth created a literal interpretation of the Fullcircle brand. A 'floating' white architectural box, set within the envelope of the existing space, was cut away to reveal a dramatic optical illusion that, when viewed from the entrance, describes a circle (12 m in diameter) at the rear of the store. Stark juxtapositions of overlapping materials and colours blur distinctions between floor, walls and ceiling. Beyond the crisp new box, rough-rendered grey walls and a ceiling fixture of mirror-finish stainless steel add contrast to the theme of 'revealed', which marks this space. A similar dramatic effect - visible to visitors leaving the shop - was created with the application of one-way reflective film to the display window. The dual optical illusion of both 'full circles' can be viewed from specific spots within the store, only to be distorted visually as the customer moves through the space. The strong, contrasting lines of the menswear collection and the softer, more textural contours of the women's collection appear on either side of the store, accentuated by a variety of materials and backdrops, while beautifully detailed contemporary fixtures and furniture seamlessly unite the two areas. Brinkworth collaborated with furniture company twentytwentyone, which supplied pieces by key British designers such as Tom Dixon, Matthew Hilton and Jasper Morrison, thus underpinning the British design ethos at the heart of the Fullcircle brand.

Brinkworth
4-6 Ellsworth Street
London E2 0AX
United Kingdom

T +44 (0)20 7613 5341
E info@brinkworth.co.uk
W www.brinkworth.co.uk

Photography: Alex Franklin and Louise Melchior

01

02

01   The different materials used for the floor accentuate the optically illusionary 'full circle'.

02   The detailed clothes rack is made from stainless steel with a mirror polished finish.

03   A variety of materials and backdrops were used to distinguish the women's department from the menswear section.

04   Felt Shade pendants, designed by Tom Dixon, enhance the fitting rooms.

05   The detailed clothes rack is made from stainless steel with a mirror polished finish.

H&M
Universal Design Studio

01

WHERE:	LOS ANGELES, CA, USA
WHEN:	AUGUST 2008
CLIENT:	H&M
ARCHITECT:	TEK ARCHITECTS

||||||||||||||||||||||||||||||||||||

UNIVERSAL DESIGN STUDIO IS A LONDON–BASED ARCHITECTURE, INTERIOR– AND INDUSTRIAL– DESIGN STUDIO SPECIALIZING IN SPATIAL IDEN– TITY AND BRANDED ENVIRONMENTS. FOUNDED IN 2001 BY EDWARD BARBER AND JAY OSGERBY, THE COMPANY OPENED A MELBOURNE OFFICE IN 2008. UNIVERSAL DESIGN STUDIO HAS UNDER– TAKEN PROJECTS FOR CLIENTS SUCH AS STELLA MCCARTNEY, VIRGIN ATLANTIC, UNITED ARROWS, SELFRIDGES AND THE V&A MUSEUM.

||||||||||||||||||||||||||||||||||||

Universal Design Studio has been working with H&M since 2007 to create a new architectural identity. The studio was originally asked to de- sign a new brand image to launch the brand's first flagship stores in Asia but the design proved so successful, that it is now being applied to H&M stores worldwide.
The seemingly random and unstructured design used to create both façade and interior of the retail space, is actually based on a rigid, geo- metric pattern, which can be repeated in numer- ous combinations to produce the illusion of a free following form. The Sunset Boulevard H&M store in Los Angeles is the first implementation of the concept. The dramatic, three–dimensional façade is constructed of aluminium panels with a painted finish. Each panel was folded into a modular re- lief in one of two variations. The studio achieved an irregular pattern, without the need for com- plicated fabrication, by rotating and staggering the panels. The façade panels feature interesting areas of perforation that, when lit from behind, reveal the irregular form beautifully after dark.

Universal Design Studio
35 Charlotte Road
London EC2A 3PG
United Kingdom

T +44 (0)20 7033 3881
E mail@universaldesignstudio.com
W www.universaldesignstudio.com

Photography: John Edward Linden

01   The H&M façade is clad in powder—coated aluminium panels.

02   The perforated, aluminium façade is lit from behind ensuring the store is clearly visible both during the day and at night.

03   H&M on Sunset Boulevard was the first store completed under Universal Design Studio's design direction, launching H&M's new brand identity.

Hugo Boss
Special Concept Store
Matteo Thun & Partners

WHERE:	NEW YORK, NY, USA
WHEN:	OCTOBER 2008
CLIENT:	HUGO BOSS
SHOP CONSTRUCTOR:	HUGO BOSS SHOP CONSTRUCTION TEAM
TOTAL FLOOR AREA (M²):	350

||||||||||||||||||||||||||||||||||||||||||||||||||

MATTEO THUN (BOLZANO, ITALY, 1952) STUDIED AT THE SALZBURG ACADEMY UNDER OSKAR KOKOSCHKA, TOOK HIS DEGREE IN ARCHITECTURE IN FLORENCE WITH ADOLFO NATALINI AND MOVED TO MILAN IN 1978, WHERE HE MET AND WORKED WITH ETTORE SOTTSASS. THUN AND HIS STAFF OF 50 PROFESSIONALS OFFER SERVICES IN ARCHITECTURE, INTERIOR DESIGN, PRODUCT DESIGN, COMMUNICATION AND STYLING.

||||||||||||||||||||||||||||||||||||||||||||||||||

The design of the Hugo Boss concept store in New York reflects the theme of the brand's Swiss subsidiary: 'mastering fashion flow'. Exemplifying a new merchandising concept, the store combines the four Boss lines and the Hugo brand to create a 'total look' that includes shoes and accessories.

Designed by Matteo Thun, the interior features a trelliswork shell of blanched oak, a reference to the superstructure of the brand's subsidiary and a reinforcement of its corporate identity. Lighting was designed in collaboration with A.J. Weissbard. Divided into two areas, the interior has a retail zone where fashions appear in burnished-steel and dark-brown lacquered displays, while showcases of glass and leather hold accessories. Customers enjoy refreshments at a Corian counter. The softer, warmer atmosphere of the fitting-room area relies on rugs, red velvet curtains, wood and a golden ceiling. The interior assimilates the anima of the surrounding Meatpacking District, embracing an austere aesthetic attuned to the *genius loci*.

Matteo Thun & Partners
Via Appiani 9
20121 Milan
Italy

T +39 02 6556 911
E info@matteothun.com
W www.matteothun.com

Photography: Paul Warchol for Hugo Boss

01   An LED system immerses the store's left and right walls in white light during the day, while providing more theatrical lighting at night.

02   The large blanched-oak structure, manufactured in Germany, is the basis of a flexible merchandising system. The same plug-in system is used for shelves, hooks and front-hanging solutions.

03   Wishing to preserve the link between the store and its surroundings - New York's famed Meatpacking District - the designers left the orignal concrete floor, columns and red-brick wall intact.

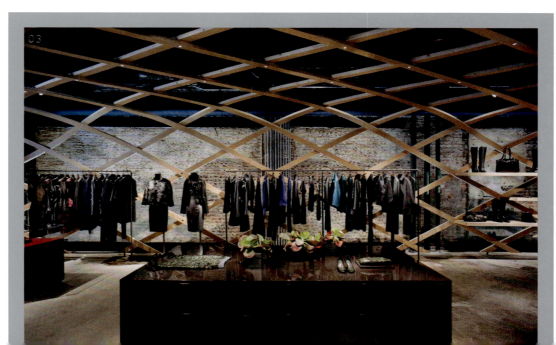

Irma Mahnel
d e signstudio regina dahmen–ingenhoven

WHERE:	MUNICH, GERMANY
WHEN:	NOVEMBER 2007
CLIENT:	IRMA MAHNEL
SHOP CONSTRUCTOR:	HEIKAUS
TOTAL FLOOR AREA (M²):	300

||||||||||||||||||||||||||||||||||||||||||||||||||||||||||||||||

HAVING COMPLETED HER STUDIES IN ARCHITEC-TURE AND ART, IN 2001 REGINA DAHMEN–IN-GENHOVEN FOUNDED THE DESIGN STUDIO THAT BEARS HER NAME. BASED IN DÜSSELDORF, SHE CURRENTLY WORKS WITH A STAFF OF FIVE AR-CHITECTS AND DESIGNERS. THE MAIN OBJECTIVE OF THE TEAM - WHICH SPECIALIZES IN HEALTH, WELLNESS, BEAUTY AND FASHION DESIGN - IS 'TO MAKE PEOPLE HAPPY'.

||||||||||||||||||||||||||||||||||||||||||||||||||||||||||||||||

The Munich store occupied by Irma Mahnel, an exclusive fashion label for larger sizes, is a cross section of concepts: exhibition, installation and shopping. Its look is inspired by the client, who highlights the sensuality of the female body in apparel that emphasizes curves. Consequently, the atmosphere here is sparkly, curvaceous and glamorous.
Designer Regina Dahmen-Ingenhoven has spot-lighted the woman who shops at Irma Mahnel by producing a retail interior that fits her like a second skin and makes her feel comfort-able. Trying on clothes here creates a relation-ship between the body and surrounding space. Thousands of reflections in a collage of circular mirrors on the wall reveal fascinatingly fragment-ed images, stimulating customers to rediscover themselves. Rather than tucking fitting rooms into a far corner, the designer has placed them in the middle of the room, all with an eye to making the customer the star of the show and giving her the attention she deserves.

d e signstudio regina dahmen–ingenhoven
Plange Mühle 1
40221 Düsseldorf
Germany

T +49 (0)211 3010 101
E info@drdi.de
W www.drdi.de

Photography: Studio Holger Knauf

01   Frank O. Gehry's Cloud lamps hover above the oval cash desk.

02   The fitting room is reflected in a mirror mounted on a parti-tion wall. Circles of different sizes have been cut out of a felt curtain to match the circular mirrors that form a collage on one wall of the interior.

03   Sparkly wallpaper covers the cash desk.

01

Jill by JillStuart
Line-Inc

WHERE:	TOKYO, JAPAN
WHEN:	AUGUST 2008
CLIENT:	SANEI INTERNATIONAL
SHOP CONSTRUCTOR:	MESSE
TOTAL FLOOR AREA (M²):	126

|||||||||||||||||||||||||||||||||||||||||||||||

TAKAO KATSUTA (1972) IS A JAPANESE DESIGNER AND A FORMER PARTNER OF EXIT METAL WORK SUPPLY. IN 2002 HE SET UP AN INDEPENDENT COMPANY, LINE-INC, WHICH SPECIALIZES IN THE DESIGN OF RETAIL INTERIORS BOTH AT HOME AND ABROAD. IN 2004 TAKAO KATSUTA ESTABLISHED ANOTHER CREATIVE ORGANIZATION, LINE-PRODUCTS.

|||||||||||||||||||||||||||||||||||||||||||||||

Jill by JillStuart debuted as the label's new casual brand in 2008. The interior design of the Jill shop in Shibuya, Tokyo, is a continuation of this stylish line of smart leisure-wear. Line-Inc created a repetitive motif based on octagons and used the pattern throughout the shop. The window frame that features this octagonal motif gives the shop a cosy, intimate atmosphere. Passerś-by spotting the window are curious about what's going on inside, while shoppers already in the store are made to feel snug and secure. Mosaic tiles, also highlighted by an octagonal pattern, have been used to clad columns and cash desk. Colours used for these tiles, as well as for flooring and furnishings, are warm brown, off-white and gold. At ground level, the rear wall features glass tiles with a pattern that evokes water and imbues the space with a light, refreshing touch of the outdoors.

Line-Inc
Kazami Bldg 2F+3F
1-1-6 Higashiyama Meguro-ku
153-0043 Tokyo
Japan

T +81 (0)3 5773 3536
E line@line-inc.co.jp
W www.line-inc.co.jp

Photography: Kozo Takayama

01   Tulip armchairs, the work of designer Eero Saarinen, are found throughout the shop.

02   A palette of calm, neutral colours - brown, off-white and gold - imbues the interior with a warm, serene ambience.

03   Line-Inc created a repetitive motif based on octagons and used the pattern to give the store a sense of coherence.

02

03

1 Showroom
2 Lingerie area
3 Lounge area
4 Fitting room
5 Cash desk
6 Storage

First floor

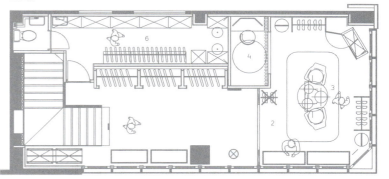

Ground floor

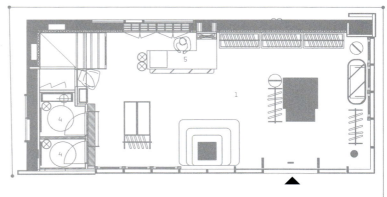

Laurèl
Plan2Plus design

WHERE: HAMBURG, GERMANY
WHEN: JANUARY 2007
CLIENT: LAURÈL
SHOP CONSTRUCTOR: KORDA
TOTAL FLOOR AREA (M²):   330
BUDGET (€):   650,000

PLAN2PLUS DESIGN HAS BEEN WORKING WITH PROMINENT COMPANIES ON AN INTERNATIONAL BASIS SINCE 1996. SPECIALIZING IN ARCHITECTURE AND INTERIOR DESIGN, PLAN2PLUS EMPLOYS AN ARTICULATE DESIGN LANGUAGE AND TIMELESS ARCHITECTURAL ELEMENTS TO CREATE UNIQUE, TRENDSETTING INTERIORS. THE CONCEPTUAL EXACTITUDE THAT GOES INTO THESE PROJECTS CONVEYS EMOTION WHILE PRODUCING INSPIRING SPACES AND ATMOSPHERES.

Situated on Hamburg's smartest shopping street, Laurèl's flagship store offers customers premium fashions in a retail interior conceived and realized by Plan2Plus design.
Plan2Plus design stripped the existing premises to create an unobstructed view that extends from the street to the very back of the retail interior. The spacious loft-like atmosphere is generated in part by a large skylight that fills the shop with natural light. To accentuate Laurèl's feminine character, the designers opted for elegantly curved elements, such as overhead openings at mezzanine level and sweeping glass balustrades. Lending structure to the interior are freestanding walls clad in jacaranda, and organically designed fitting rooms. Illuminated alcoves and extra-tall display units for accessories provide a setting for Laurèl's exclusive collections. A double-height lounge area occupies the rear of the shop, beyond which the Alster River runs. A VIP area at mezzanine level features a bar and a discrete lounge for preferred customers.

Plan2Plus design
Ralf Peter Knobloch and Tina Assmann
Friedrich-Herschel-strasse 3
81679 Munich
Germany

T +49 (0)89 6120 9090
E info@plan2plus.com
W www.plan2plus.com

Photography: Angelo Kaunat

01

1 Fitting room
2 Lounge area
3 Cash desk

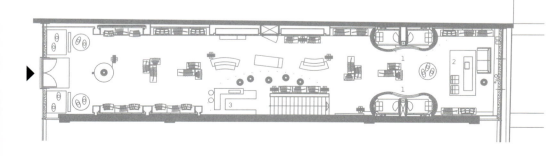

02

03

01 A huge skylight above the stairwell fills the shop with daylight.

02 A white-limestone floor and white furniture make a striking contrast to the dark wood used for balustrade and counter.

03 Illuminated alcoves feature rectangular polished stainless-steel hanging racks, one of the few elements in the shop without organic contours.

Le Ciel Bleu
Noriyuki Otsuka
Design Office

WHERE: TOKYO, JAPAN
WHEN: SEPTEMBER 2007
CLIENT: LE CIEL BLEU
SHOP CONSTRUCTOR: HASEGAWA
TOTAL FLOOR AREA (M²):   386

NORIYUKI OTSUKA DESIGN OFFICE WAS FOUNDED
1990 BY INTERIOR DESIGNER NORIYUKI OTSUKA.
THE MAJORITY OF OTSUKA'S WORK INVOLVES
INTERIORS FOR BOUTIQUES, RESTAURANTS AND
PRIVATE RESIDENCES. ALTHOUGH MUCH OF THE
WORK MAY APPEAR ALMOST TOO SIMPLE AT
FIRST GLANCE, HIS PROJECTS ARE NOTED FOR
THEIR DELICATE FEATURES AND THE RICHLY
SUBTLE NUANCES.

The Le Ciel Bleu boutique in Tokyo's chic Shibuya
ward was designed by the Noriyuki Otsuka
Design Office. Inside the shop, some 5000
original, smartly bound books are tightly packed
in rows on shelves along the walls. Unobtru-
sively embossed into the blue and black covers
of these volumes is the name of the store. In this
rather dim interior, lighting plays a major role.
One example is lighting that has been integrated
into the undersides of tabletops belonging to
two black-lacquered display tables near the
entrance. Clothes racks recessed into walls on
both sides of the shop are lit from above,
providing the space with a warm glow. Covering the suspended ceiling are lustrously finished
panels arranged in a random pattern. In an
abstract way, these panels blend with the
products, customers and furniture directly
beneath them, conveying the comings and goings
of shoppers and the flickering light in dreamlike
reflections. The carefully crafted colour scheme
used throughout the premises is dominated by
shades of blue and black, which express and
underpin the elegance of Tokyo. Black conjures
up images of cool fashions on the cutting edge
of contemporary design, while blue gracefully
articulates the ongoing passage of time. It's an
intriguing contrast, which Noriyuki Otsuka
has used to design an interior whose spatial
dimensions embrace the character of this
sophisticated metropolis, and particularly the
trendy streets of Shibuya.

Noriyuki Otsuka Design Office
6-13-5-401 Minamiaoyama Minato-Ku
107-0062 Tokyo
Japan

T +81 (0)3 3406 6341
E nodo@blue.ocn.ne.jp
W www.nodo.jp

Photography: Hiroyuki Hirai

01   The brightly illuminated shop
window between the first and the
second levels stands out at night.

02   Melamine-veneered panels
cover the ceiling and give it
a reflective finish.

03   Noriyuki Otsuka Design
Office designed the shelving that
holds row after row of books with
embossed covers. Moon Crow
Studio designed the bookbinding.

01

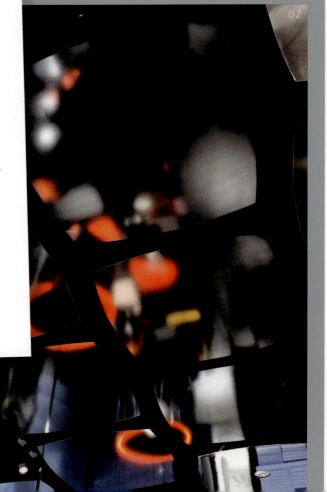

02

03

1 Display tables
2 Lounge area
3 Fitting room
4 Cash desk
5 Storage

04

04   Large display tables with integrated lighting are crucial to the ambience created by Noriyuki Otsuka Design's dreamily dim interior.

Levi's®
Checkland
Kindleysides

01

WHERE:	BERLIN, GERMANY
WHEN:	SEPTEMBER 2008
CLIENT:	LEVI STRAUSS & CO
SHOP CONSTRUCTOR:	GGP ARCHITEKTEN
TOTAL FLOOR AREA (M²):	550

||||||||||||||||||||||||||||||||||||

JEFF KINDLEYSIDES ESTABLISHED HIS COMPANY, CHECKLAND KINDLEYSIDES (CK), IN 1979. OVER THE PAST 30 YEARS, THE COMPANY HAS DEVELOPED A UNIQUE CULTURE AND LONG-STANDING RELATIONSHIPS WITH CLIENTS. AT CK CREATIVITY IS DRIVEN BY ROBUST CUSTOMER, DESIGN AND MARKET INSIGHT AND AN ABILITY TO MAKE THINGS WORK AESTHETICALLY, PHYSICALLY AND COMMERCIALLY. CLIENTS INCLUDE CONVERSE, SONY PLAYSTATION AND TIMBERLAND.

||||||||||||||||||||||||||||||||||||

Both designer and client envisioned this store as an environment in which customers could immerse themselves in the pioneering spirit of Levi's®. Located in the heart of Berlin, the store has a striking façade of arched windows spanning the building's three-storey height. Checkland Kindleysides (CK) wanted to produce a space that would nurture Levi's® relationships with artists, musicians and filmmakers while generating a youthful mix of global and local creativity. A beautiful curved staircase serves as both a central feature and a journey between floors. It's set against a graphic backdrop that portrays Levi's® timeline, presenting imagery from the brand's early roots to the present day. In a gallery on the ground floor, the 'innovation' of Levi's® products can be exhibited, along with the work of local creatives. Levi's® Blue is presented on the first floor, where simple white fixtures display the range with clarity, and feature garments in burnt orange punctuate the space. On the second floor, with its 3-m-high vaults, shoppers find Levi's most collectable apparel sourced from around the world. Privileged customers are led to a hidden room - an exclusive space accessible by invitation only - that contains the rarest of products, making it a mecca for denim aficionados. The store conveys the various personalities of the brand, creates a strong definitive area for each, and brings it all together in a retail space that is the ultimate expression of Levi's®.

Checkland Kindleysides
Charnwood Edge, Cossington
Leicester LE7 4UZ
United Kingdom

T +44 (0)116 2644 700
E info@checklandkindleysides.com
W www.checklandkindleysides.com

Photography: Daniel Grund

01 The striking façade of this Berlin shop attracts passers-by.

02 The centrepiece of the store is a curving staircase that features white-painted steel and concrete treads.

1 Menswear
2 Womenswear
3 Accessories
4 Library
5 Fitting rooms
6 Elevator
7 Storage

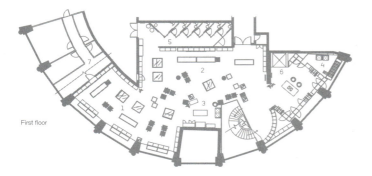

First floor

04

05

03   Hanging on chains, jeans appear in a display unit against a wall finished in copper panelling.

04   Walls were stripped to expose the building's original brick surfaces.

05   The combination of herringbone parquet floor and industrial wall system gives the space a rugged yet stylish ambience.

Levi's® Blue Lab Temporary Store
Liganova

WHERE: COLOGNE, GERMANY
WHEN: MARCH–MAY 2008
CLIENT: LEVI STRAUSS
TOTAL FLOOR AREA (M²):   90

LIGANOVA SPECIALIZES IN BRAND AND RETAIL MARKETING. BY INTERLINKING THE WORK OF ITS VARIOUS DEPARTMENTS - BRAND & VISUAL COMMUNICATION, RETAIL ARCHITECTURE, VISUAL MARKETING AND EVENT DESIGN - LIGANOVA HAS WHAT IT TAKES TO CREATE AND REALIZE WELL-INTEGRATED CONCEPTS. AMONG THE FIRM'S CLIENTS ARE INTERNATIONAL COMPANIES WITHIN THE FASHION, LIFESTYLE AND LUXURY-GOODS SECTORS SUCH AS ADIDAS, HUGO BOSS, LEVI STRAUSS, TOMMY HILFIGER, CARTIER, JOOP! AND MANY MORE. THE COMPANY WAS FOUNDED IN 1996 BY BODO VINCENT ANDRIN AND MICHAEL HAISER. THE FIRM HAS OFFICES IN BOTH STUTTGART AND BERLIN.

Levi Strauss approached Liganova with a request for a temporary store that would present the philosophy and feel of Levi's® Blue brand in an unconventional way. The client wanted a brand world that would both reflect and identify with the target customer.

In keeping with the avant-garde spirit of the label, Liganova's core idea - Fashion meets Art - became the primary concept. The store served as a platform for the communication of fashion and art, a melting pot that fused two aspects of the world of Levi's® Blue. Finding the right location was a major challenge, but an old Chinese restaurant no longer in use perfectly filled the bill. Located in Cologne's trendiest district, the space was quickly transformed into the world of Levi's® Blue. Working around the existing architectural features, Liganova opted to preserve white-tiled surfaces, to spray-paint the original ceiling black and to carpet part of the floor in white. Furniture, spotlights and a light installation of spherical pendants completed the picture. The shop remained open for three months. Thanks to both the interior design and an experimental approach to product display - the work of progressive young artists - fashion was presented as part of an evolving work of art. A selection of garments hung from ceiling-mounted chains, paintings and posters adorned the walls, and a video-cube installation greeted customers entering the store. Continually changing exhibitions, installations and events resulted in a unique lifestyle and shopping experience. The store functioned more as a brand and lifestyle space than as a conventional retail environment.

Liganova
The BrandRetail Company
Herdweg 59
70174 Stuttgart
Germany

T +49 (0)711 65220 201
E info@liganova.com
W www.liganova.com

Photography: Liganova

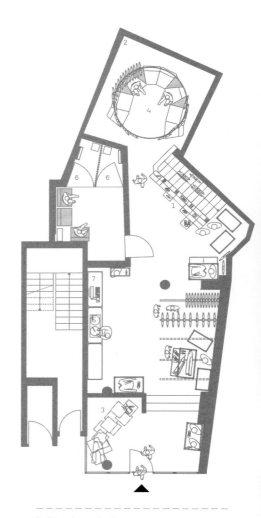

1 Display shelves
2 Exhibition wall
3 Video-cube installation
4 Lounge
5 DJ stand
6 Fitting room
7 Cash desk

01   A mirror in the fitting room offers to be your friend for the day.

02   A former Chinese restaurant houses the temporary shop.

03   A set of white flight cases functions as a cash desk and DJ stand.

05

04   Original wall tiles from the
Chinese restaurant have been left
intact.

05   A video-cube installation
that greets customers at the
entrance of the shop corresponds
to the retail concept: Fashion
meets Art.

06   Chains hanging from the
ceiling display the fashion
collection.

06

01

02

Mad Child's Dollhouse
No Picnic

WHERE:	STOCKHOLM, SWEDEN
WHEN:	DECEMBER 2007
CLIENT:	WEEKDAY
SHOP CONSTRUCTOR:	NÄSSJÖ INREDNINGAR
TOTAL FLOOR AREA (M²):	1500

SCANDINAVIAN DESIGN COMPANY NO PICNIC WAS FOUNDED IN 1993 BY PARTNERS WHO STILL RUN THE FIRM. THE MULTIDISCIPLINARY TEAM OF ARCHITECTS, INDUSTRIAL DESIGNERS, GRAPHIC DESIGNERS, DESIGN ENGINEERS, STRATEGISTS, TREND ANALYSTS AND PROJECT MANAGERS HAS COMPLETED OVER 750 PROJECTS FOR CLIENTS WORLDWIDE, INCLUDING ASTRA TECH, BOSCH, ERICSSON, OTTO BOCK, SAS, SONY, SONY ERICSSON, TETRA PAK, UNIBAIL-RODAMCO, UNILEVER, WEEKDAY AND KRAFT.

In 2002, Weekday - a popular Swedish brand that operates a chain of stores - opened its first shop. The brief asked for something that had never been done before. Weekday wanted its style, its fashions, its personality and its history to be transformed into a story so strong and unique that advertising would be unnecessary. That brief remained during years of cooperation between Weekday and No Picnic. Using preliminary studies and workshops, No Picnic develops a 'set design' for each new store, like a storyboard for a Weekday movie. The 'Mad Child's Dollhouse' store is one of eight remarkable results. Three colour schemes that help to tell the story are visible through the high glass façade. The entire interior - including ceiling and furniture - is based on classic optical illusions. Mirrors everywhere add to the 'distorted' atmosphere. Floor graphics were created in collaboration with Swedish graphic-design studio VÅR.

01 Furniture at Mad Child's Dollhouse creates classic optical illusions.

02 Looking through the glazed façade, passers-by have a clear view of the colours used for various floors.

03 An elongated graphic on the floor, as reflected in this mirror-panelled column, suddenly gains 'correct' proportions.

04 The yellow ceiling and some of the many mirrors used to distort the retail surroundings.

No Picnic
Ljusslingan 1
120 31 Stockholm
Sweden

T +46 (0)8 556 96 550
E info@nopicnic.se
W www.nopicnic.com

Photography: Patrik Engquist

03

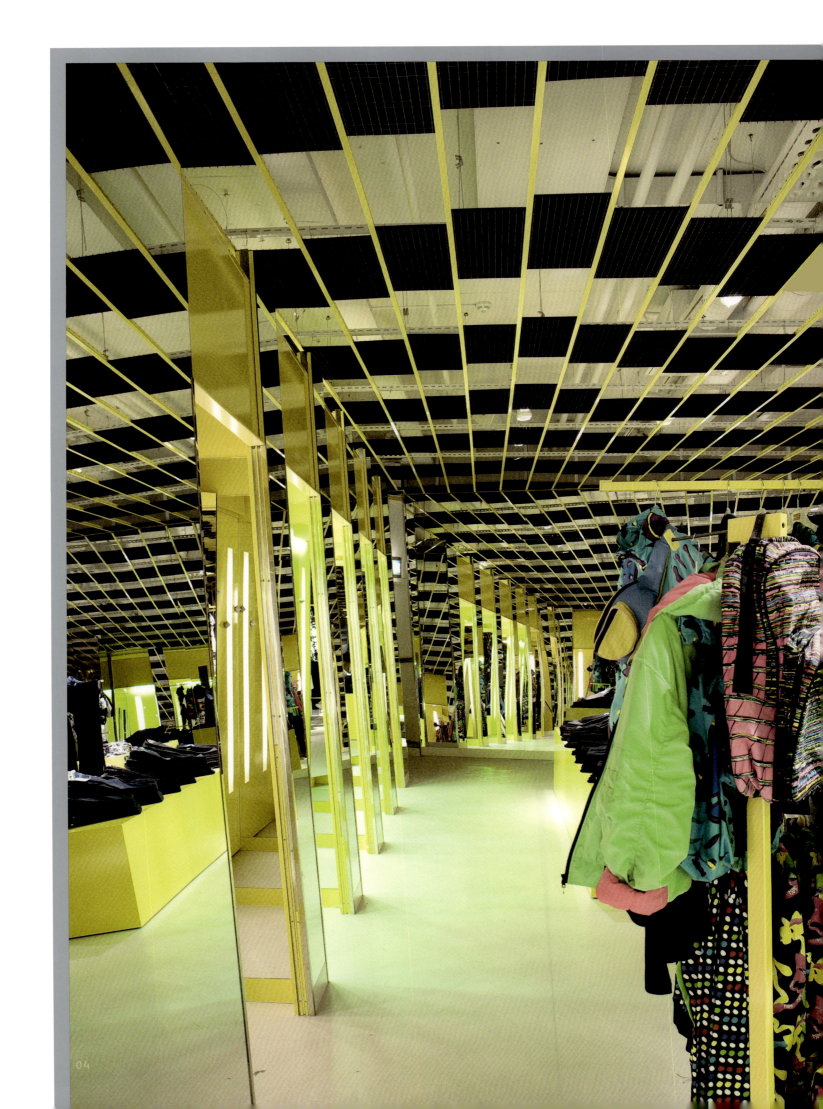

04

Masha Tsigal
AdaDesign

WHERE:	MOSCOW, RUSSIA
WHEN:	DECEMBER 2008
CLIENT:	MASHA TSIGAL STUDIO
TOTAL FLOOR AREA (M²):	44
BUDGET (€):	60,000

||||||||||||||||||||||||||||||||||||||||||||||||||||||

IN 1995 ARIADNA SHMANDUROVA COMPLETED HER INTERIOR ARCHITECTURE AT A DUTCH ART ACADEMY. AFTER WORKING FIVE YEARS FOR A DUTCH DESIGN STUDIO, IN 2000 SHMANDUROVA FOUNDED HER OWN FIRM, ADADESIGN. WORKING FROM OFFICES IN BOTH AMSTERDAM AND MOSCOW, SHE DESIGNS AND REALIZES PROJECTS THAT VARY FROM RETAIL AND HOSPITALITY INTERIORS TO PRODUCT DESIGN.

||||||||||||||||||||||||||||||||||||||||||||||||||||||

Russian fashion designer Masha Tsigal started her brand in 2001. Tsigal dresses local and international celebrities and designs theatre costumes. She asked Ariadna Shmandurova to design the interior of a Masha Tsigal boutique that opened in the heart of Moscow in 2008. Shmandurova painted the existing wooden floor white and installed custom-made clothes racks along the walls. Not merely functional, these racks are the striking highlight of the interior. They feature jagged shapes that have been laser cut from polished stainless-steel sheet. Resembling cartoon speech balloons, the reflective laser-cut frames are equipped with shelves and rails that hold Tsigal's sporty-glamorous fashions. Fluorescent-pink clothes hangers are the only splashes of colour in the interior, apart from the garments on display. Flanking a large, heart-shaped, laser-cut mirror are two fitting rooms. Shmandurova also designed the cash desk, which matches the style of all furniture that appears in the shop.

AdaDesign
Westerstraat 13-D
1015 LT Amsterdam
the Netherlands

T +31 (0)6 1709 0924
E info@adadesign.nl
W www.adadesign.nl

Photography: N. Karachev

01

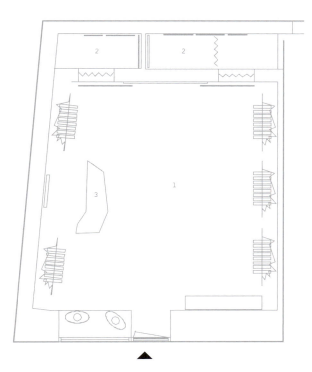

1 Retail area
2 Fitting room
3 Cash desk

01   Ariadna Shmandurova painted the existing wooden floor white.

02   The luminaires at Masha Tsigal are by Modular Lighting Instruments.

03   Laser-cut shapes made of polished stainless steel resemble cartoon speech balloons.

McGregor Women
Conix Architects

WHERE:	GHENT, BELGIUM
WHEN:	JUNE 2007
CLIENT:	MCGREGOR BELGIUM
SHOP CONSTRUCTORS:	AABLOS AND VIRTUS
TOTAL FLOOR AREA (M²):	330
BUDGET (€):	580,000

CONIX ARCHITECTS, FOUNDED IN 1979 AND LOCATED IN ANTWERP AND BRUSSELS, CONSCIOUSLY DECIDES NOT TO FOCUS ON ONE SPECIFIC TYPOLOGY. EACH PROJECT, FROM SMALL INTERIOR TO URBAN DESIGN, OFFERS ITS OWN CHALLENGES. THE GUIDELINES FOR INTERIOR DESIGNS BY CONIX ARCHITECTS ARE BASED ON HUMAN SCALE, FUNCTIONALISM, SUSTAINABILITY AND MINIMALISM.

The brief that McGregor gave Conix Architects asked for an interior concept for the McGregor Women flagship store in Ghent: a retail space situated in a listed building, the Wool Weavers' Chapel.

Respect for this unique setting was Conix's point of departure. The shop had to exude class. Transparency, minimalism and timelessness were introduced to ensure integration of the concept into its surroundings. The layout references the traditional floor plan of a church: a central area bordered by a circulation zone. Within this space, a painted steel structure - featuring bands of leather that generate an air of intimacy - successfully bridges the disparity between a retail space and a religious interior. Conix covered the existing concrete floor with a herringbone walnut parquet. A palette of ochre and cream reinforces the patina of the high columns and the chapel walls. Newly designed furniture juxtaposed with several antique showpieces adds a touch of finesse that stresses the craftsmanship of the chapel.

Conix Architects
Cockerillkaai 18
2000 Antwerp
Belgium

T +32 (0)3 259 11 30
E info@conixarchitects.com
W www.conixarchitects.com

Photography: Serge Brison

01-03 Because the shop is housed in a listed building, the Wool Weavers' Chapel, the architects were prevented from attaching anything to walls and ceiling. Freestanding display units made of glass are visually absorbed by their surroundings.

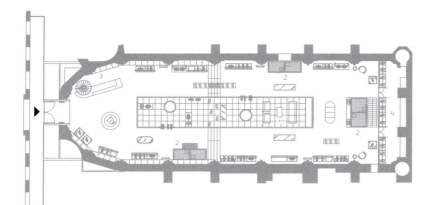

1 Lounge area
2 Fitting rooms
3 Cash desk
4 Storage

03

Miffy Shop-in-Shop
UXUS

WHERE:	AMSTERDAM, THE NETHERLANDS
WHEN:	MARCH 2007
CLIENTS:	MERCIS AND V&D
TOTAL FLOOR AREA (M²):	75

||||||||||||||||||||||||||||||||||||||||||||||

FOUNDED IN AMSTERDAM IN 2003, UXUS IS AN INDEPENDENT AWARD WINING DESIGN CONSULTANCY SPECIALIZING IN STRATEGIC DESIGN SOLUTIONS FOR RETAIL, COMMUNICATION, HOSPITALITY, ARCHITECTURE AND INTERIORS. UXUS CREATES 'BRAND POETRY', FUSING TOGETHER ART AND DESIGN, AND CREATING NEW BRAND EXPERIENCES FOR ITS CLIENTS WORLDWIDE. THEY DEFINE 'BRAND POETRY' AS AN ARTISTIC SOLUTION FOR COMMERCIAL NEEDS. ARTISTIC SOLUTIONS TARGET EMOTIONS; EMOTIONS CONNECT PEOPLE IN A MEANINGFUL WAY. DESIGN GIVES FUNCTION, ART GIVES MEANING, POETRY EXPRESSES THE ESSENCE.

||||||||||||||||||||||||||||||||||||||||||||||

01   Most of the merchandise is displayed on the back wall of this shop-in-shop.

02   One giant plush Miffy welcomes customers to the shop.

03   UXUS purpose-designed all graphic display units featured in the Miffy shop-in-shop concept.

Mercis and V&D asked UXUS to design the world's first official Miffy shop-in-shop for leading Dutch department store V&D. The retail space was to be featured in the chain's main Amsterdam location. UXUS based the 'Miffy Goes Shopping' experience on the concept of a colouring-book village that comes to life: the shop-in-shop is an appealing environment that reflects in every way the graphic style of Miffy's creator, Dick Bruna. In this imagination-filled world, whimsical display units in the form of houses, flowers and picket fences not only present the merchandise in a highly efficient way, but also clearly echo Bruna's bright, bold drawings. A giant 'real life' interactive Miffy greets children and invites them to play.

UXUS
Keizersgracht 174
1016 DW Amsterdam
the Netherlands

T +31 (0)20 6233 114
E europe@uxusdesign.com
W www.uxus.com

Photography: Dim Balsem

nijntje
gaat
winkelen

01

nijntje gaat winke

nijntje gaat winkelen

01

02

Monki: City of Oil and Steel
Electric Dreams

WHERE:	NORRKÖPING, SWEDEN
WHEN:	FEBRUARY 2008
CLIENT:	MONKI
SHOP CONSTRUCTOR:	NÄSSJÖ INREDNINGAR
TOTAL FLOOR AREA (M²):	200

||||||||||||||||||||||||||||||||||||||||||||||||

JOEL DEGERMARK (PRODUCT DESIGNER) AND CATHARINA FRANKANDER (ARCHITECT) ESTABLISHED ELECTRIC DREAMS, A STOCK-HOLM-BASED ARCHITECTURE AND DESIGN FIRM, IN 2006. DEGERMARK STUDIED AT BECKMANS SCHOOL OF DESIGN, THE ROYAL COLLEGE OF ART AND DANMARKS DESIGNSKOLE. FRANKANDER WAS EDUCATED AT THE ARCHI-TECTURAL ASSOCIATION KTH AND KUNGLIGA KONSTHÖGSKOLAN. THEY SPECIALIZE IN BRAND ENVIRONMENTS AND PRODUCT DESIGN.

||||||||||||||||||||||||||||||||||||||||||||||||

Monki, a Swedish fashion brand for teenage girls, has many exciting shops throughout Sweden. In 2006, design firm Electric Dreams assumed responsibility for the interior design of Monki's new retail locations.
A 'Monki' is a cute little creature - but looks can be deceiving! - who lives with friends in a magical, mysterious world parallel to ours. The new realm that Electric Dreams created for them, 'City of Oil and Steel', is dark and filled with machinery, broken skyscrapers, swamps and huge strands of pearls. Pearls covering part of the ceiling and stretching from ceiling to floor provide illumination, while those on the floor function as seating or display units. The swamp, which doubles as a shoe display, is reflected in a mirror-clad wall. Although the interior design clearly relates the Monki story, shoppers experience it in other ways as well: the Monki motif appears on clothing and in other forms of brand communication.

Electric Dreams
Alsnögatan 3
11641 Stockholm
Sweden

T +46 (0)736 5532 92
E info@electricdreams.se
W www.electricdreams.se

Photography: Fredrik Sweger

1 Strand of pearls
2 Seating element
3 Shoe display
4 Fitting room
5 Cash desk

01   Fitting rooms.

02   The interior of the Monki shop is dominated by coloured strings of jumbo 'pearls', machine parts and swamps - all elements of the whimsical world inhabited by Monki and his friends.

03   Shop windows promise passers–by an exiting experience inside. All the Monki shops together form an entity that combines recognition, repetition and always surprise.

Napapijri Gallery Store
Studio DeCarloGualla

WHERE:	MILAN, ITALY
WHEN:	JUNE 2008
CLIENT:	NAPAPIJRI
SHOP CONSTRUCTOR:	IMPRESA MULTICOLORE
TOTAL FLOOR AREA (M²):	450
BUDGET (€):	1.7 MILLION

FOUNDED IN THE YEAR 2000, ARCHITECTURE AND DESIGN STUDIO DECARLOGUALLA IS HEADED BY JACOPO DE CARLO (AVIANO, 1965) AND ANDREA GUALLA (MILAN, 1965), BOTH OF WHOM STUDIED ARCHITECTURE AT THE POLITECNICO DI MILANO. AMONG THEIR MORE IMPORTANT PROJECTS IS THE DESIGN AND REALIZATION OF VF INTERNATIONAL'S EUROPEAN HEADQUARTERS IN LUGANO, SWITZERLAND. THIS PROJECT LED TO THE DEVELOPMENT OF NUMEROUS NAPAPIJRI CONCEPT STORES WORLDWIDE, AN EVOLUTION THAT CULMINATED IN NAPAPIJIRI'S FIRST FLAGSHIP STORE IN NEW YORK CITY, FOLLOWED BY STORES IN MIAMI, PARIS, BERLIN, MADRID, OSAKA AND MILAN.

In 2008 Studio DeCarloGualla designed and realized a flagship store in Milan for outdoor-inspired sportswear brand Napapijri. The 450-m² space occupies two floors of a building on Via Manzoni. According to the architects, the point of departure was 'partly gallery, partly sales area'. The atmosphere throughout the store is warm and welcoming. Art and photography can be admired at both ends of the upper level. Stairs leading to this permanent gallery are found in several areas of the store where the brand's sportswear collection is displayed. The ground-floor sales area is divided into several zones, the first of which is close to the entrance and focuses on dynamism and communication. Projected on two large cubes hanging from the ceiling are scenic images of the great outdoors. Walls covered in metal panelling feature horizontal cross sections of tree trunks, showing annual growth rings in relief. Interrupting the metallic surface are deep niches for the display of Napapijri fashions. In the second zone, which is devoted wholly to accessories, burnished brass-plated panelling covers walls and ceiling. The highly flexible display system in this area relies on teak boxes of various sizes, which can be moved freely along the monochrome walls thanks to magnets. The third zone, devoted to clothes for kids, consists of a room with plastered walls painted in a warm olive green, colourful garden gnomes and plants.

01   Scenic images are projected on two big cubes near the entrance.

02   At the back of the store, a huge metallic sphere and several small globes below it refer to the connection between Napapijri and travel.

1 Communication zone
2 Accessories zone
3 Kids' clothes zone
4 Sales area
5 Amphitheatre
6 Fitting rooms
7 Cash desk
8 Projection cubes
9 Permanent gallery
10 Lavatories

02

Shoppers passing through the children's section reach the concluding and most spectacular zone, which features three architectural elements on one vertical axis: a large skylight, the huge metallic sphere suspended below it and, at floor level, an amphitheatre furnished with several globes. Steps ascending from the exhibition gallery lend access to the hollow sphere.

Studio DeCarloGualla
Via C.M. Maggi 6
20154 Milan
Italy

T +39 02 3492 576
E info@decarlogualla.com
W www.decarlogualla.com

Photography: Santi Caleca

03

03   A footbridge with a glass balustrade provides shoppers with a glimpse of the permanent exhibition gallery upstairs.

04   Stairs ascending from the gallery lend access to the interior of the large hollow sphere.

05

05   In contrast to the rest of
the shop, the children's section
features garden gnomes and
plastered walls painted green.

06   Metal plates that cover
the wall feature horizontal cross
sections of tree trunks, another
link to the outdoors.

07   Teak boxes can be moved
freely along the wall thanks to
magnets.

06

07

Napapijri Totem Concept Store
Wagner Associati

WHERE:	LUGANO, SWITZERLAND
WHEN:	DECEMBER 2007
CLIENT:	VF INTERNATIONAL SAGL
SHOP CONSTRUCTOR:	F.LLI BIANCHI
TOTAL FLOOR AREA (M²):	80
BUDGET (€):	160,000

||||||||||||||||||||||||||||||||||||||||||||||||

WAGNER ASSOCIATI IS A DESIGN COMPANY ESTABLISHED AND OWNED BY STEFANO BIZZOTTO AND ENRICO TOSO. THE FIRM WAS FOUNDED IN 1992, AND MOST OF ITS PROJECTS INVOLVE EXHIBITION AND RETAIL DESIGN. WAGNER ASSOCIATI SERVES AS A CONSULTANT TO NAPAPIJRI, NORTH SAILS, 7 FOR ALL MANKIND, EVISU AND VIVIENNE WESTWOOD.

||||||||||||||||||||||||||||||||||||||||||||||||

In December 2007 Wagner Associati designed a new store in Lugano for outdoor-sportswear brand Napapijri. The concept is an iconographic and linguistic interpretation of the brand's roots. Totem poles, which tell the story of Napapijri's history and philosophy, represent the destinations of a journey into the character of Napapijri; each totem pole and its laser-carved markings indicate a place to pause and explore.
The wooden poles double as units for display and storage. Shoppers are encouraged to open drawers in each of these 'landmarks' to view items from Napapijri's latest collection. The back wall consists of tip-up shelves, further enhancing an interior designed for interaction between visitor and merchandise. Wagner Associati has imbued the space with fine finishes and materials and excellent craftsmanship. Laser work, the play of light, and a multiplicity of drawers and shelves combine to reveal an attention to detail and construction that echoes that of Napapijri's handmade products.

Wagner Associati
Viottolo Pagnana 35
31033 Castelfranco Veneto (TV)
Italy

T +39 0423 467 975
E info@wea.it
W www.wea.it

Photography: André Lucat

01

02

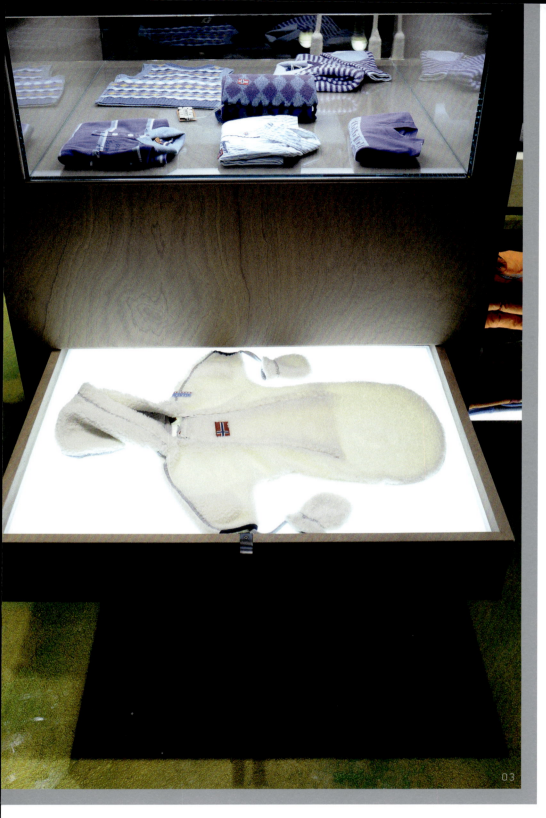

01   Display shelves are equipped with built-in lighting.

02   The back wall of the shop consists of tip-up shelves.

03   Totem poles used for display purposes feature shelves, glass cases and drawers.

04   The clever use of lighting, paired with a gleaming floor, makes the totem-pole display unit appear to float in midair.

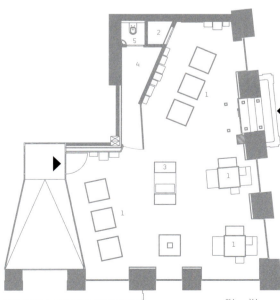

1 Display
2 Fitting room
3 Cash desk
4 Storage
5 Lavatory

0M   1M

Nau
Skylab
Architecture

WHERE:	BOULDER, CO, USA
WHEN:	JUNE 2007
CLIENT:	NAU
TOTAL FLOOR AREA (M²):	185.8

SKYLAB ARCHITECTURE WAS FOUNDED IN 1999 AS 'A LABORATORY TO EXPLORE A SMALL DEPARTURE FROM AN INDUSTRY OF MOUNTING STANDARDIZATION'. BASED IN PORTLAND, OREGON, THE FIRM IS HEADED BY PRINCIPAL JEFF KOVEL. SKYLAB ARCHITECTURE'S PROJECTS INCLUDE RESIDENTIAL, RETAIL, AND RESTAURANT DESIGN.

The brand principles of apparel company Nau are beauty, performance and sustainability. Nau's retail locations, called 'webfronts', add a third dimension to the company's primary sales channel: the internet. Skylab Architecture was asked to bring Nau's defining principles and alternative retail strategies to life in the built environment. In designing the webfronts, Skylab employed beauty as concept, performance as functionality and sustainability as opportunity. Beauty is evident in an organic landscape of Medite modules, the backdrop of the retail environment. Performance relies largely on the integration of technology. After selecting clothes, shoppers can use one of the store's touchscreens to gain more product knowledge or have them shipped home, making it easy for the customer but also for the store, which needs to keep only limited stock on hand. Sustainability is achieved through the reuse of existing spatial attributes and the introduction of a prefabricated environment: Medite modules, for example, can be rearranged or reused in other stores.

Skylab Architecture
1221 SW Alder Street
Portland, OR 97205
USA

T +1 503 525 9315
E info@skylabarchitecture.com
W www.skylabarchitecture.com

Photography: Steve Cridland

02

01   Customers can use a touch-screen to order clothes and have them sent home.

02   Interior view of a fitting room at the back of the store.

03   Entrance doors are made from reclaimed hardwood, most of which was salvaged from dismantled factories and barns.

04   Medite modu.es (1.2 x 3 m) form the backbone of the retail environment.

Nike 1928
Pop-Up Store
....,staat

WHERE:	AMSTERDAM, THE NETHERLANDS
WHEN:	AUGUST 2008
CLIENT:	NIKE SPORTSWEAR
SHOP CONSTRUCTORS:	FOUND AND SHIVERS
TOTAL FLOOR AREA (M²):	300

|||||||||||||||||||||||||||||||||||

AMSTERDAM-BASED ....,STAAT IS A CREATIVE AGENCY FOUNDED BY JOCHEM LEEGSTRA IN THE MAGIC YEAR '00. LEEGSTRA WORKS TOGETHER WITH PARTNERS JULIA KORTEKAAS, MICHIEL STEYN AND MARTIJN TAMBOER. THEIR INTERNATIONAL STAFF OF 25 INCLUDES AN INSPIRING MIX OF ART DIRECTORS, DESIGNERS, STRATEGISTS, PROJECT MANAGERS AND COPY-WRITERS, WHO WORK WITH CLIENTS WORLDWIDE. PROJECTS RANGE FROM FASHION, ADVERTISING AND BRAND-BUILDING TO RETAIL, INTERIOR, ENVIRONMENTAL AND GRAPHIC DESIGN.

|||||||||||||||||||||||||||||||||||

Nike commissioned ....staat to design a pop-up store for its launch of a special Nike Sports-wear collection. The location was a unique retail environment in Amsterdam. Nike chose August 8, 2008, as the day of the opening to coincide with the opening of the Beijing Games. On August 8, Nike's collection of eight iconic products was unveiled in eight concept stores in eight Olym-pic cities: London, Paris, Barcelona, Rome, Berlin, Moscow, Stockholm and Amsterdam. Erected on the grounds of Amsterdam's popular Westergas-fabriek, ...staat's stand-alone cube employed light to make its eye-catching statement. Inside, original elements from high-school gyms of the past were used to create artistic installations that evoked images of aspiring gymnasts of yesteryear. Even the lighting - also from school gymnasiums - contributed to an atmosphere of exercise and strenuous sports. Separate areas featured the Olympics and a NikeID studio. Behind the temporary shop, an inconspicuous door opened to reveal a surrealistic gallery dedicated to Nike Sportswear.

....,staat
De Ruyterkade 143
1011 AC Amsterdam
the Netherlands

T +31 (0)20 5721 388
E info@staatamsterdam.nl
W www.staatamsterdam.nl

Photography: Joachim Baan and ....,staat

01

01   For the interior design of the shop, traditional gymnastic equipment was remastered for live.

02   Dominating the space is a shade of aqua originally found in American high-school gyms. The lighting in this temporary store was done by Jurlights and Vasco Showtechniek.

03   The stand-alone cube uses an enormous LED wall to make a bold statement that attracts passers-by. Video art + motion graphics are to be credited for this addition to the shop.

04   Original pieces of gym equipment serve as display units: the climbing wall is used as a clothing rack and the vaulting box as a display table.

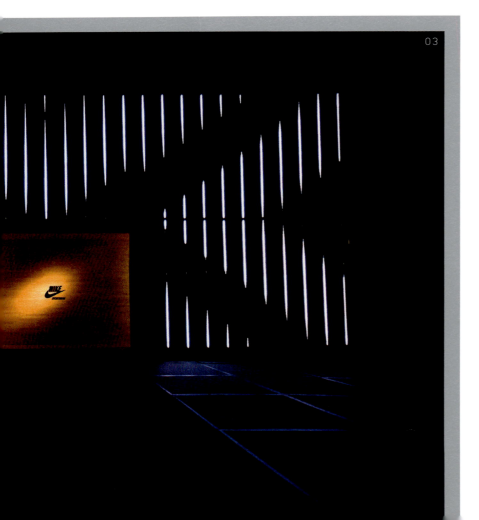

Oasis
Household Design

WHERE:	LONDON, UNITED KINGDOM
WHEN:	NOVEMBER 2008
CLIENT:	OASIS
SHOP CONSTRUCTORS:	POWELLS GROUP AND ERI
TOTAL FLOOR AREA (M²):	240

FOUNDED IN 2004, HOUSEHOLD DESIGN IS A LONDON-BASED DESIGN CONSULTANCY SPECIALIZING IN CREATING MEMORABLE BRAND EXPERIENCES AND IN OFFERING BRAND STRATEGY AND INTERIOR DESIGN FROM CONCEPT TO IMPLEMENTATION. HOUSEHOLD HAS PARTNERED WITH BRANDS SUCH AS ASOS. COM, BOOTS, MARKS & SPENCER, OASIS, TESCO, VIRGIN BRANDS AND LUXURY BOUTIQUE BRAND SOHO HOUSE GROUP.

The brief that Oasis gave to Household Design asked for an evolving, revitalized image that would make Oasis not only dynamic but the leading fashion boutique on the high street. The brand wanted to increase its appeal to fashion-conscious women in their late 20s. Household Design's branding concept revolves around a series of key customer experiences. The first is 'brand truths', created to revive pace and energy and to link the various Oasis stories. This experience was translated into attractive shop windows. The second, tagged 'unexpected moments', features miniature pop-up fashion houses within the shop, which introduce and showcase new collections. 'Meaningful pauses' consists of messages planted in unexpected places to communicate with visitors in a fun but expert way. Last but not least, 'loyalty factors' reflects innovative customer-service amenities, including spacious and luxurious fitting rooms, as well as single-payment pods modelled on concierge desks to generate 'intimacy' rather than 'transaction'.

Household Design
135 Curtain Road
London EC2A 3BX
United Kingdom

T +44 (0)20 7739 6537
E michelle@household-design.com
W www.household-design.com

Photography: Julian Abrams

01 Gloss-lacquered cash pods have been furnished with hand-blown glass lanterns.

02 Individually crafted, mechanically jointed flowers made of anodized aluminium decorate the shop front.

03 Each fitting room is furnished with a pure-silk panel and a heavy curtain of rippled velvet. These luxurious rooms have been designed to reflect the impeccable customer service provided by Oasis.

04 Fret-cut, anodized-aluminium screens divide the retail area into several sections.

01

02

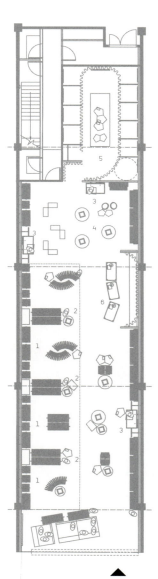

1 Fashion collection
2 Collection highlight
3 Pop-up fashion house
4 Shoe lounge
5 Fitting rooms
6 Cash desk

03

04

Oilily
UXUS

WHERE:	NEW YORK, NY, USA
WHEN:	MARCH 2007
CLIENT:	OILILY
TOTAL FLOOR AREA (M²):	410
BUDGET (€):	500,000

||||||||||||||||||||||||||||||||||||||||||||||

FOUNDED IN AMSTERDAM IN 2003, UXUS IS AN INDEPENDENT AWARD WINING DESIGN CONSULTANCY SPECIALIZING IN STRATEGIC DESIGN SOLUTIONS FOR RETAIL, COMMUNICATION, HOSPITALITY, ARCHITECTURE AND INTERIORS. UXUS CREATES 'BRAND POETRY', FUSING TOGETHER ART AND DESIGN, AND CREATING NEW BRAND EXPERIENCES FOR ITS CLIENTS WORLDWIDE. THEY DEFINE 'BRAND POETRY' AS AN ARTISTIC SOLUTION FOR COMMERCIAL NEEDS. ARTISTIC SOLUTIONS TARGET EMOTIONS; EMOTIONS CONNECT PEOPLE IN A MEANINGFUL WAY. DESIGN GIVES FUNCTION, ART GIVES MEANING, POETRY EXPRESSES THE ESSENCE.

||||||||||||||||||||||||||||||||||||||||||||||

UXUS designed and realized Oilily's New York City flagship store, which is located in SoHo's Cast Iron Historic District.
Inspired by Oilily's muse - 'A woman who lives her entire life as a work of art' - UXUS crafted a retail experience modelled after the world and the atelier of an artist. The objective was a unique, exciting brand embassy and cultural hub aimed at communicating the total Oilily brand experience. The shop interior is raw and exposed, much like an artist's studio. Inserted into the space are a series of custom fixtures made from found objects and grafted to more luxurious elements, creating one-of-a-kind displays and enhancing the effect of an 'atelier'. These fixtures not only hold products, but also incorporate secret play areas and cosy corners for kids to explore.
The concept is flexible and easily adapted to other retail contexts, forging a new, unique and powerful Oilily brand experience.

UXUS
Keizersgracht 174
1016 DW Amsterdam
the Netherlands

T +31 (0)20 6233 114
E europe@uxusdesign.com
W www.uxus.com

Photography: George Gottl

01

01   An arrangement of stacked wooden chairs painted in bright, cheerful colours serves as a display for bags.

02   A wall filled with an array of vintage cabinets, one atop the other, creates a special display unit for clothes and accessories, while also inviting kids to make this area their playhouse.

03   Painted brick walls give the interior a rustic look and feel.

Pimkie
::dan pearlman

WHERE:	LINZ, AUSTRIA
WHEN:	MARCH 2007
CLIENT:	PMD MODEN
SHOP CONSTRUCTOR:	RUPPEL LADENBAU
TOTAL FLOOR AREA (M²):	335
BUDGET (€):	335,000

IN 1999 NICOLE SROCK-STANLEY, VOLKER KATSCHINSKI, MARCUS FISCHER AND KIERAN STANLEY FOUNDED ::DAN PEARLMAN, AN AGENCY WITH A FOCUS ON BRAND ARCHITECTURE AND EXPERIENCE ARCHITECTURE. THE BERLIN-BASED FIRM RESPONDS TO THE VARIOUS COMMUNICATION-RELATED OBJECTIVES OF ITS CLIENTS BY MEANS OF FOUR INDEPENDENT SPECIALIST UNITS: STRATEGY, RETAIL, EXHIBITION AND MEDIA.

As part of Group Mulliez of France, Pimkie opened its first fashion shop in France in 1972. Today the brand operates more than 650 stores across Europe; the target group is young women from 15 to 25 years of age. Pimkie asked ::dan pearlman to create a new retail concept. The designers came up with a scheme that revolves around the tagline 'Feel Pimkie', which underlines the philosophy of a brand that offers clients more than just a product. The heart of the strategy - the metaphoric structure of backstage and front stage - combines the intimacy of best friends with the dream of public celebrity. Backstage is about trying on clothes together behind the scenes, with music, drinks and cosy, stylish interiors in the form of spacious fitting rooms. Front stage represents a glamorous runway leading to 'life in the limelight'; here fashions are displayed on catwalk-like pieces of furniture.

::dan pearlman
Kiefholzstrasse 1
12435 Berlin
Germany

T +49 (0)30 5300 0560
E office@danpearlman.com
W www.danpearlman.com

Photography: diephotodesigner.de

01

02

03

01 & 02 The store's 'front stage' area - where merchandise is dis—played - features grey walls and grey ceramic tiles. Black and white laminated plastics, along with chrome, dominate the palette of materials used for furniture.

03   Taking priority 'backstage' - where fitting rooms are located - is Pimkie's corporate pink. Pink wallpaper displays white silhou—ettes of landmarks associated with the store location.

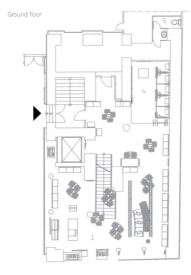

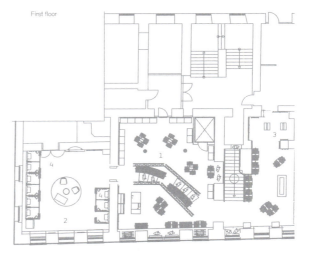

1 Front stage
2 Backstage
3 Accessories
4 Fitting rooms
5 Lavatory

QS by s.Oliver
plajer & franz studio

WHERE:	OBERHAUSEN, GERMANY
WHEN:	MARCH 2008
CLIENT:	S.OLIVER BERND FREIER
SHOP CONSTRUCTOR:	SCHLEGEL
TOTAL FLOOR AREA (M²):	260

|||||||||||||||||||||||||||||||||||||||||||||

FOUNDED IN 1996 BY ALEXANDER PLAJER AND WERNER FRANZ, BERLIN-BASED PLAJER & FRANZ STUDIO IS AN INTERNATIONAL, INTERDISCIPLINARY TEAM OF 45 ARCHITECTS, INTERIOR ARCHITECTS AND GRAPHIC DESIGNERS. ALL PHASES OF A PROJECT - FROM CONCEPT TO DESIGN TO ROLL-OUT SUPERVISION - ARE CARRIED OUT IN-HOUSE. FROM PRIVATE YACHTS AND TRADE STANDS TO BARS AND APARTMENTS, PLAJER & FRANZ STUDIO EXPLORES AND FUSES DISCIPLINES AND NEW AREAS OF EXPERIENCE. THE STUDIO HAS A STERLING REPUTATION IN EUROPE AND ASIA IN THE LUXURY RESIDENTIAL AND HOTEL SECTORS. CLIENTS INCLUDE GALERIES LAFAYETTE, S.OLIVER, BMW, TIMBERLAND AND OTHERS.

|||||||||||||||||||||||||||||||||||||||||||||

The s.Oliver label QS targets young trendsetters. To express the brand's singularity, plajer & franz studio was asked to develop a holistic design concept that would clearly illustrate the modern, up-to-date identity of QS as an integral part of the s.Oliver portfolio.

The designers opted for contemporary 'urban' materials in a bid to grab the attention of a youthful target group. Tagging the design vocabulary of QS are cool choices like stainless steel, perforated metal plates and recycled rubber. Although the concept is suitable for stand-alone stores, it can be easily implemented for shop-in-shop outlets as well. For visual merchandising and calculated stylistic clashes, the designers used imprinted truck tarp with eyelets and iron cramps, along with equipment typically found in automotive workshops, such as suspended chains and inspection lamps. The lighting concept features all-black ceiling-mounted track lighting and light cubes of perforated-metal, which draw customers into the store and round out the young concept. The backs of both cash desk and fitting rooms resemble small freight containers. The store is defined by an open ceiling in anthracite grey. Concrete tiles and oiled blanched oak have been used as flooring materials. A suspended ceiling and corresponding carpet made of recycled rubber mark the lounge area, which is furnished with Massaud's Truffle armchair.

>>

01   An animated light wall featuring a red QS logo plays a starring role in the interior design. A small lounge area (on the right) separates the men's and women's sections.

02   Here in Oberhausen, the QS retail concept has been used in the design of a stand-alone store, but it can also be applied to (future) shop-in-shop outlets.

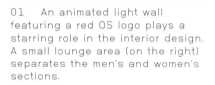

02

01

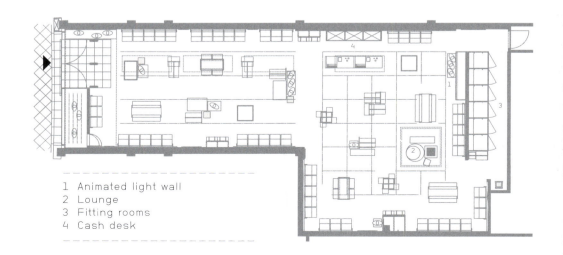

1 Animated light wall
2 Lounge
3 Fitting rooms
4 Cash desk

All furniture has a strong, youthful image that underlines the QS brand identity in a fresh way. The focal point of the store is a large animated light wall made of satinized acrylic glass. The designers made an eye-catching QS logo at the top half of this wall, using an aluminium grid covered by a glass panel to produce a striking pixellated effect. 'Artwork' wallpaper purpose-designed for QS by plajer & franz studio appears in two versions - coloured and monochrome - one indicating the men's section and the other the women's department. Wallpaper graphics reappear in chrome-laminated shapes finished in black and illuminated from behind with red light; these abstract forms float like clouds above a polished stainless-steel shelving system.

plajer & franz studio
Erkelenzdamm 59-61
10999 Berlin
Germany

T +49 (0)30 616 558 0
E studio@plajer-franz.de
W www.plajer-franz.de

Photography: diephotodesigner.de

03

04

05

03   Black forms lit from
behind mimic the graphic motif
on the purpose-designed
wallpaper. Orange/red wallpaper
marks the women's section,
while a monochrome version
covers the walls in menswear.

04&05   As fitting rooms,
plajer & franz studio used small
freight containers similar to those
stacked behind the cash desk.
They add to the shop's contemporary urban feel - an atmosphere
meant to grab the attention of
the label's young target group.

06   Overview of the shop.

Raffinalla
BlazysGérard

WHERE: MONTREAL, CANADA
WHEN: MAY 2007
CLIENT: STEVEN SALPETER
SHOP CONSTRUCTOR: RENDA CONSTRUCTION
TOTAL FLOOR AREA (M²):   65
BUDGET (€):   70,000

||||||||||||||||||||||||||||||||||||

IN 2003, ALEXANDRE BLAZYS AND BENOIT GERARD COMBINED THEIR TALENTS AND KNOWLEDGE TO CREATE AN OFFICE OF DESIGN AND ARCHITECTURE. THEIR GOAL IS TO CREATE BALANCED, FUNCTIONAL AND USEFUL HUMAN ENVIRONMENTS THAT OFFER USERS A NEW EMOTIONAL AND ARTISTIC APPRECIATION OF THEIR PHYSICAL AND BUILT SURROUNDINGS.

||||||||||||||||||||||||||||||||||||

Situated in Ogilvy's shopping mall in Montreal, the Raffinalla boutique drew conceptual inspiration from the folding and unfolding of a garment. The interior has been divided in two. The main retail area, where shoppers find the current collection, has a linearly patterned wooden floor stained in a charcoal grey for depth and contrast. The second, a service area immersed in white, features white-tiled flooring and walls with a glossy finish that reflects images of browsing shoppers and, thanks to its mirror-like effect, makes the space seem larger. The matte-surfaced retail area has a more architectural feel, providing a soft backdrop for fashions intended for a female clientele. Garments hang from an airy system of angular rails that leaves the floor of this 65-m2 space free of clutter. This sculptural display solution doubles as a sequence of linear geometry that lures the shopper towards the back of the shop, where she finds fitting rooms for trying on the items of her choice.

BlazysGérard
4211 de Rouen no. D-108
Montreal, QC H1V 1G7
Canada

T +1 514 5226 380
E blazysgerard@videotron.ca
W www.blazysgerard.com

Photography: Steve Montpetit

01

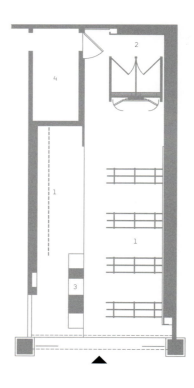

1 Display area
2 Fitting rooms
3 Cash desk
4 Storage

01   Like the entire retail space at Raffinalla, the floor is also based on duality: small, white, rectangular tiles have been used in the service area, while the rest of the store has a patterned wood floor stained a charcoal grey.

02&03   Brushed—metal racks suspended from the ceiling enable shoppers to view the clothing from all directions.

Rajesh Pratap Singh
Lotus

WHERE: NEW DELHI, INDIA
WHEN: OCTOBER 2008
CLIENT: RAJESH PRATAP SINGH
SHOP CONSTRUCTOR: BUILTKRAFT INDIA
TOTAL FLOOR AREA (M²):   85

|||||||||||||||||||||||||||||||||||||||||

FOUNDED IN 2002, LOTUS - HEADED BY AMBRISH ARORA, SIDHARTHA TALWAR, ANKUR CHOKSI AND ARUN KULLU - HAS A 20-MEMBER MULTIDISCIPLINARY TEAM OF ARCHITECTS, INTERIOR DESIGNERS, GRAPHIC DESIGNERS, FURNITURE DESIGNERS AND EXHIBITION DESIGNERS. SPECIALIZING IN HOSPITALITY AND RETAIL PROJECTS, THE FIRM PRIDES ITSELF ON CREATING EXPERIENTIAL SPACES THAT BLUR THE BOUNDARIES BETWEEN VISUAL COMMUNICATION AND ARCHITECTURE.

|||||||||||||||||||||||||||||||||||||||||

Rajesh Pratap Singh's fashion collections are for sale in six India-based flagship stores and several international multi-brand boutiques. For his flagship store in New Delhi, the fashion designer wanted a simple, clean, distinctive design concept. He asked the team at Lotus to craft an interior that would interpret his ideas. Lotus gave the space 'personality' by using scissors - an obvious tailor's tool - as a starting point for the design concept, arranging real scissors to form an intriguing pattern. Welded together on a metal frame and painted white, scissors generate a lacelike surface which has been used to produce an enclosure that fills the entire space. Thousands of pairs of scissors had to be located for this purpose; most were found at local markets. Integrated into the mesh of scissors are fittings made to hold shelves and hanging displays. Shot-blasting and brushing the grey sandstone floor gave the surface added texture.

Lotus
185 Anupam Apts
M B Road, Saket
110030 New Delhi
India

T + 91 (0)11 2953 6354
E ankur@lotslink.in
W www.lotuslink.in

Photography: Shailan Parker

01   The central display block, which runs the entire length of the store, features the same type of grey sandstone used for both floor and cash desk.

02   Thousands of pairs of scissors had to be collected before the lacy enclosure could be created.

03   To reinforce the simplicity and rawness of the design, Lotus used basic Par38 lamps, which hang from the ceiling and pass through the scissor-laced mesh.

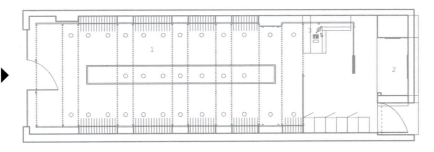

1 Retail area
2 Fitting room
3 Cash desk

0M   10M

Roar
Ito Masaru Design Project / SEI

WHERE:	TOKYO, JAPAN
WHEN:	JULY 2007
CLIENT:	MACNEEL CORPORATION
SHOP CONSTRUCTOR:	HEARTS
ARCHITECT:	SAVOR
TOTAL FLOOR AREA (M²):	95

||||||||||||||||||||||||||||||||||||||||||||||||||

A MAN WITH A SHARP SENSE OF FASHION, MASARU ITO WAS BORN IN OSAKA, JAPAN, IN 1961. AFTER GRADUATING FROM TOKYO ZOKEI UNIVERSITY IN 1987, HE ESTABLISHED ITO MASARU DESIGN PROJECT / SEI, A FIRM WITH A STRONG FOCUS ON RETAIL SPACES. MASARU ITO'S MOTTO IS: 'ALWAYS CONSIDER AN INTERIOR DESIGN FROM THE CONSUMER'S POINT OF VIEW.'

||||||||||||||||||||||||||||||||||||||||||||||||||

Distressed T-shirts featuring a crossed-guns logo are the trademark of Roar, a clothing label whose Tokyo flagship store was designed by Ito Masaru Design Concept / SEI. The designers were asked to produce a highly artistic space with a 'garage' look and feel.
To enter Roar is to experience a miniature adventure. After spotting the Roar sign, shoppers walk along a passage finished in steel panel-ling, go through a black-metal gate and reach a sliding door that opens automatically as they approach. The next part of their journey takes place in a dark, curving tunnel illuminated only by overhead light. The tunnel leads to a long, narrow, 95-m² retail interior dominated by a huge chandelier made of streetlights. Brick walls in the shop have undergone an ageing treatment, while evenly placed shutters on both sides of the space create a look of symmetry. These shut-ters function as the doors of 'closets' for hang-ing clothes belonging to Roar's current collec-tion. Recycled timber scaffolding has been used to make the closets, as well as the floor, which is covered with clear glass and lit with indirect lighting. A 3-m-long handcrafted table made of steel occupies the centre of the store. At one end of the interior, a steel gate sporting an array of antique locks adds a finishing touch to the retail concept. An atmosphere generated by well-used materials combined with cutting-edge technology radiates the spirit of the Roar brand.

Ito Masaru Design Project / SEI
#101 Daikanyama Tower
1-35-11, Ebisunishi, Shibuya-ku
150-0021 Tokyo
Japan

T +81 (0)3 5784 3201
E sei@itomasaru.com
W www.itomasaru.com

Photography: Kozo Takayama

01 Out of respect for the past, the designers used old scaffolding as flooring, simulated aged bricks on the walls, and handcrafted steel for elements such as table and gate.

02 Roll-up shutters designed to cover clothes racks give the boutique a 'garage' feel.

03 Carpeting used in the front part of the shop extends up the walls of the fitting rooms.

01

02

03

1 Display tables
2 Display shelves
3 Fitting room
4 Seating area
5 Cash desk
6 Storage
7 Lavatory

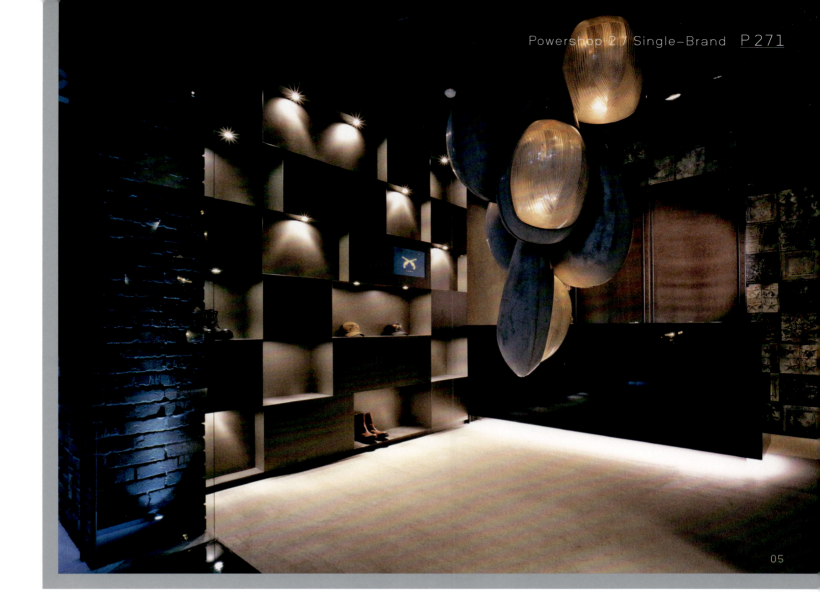

05

06

04   A huge chandelier made of streetlights welcomes visitors to the shop.

05   Next to the counter, a display area for accessories features Roar's famous crossed-guns logo.

06   A steel gate with an array of antique locks highlights one end of the shop.

Roen
Ito Masaru Design Project / SEI

WHERE:	TOKYO, JAPAN
WHEN:	OCTOBER 2007
CLIENT:	ROEN
SHOP CONSTRUCTOR:	AIM CREATE
ARCHITECT:	HARAKIRI
TOTAL FLOOR AREA (M²):	92

||||||||||||||||||||||||||||||||||||||||||

A MAN WITH A SHARP SENSE OF FASHION, MA-
SARU ITO WAS BORN IN OSAKA, JAPAN, IN 1961.
AFTER GRADUATING FROM TOKYO ZOKEI UNI-
VERSITY IN 1987, HE ESTABLISHED ITO MASARU
DESIGN PROJECT / SEI, A FIRM WITH A STRONG
FOCUS ON RETAIL SPACES. MASARU ITO'S MOT-
TO IS: 'ALWAYS CONSIDER AN INTERIOR DESIGN
FROM THE CONSUMER'S POINT OF VIEW.'

||||||||||||||||||||||||||||||||||||||||||

According to fashion designer Hiromu Takahara,
clothes by Japanese brand Roen are for the 'mature and classy' guy. For the interior of Roen's
first indoor shop, Takahara turned to Ito Masaru
Design Project / SEI. The brief that he gave the
designers requested a retail concept inspired by
two terms: 'tunnel' and 'a floating feeling'.
The design team used a centrally positioned
black-glass tunnel to create three circulation
zones. The main zone, in the middle, opens wide
towards the entrance. A custom-made Swarovski-
crystal chandelier above this area sparkles like
a waterfall. A smaller space to one side functions as the 'antechamber' to a fitting room. Here
a glazed floor illuminated by built-in, digitally
controlled LEDs sports a lively leopard-skin pattern. Concluding the trio is a minimalist cashier
zone, which reflects the look and feel of Roen
streetwear. In addition to the chandelier, titanium
skulls intensify the atmosphere of this intriguing
retail interior.

Ito Masaru Design Project / SEI
#101 Daikanyama Tower
1-35-11, Ebisunishi, Shibuya-ku
150-0021 Tokyo
Japan

T +81 (0)3 5784 3201
E sei@itomasaru.com
W www.itomasaru.com

Photography: Kozo Takayama

01 Passers-by often stop to
gaze at the Swarovski chandelier hanging at the centre of the
shop.

02 Black carpeting and walls
and ceiling of black glass give
shoppers the sense of walking
through a tunnel..

03 By positioning the cashier zone next to the diagonally
placed 'tunnel', the designers
gave the cash desk a jaunty, angular look.

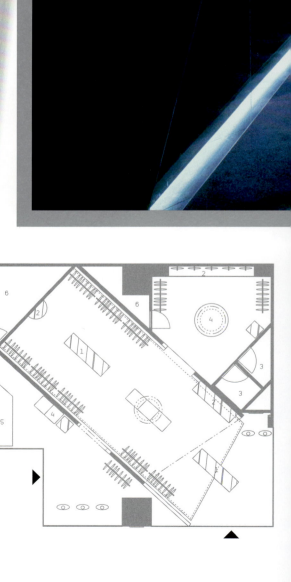

01

02

1 Display tables
2 Display shelves
3 Fitting room
4 Seating area
5 Cash desk
6 Storage

03

01

Rohit Bal
Lotus

WHERE:	NEW DELHI, INDIA
WHEN:	SEPTEMBER 2008
CLIENT:	ROHIT BAL
SHOP CONSTRUCTOR:	BUILDKRAFT INDIA
TOTAL FLOOR AREA (M²):	110
BUDGET (€):	160,000

||||||||||||||||||||||||||||||||||||||||

FOUNDED IN 2002, LOTUS - HEADED BY AMBRISH ARORA, SIDHARTHA TALWAR, ANKUR CHOKSI AND ARUN KULLU - HAS A 20-MEMBER MULTIDISCIPLINARY TEAM OF ARCHITECTS, INTERIOR DESIGNERS, GRAPHIC DESIGNERS, FURNITURE DESIGNERS AND EXHIBITION DESIGNERS. SPECIALIZING IN HOSPITALITY AND RETAIL PROJECTS, THE FIRM PRIDES ITSELF ON CREATING EXPERIENTIAL SPACES THAT BLUR THE BOUNDARIES BETWEEN VISUAL COMMUNICATION AND ARCHITECTURE.

||||||||||||||||||||||||||||||||||||||||

Located in New Delhi's Emporio shopping mall, fashion designer Rohit Bal's store was created by Lotus. The brief stipulated a men's section well separated from the women's section. Lotus responded to this request with a centrally positioned salon that divides the rectangular space into a women's collection, on the side closest to the entrance, and a men's collection that extends from the salon to the back of the store. A purpose-designed, blown-glass chandelier illuminates the salon, which is bordered by rusted metal *jaalis* (latticed screens) adorned with Rohit Bal's signature lotus motif, a floral reference used extensively in his fashions. Brass inlays in the blue concrete floor also feature the lotus. Walls and ceiling are finished in a pewter colour. A suspended display system of flame-treated metal supports garments on hangers. Using layers and an interplay of raw and elaborately detailed elements, the designers crafted an exceptionally rich, mysterious and warm space.

Lotus
185 Anupam Apts
M B Road, Saket
110030 New Delhi
India

T + 91 (0)11 2953 6354
E ankur@lotslink.in
W www.lotuslink.in

Photography: Eye Piece

01   A centrally placed salon divides the store into two sections: one for menswear and the other for women's fashions.

02   Suspended metal system for displaying clothes.

03   The lotus motif, which is used extensively in fashions designed by Rohit Bal, also features in the brass inlays that appear in the blue concrete floor.

04   The walls of the salon are made of CNC-cut rusted metal jaalis (lattice screens) with lotus motif.

03

02

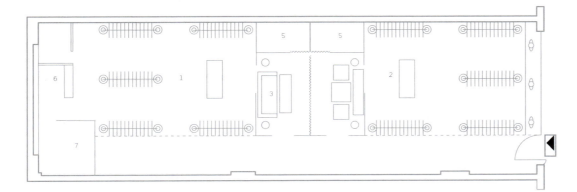

1 Men's section
2 Women's section
3 Men's salon
4 Women's salon
5 Fitting room
6 Cash desk
7 Storage

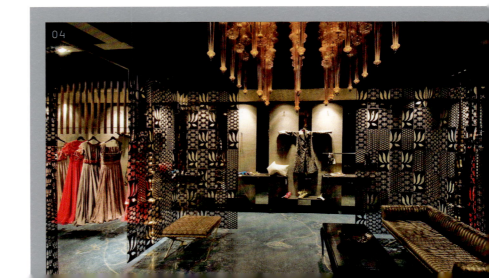

Romanticism 2
SAKO Architects

WHERE:	HANGZHOU, CHINA
WHEN:	AUGUST 2007
CLIENT:	ROMAN ISSIN
SHOP CONSTRUCTOR:	ROMAN ISSIN
TOTAL FLOOR AREA (M²):	1142
BUDGET (€):	220,000

||||||||||||||||||||||||||||||||||||||||||||||||||

AFTER GRADUATING FROM THE TOKYO INSTITUTE OF TECHNOLOGY IN 1996, KEIICHIRO SAKO (1970) JOINED THE OFFICE OF RIKEN YAMAMOTO & FIELD SHOP. IN 2004 HE ESTABLISHED SAKO ARCHITECTS IN BEIJING, CHINA. CURRENTLY THE FIRM HAS OFFICES IN BOTH BEIJING AND TOKYO. SAKO ARCHITECTS IS INVOLVED IN A WIDE RANGE OF PROJECTS, FROM RESIDENTIAL HIGH-RISE TOWERS TO COMMERCIAL INTERIOR DESIGNS. MOST OF THE WORK IS BEING CARRIED OUT IN CHINA, JAPAN AND SOUTH KOREA.

||||||||||||||||||||||||||||||||||||||||||||||||||

The 1142-m² flagship store that Keiichiro Sako designed for Romanticism 2 is a unique retail establishment at the centre of the sub-provincial city of Hangzhou, China. What makes it so unique is, among other things, its size: most of the brand's 500 stores, all located in China, occupy spaces of about 80 m². To create a neutral background for Romanticism's colourful collections of casual clothes for young women, Sako gave the retail interior an all-white atmosphere crafted from painted plasterboard and artificial marble floors. The result is a soft, dreamlike space. The architect connected ground floor and basement with the use of a fluidly shaped structure that looks like an amorphous, bone-like mesh. The sight of the structure, with its polished epoxy-resin finish, draws people from the street into the shop and, ultimately, all the way down to the 780-m² retail space in the basement. The architect describes the mesh as a 'third skin': the first is the shopper's human skin, the second is the garment she takes from the rack, the third is the mesh and 'the walls of the building itself are the fourth skin', according to Sako, who adds that 'the net forms the soft layer in between space and clothes'. Here at Romanticism 2, Sako's third skin occasionally serves as a partition or as an odd though functional piece of furniture, such as a cash desk.

Text by Cathelijne Nuijsink

SAKO Architects
1801, Tower8, JianWaiSOHO, No.39
East 3rd Ring Road, Chaoyang
100022 Beijing
China

T +86 (0)10 5869 0901
E info@sako.co.jp
W www.sako.co.jp

Photography: Nacása & Partners

01

01   Reflected in the artificial marble floor is an illuminated niche in the wall containing a draped length of scarlet fabric. Walls form the skin of a building in the same way that garments add a layer of skin to the body.

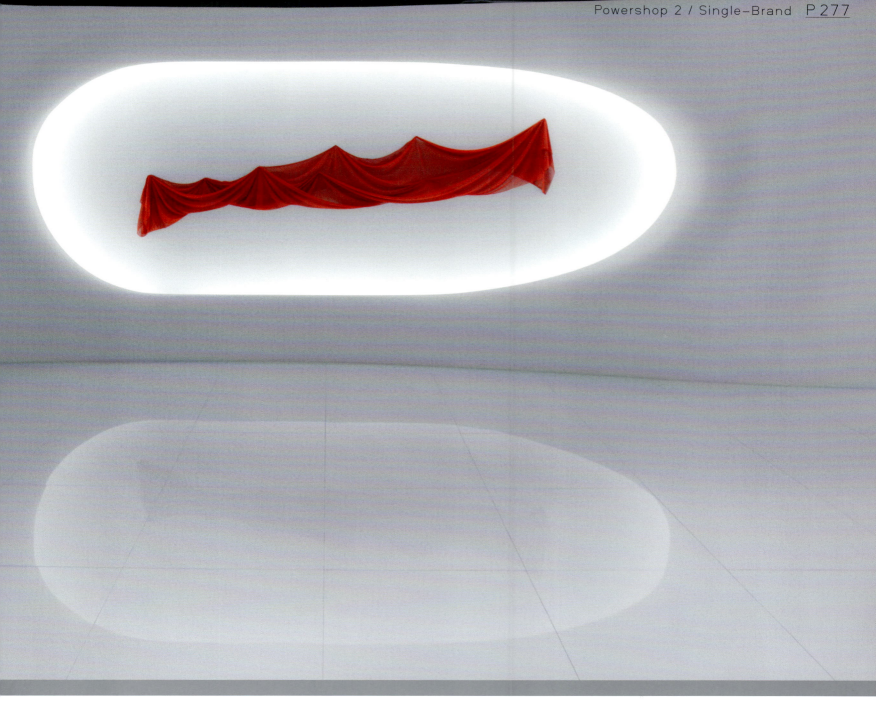

1 Display area
2 Bench
3 Fitting room
4 Cash desk
5 Café
6 Storage

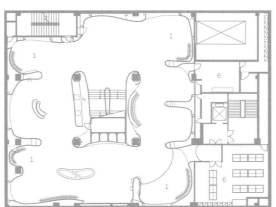

Basement

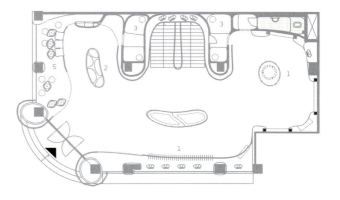

Ground floor

02   Romanticism 2 covers the
ground floor and basement level
of a building close to the centre
of Hangzhou.

03&04   To make the ceiling
appear higher, Sako gave it
a curved, metallic finish. Shoppers
looking up see reflections of
the objects around them. Seemingly afloat in an expanse of water,
the shop is filled with a dreamy,
surreal atmosphere.

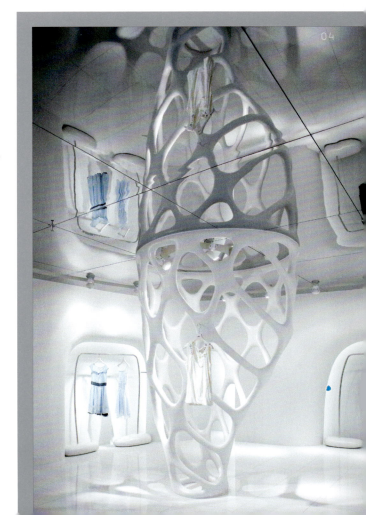

s.Oliver
Selection Store
plajer & franz
studio

WHERE:	KOBLENZ, GERMANY
WHEN:	SEPTEMBER 2008
CLIENT:	S.OLIVER BERND FREIER
SHOP CONSTRUCTOR:	KONHÄUSER
TOTAL FLOOR AREA (M²):	130

||||||||||||||||||||||||||||||||||||||||||||

FOUNDED IN 1996 BY ALEXANDER PLAJER AND WERNER FRANZ, BERLIN-BASED PLAJER & FRANZ STUDIO IS AN INTERNATIONAL, INTERDISCIPLINARY TEAM OF 45 ARCHITECTS, INTERIOR ARCHITECTS AND GRAPHIC DESIGNERS. ALL PHASES OF A PROJECT - FROM CONCEPT TO DESIGN TO ROLL-OUT SUPERVISION - ARE CARRIED OUT IN-HOUSE. FROM PRIVATE YACHTS AND TRADE STANDS TO BARS AND APARTMENTS, PLAJER & FRANZ STUDIO EXPLORES AND FUSES DISCIPLINES AND NEW AREAS OF EXPERIENCE. THE STUDIO HAS A STERLING REPUTATION IN EUROPE AND ASIA IN THE LUXURY RESIDENTIAL AND HOTEL SECTORS. CLIENTS INCLUDE GALERIES LAFAYETTE, S.OLIVER, BMW, TIMBERLAND AND OTHERS.

||||||||||||||||||||||||||||||||||||||||||||

Selection is a recently launched line of premium merchandise by fashion and lifestyle brand s.Oliver. Twelve collections a year appear in exclusive mono-brand stores that cater to the smart business client. The 'Selection Story' - translated by plajer & franz studio - is aimed at today's elegant, fashion-conscious consumer: men and women who dress 'smart' even in their leisure hours. Retail interiors for Selection are high-end environments marked by distinction. The concept of the store is 'bright and subtle elegance'. Blanched oak flooring, oiled and smoked, has been combined with freestanding chrome fixtures within an interior that is enhanced by indirect lighting to achieve the desired air of refinement and exclusivity. Clearly distinguished areas for men's and women's apparel feature contrasting compositions of chic, stylish materials and finishes - matte versus glossy, light versus dark - employed to engage and please the discerning eye. Intuitively, plajer & franz studio chose a brighter look for Selection Women, where the ambience relies on contrasts conjured by glossy white surfaces, gold highlights and pale fabrics. The darker colour scheme of Selection Men is characterized by bronze surfaces and fabrics. Nevertheless, the predominant colours and textures of the retail concept are found throughout the store, in both the men's and the women's sections. A focus wall is composed of chrome bars and mirror elements arranged on a black-varnished glass panel.

>>

01

02

01   The focus wall, highlighted
by chrome and mirror elements on
a black—varnished glass backdrop,
is visible from outside the shop.

02   By combining the focus wall
with an accessory lounge, plajer
& franz studio created an ideal
cross—selling platform.

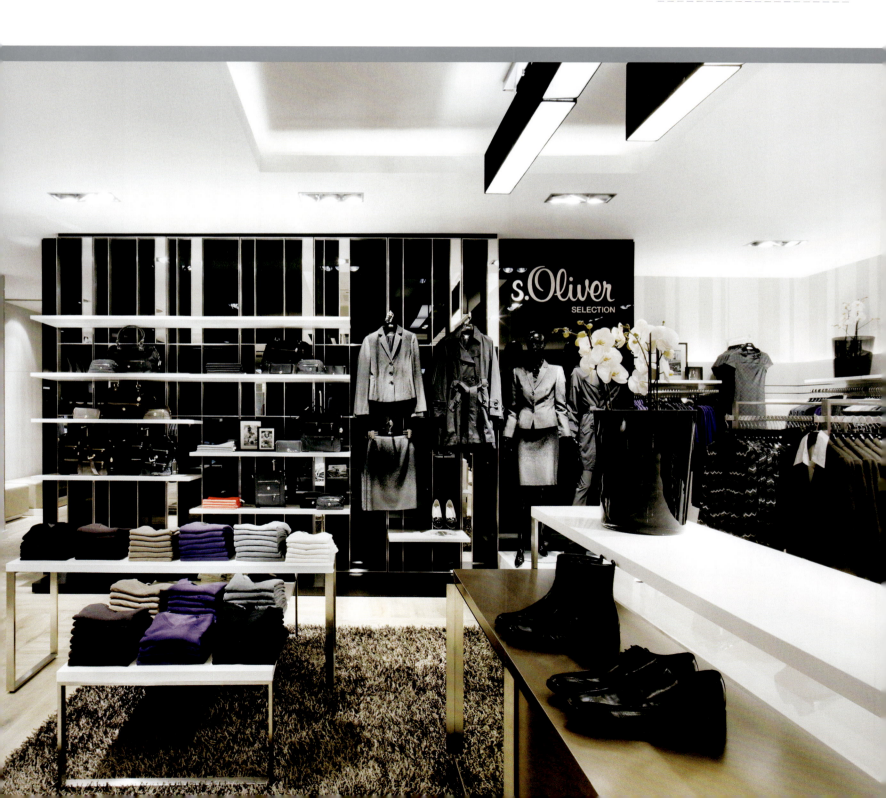

Smoked-glass panels separating various colour palettes for merchandise are used for special offers and display purposes. The wall system - a continuous panelled surface with integrated support rails - offers the utmost in flexibility and provides a perfect place for thematic presentations. Wallpaper with a motif of alternating matte and glossy stripes was designed for the store by plajer & franz studio. A lounge area with seating that matches the overall colour scheme doubles as a place where customers can try on shoes and accessories. Suspended ceiling elements signpost this corner of the store. By combining a focus wall with an accessory lounge, plajer & franz studio created an ideal cross-selling platform.

plajer & franz studio
Erkelenzdamm 59-61
10999 Berlin
Germany

T +49 (0)30 616 558 0
E studio@plajer-franz.de
W www.plajer-franz.de

Photography: diephotodesigner.de

03   Fitting rooms are at the rear of the shop, behind the black focus wall.

04   Part of the back wall, including the door to the storage room, is covered in mirrored panels.

05   Purpose-designed wallpaper with alternating matte and glossy stripes appears in both the men's and the women's sections.

05

06&07   To subtly distinguish
one area from another, the
designers chose a bright ambience for the women's section and
used darker colours and materials
for the men's section.

07

06

Sigrun Woehr
ippolito fleitz group

WHERE: KARLSRUHE, GERMANY
WHEN: APRIL 2008
CLIENT: SIGRUN WOEHR
SHOP CONSTRUCTOR: BAIERL & DEMMELHUBER
TOTAL FLOOR AREA (M²):   197

||||||||||||||||||||||||||||||||||||||||||||||

STUTTGART–BASED MULTIDISCIPLINARY
DESIGN STUDIO IPPOLITO FLEITZ GROUP
OPERATES WORLDWIDE. THE STUDIO'S CORE
CAPABILITIES - ARCHITECTURE, DESIGN AND
COMMUNICATION - INSPIRE AND COMPLEMENT
ONE ANOTHER. CALLING ITS TEAM 'IDENTITY
ARCHITECTS', IPPOLITO FLEITZ GROUP
UNDERSTANDS THE PROCESS OF TRANSLATING
COMPLEX CLIENT IDENTITIES INTO SUCCESSFUL
PROJECTS THAT INCLUDE BUILDINGS, INTERIORS,
LANDSCAPES, PRODUCTS, AND BRAND AND
COMMUNICATION STRATEGIES.

||||||||||||||||||||||||||||||||||||||||||||||

Sigrun Woehr is the premier address for high–end
footwear in the German state of Baden–Württem–
berg. The firm that designed the label's first
store in Stuttgart - ippolito fleitz group - was
also responsible for the retailer's second outlet
in Karlsruhe. This shop was to mark a new
departure for Sigrun Woehr, as the label had
recently expanded its range to include a fashion
collection and an accessory line.
The brief asked for a retail interior that would
present the client's exclusive range of goods
properly while enticing customers to cross the
threshold. The available space, located in the
city centre, was not only narrow but also nearly
25 m long. By installing a ceiling that becomes
gradually lower from front to back over the entire
length of the shop, the designers created a kind
of visual suction that is meant to pull customers
farther and farther into the space. Striking
fittings and strong ceiling motifs demarcate
individual zones. Most of the merchandise
occupies a dynamically designed wall display,
which is supplemented by several presentation
areas and centrally positioned core elements
that leave room for the customer to browse
without hindrance. The clothing line is displayed
in a dedicated area that strikes a distinct
visual note but, like everything in the shop,
is incorporated into the overall concept in a
compelling and coherent manner.

ippolito fleitz group
Augustenstrasse 87
70197 Stuttgart
Germany

T +49 (0)711 993 392 – 330
E info@ifgroup.org
W www.ifgroup.org

Photography: Zooey Braun

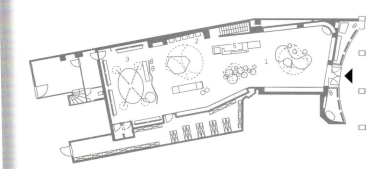

1 Shoes
2 Accessories
3 Apparel
4 Fitting room
5 Cash desk

01&02 Presented at the rear of the shop, the fashion collection is separated from the rest of the space by a smoked—glass wall that is flanked by two mannequins.

03   Four large textile lamps mounted on projecting arms emerge from the recessed, mirror—clad ceiling to span the entire fashion area.

01

02

03

04   Three circular ceiling motifs executed in violet, fuchsia and pale pink create a focal point and draw the customer's gaze towards the far end of the space.

05   The cash desk faces an ensemble of round tables. Thanks to varying heights, sizes and surface materials, they form an attractive display area for shoes, bags and accessories.

Siste's More
Bong Bong

01 A gigantic wooden reel dominates the shop.

02 Various motifs appear as perforations in the wooden structure that hides the staircase.

03 Thanks to a cladding of metal and glass, the 15-m-long counter resembles a reflective box.

WHERE:	FUNO DI ARGELATO, ITALY
WHEN:	SEPTEMBER 2007
CLIENT:	SISTE'S
SHOP CONSTRUCTOR:	SCHIAVON ARREDAMENTI
TOTAL FLOOR AREA (M²):	1000
BUDGET (€):	800,000

ARCHITECT AND DESIGNER PIETRO BONGIANA WORKED IN EUROPE AND THE USA BEFORE ESTABLISHING BONG BONG IN 1985. TODAY HIS TEAM OF INTERNATIONAL ARCHITECTS WORK ON A VARIETY OF PROJECTS THAT REFLECT THE FOUNDER'S INTERNATIONAL ORIENTATION. THE FIRM'S CURRENT FOCUS IS ON RETAIL ARCHITECTURE FOR CLIENTS SUCH AS REPLAY, PHARD, NORTHLAND, TUBES, SISTE'S, DIADORA UTILITY, LOTTO AND HENRY COTTON'S.

01

Siste's More, a brand specializing in fashions for women with generous curves, envisioned a showroom that would reflect and communicate its style: a space both distinguished and cosy, with well-defined functions. A challenging job for Bong Bong, as the original place was basically a shed. Bong Bong turned the space into a playground featuring objects that look like small works of architecture. They were inspired by potbellied musical instruments in paintings by Baschenis, as is particularly evident in the enormous wooden reel that dominates the interior. Furnishings, decorations, equipment: here everything normally found in a showroom becomes something entirely different. The counter looks like a 15-m-long reflective box. A 6-m-high screen unrolls along the perimeter and flows into a micro-perforated rhombus that hides stairs leading to offices on the first floor. This showroom is ruled by extremes and dissonances: wood and metal, smooth and rough, but also by a playful cross-reference to optical art and 17th-century baroque paintings.

Bong Bong
Via Fra' Giovanni Eremitano 12
35138 Padua
Italy

T +39 04 9661 270
E studio@bongiana.it
W www.bongiana.it

Photography: Marco Righes

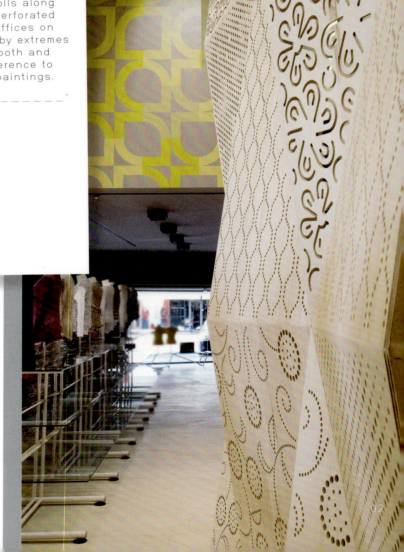

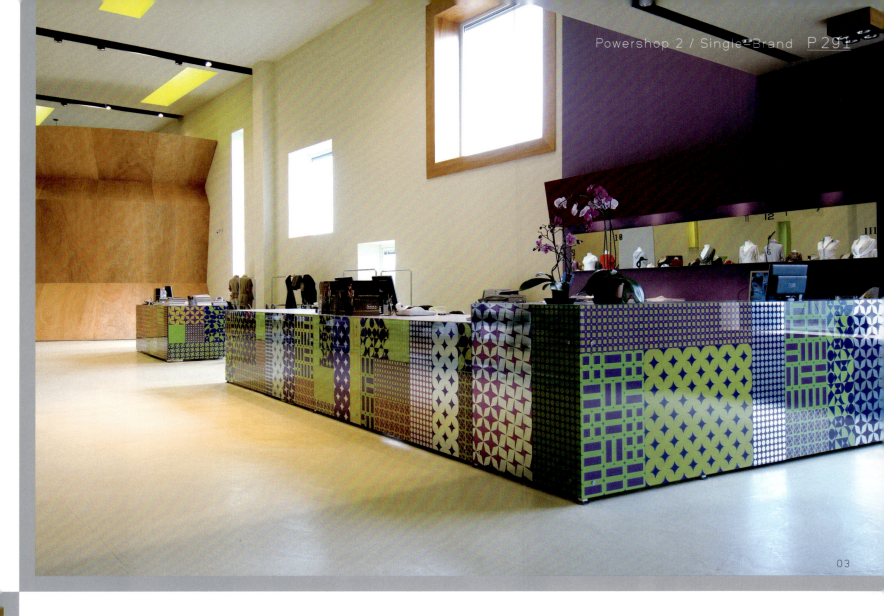

03

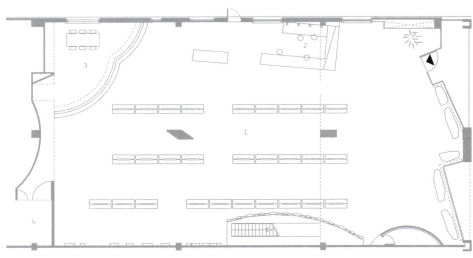

1 Sales area
2 Cash desk
3 Office
4 Storage

Sportsgirl
HMKM

WHERE: MELBOURNE, AUSTRALIA
WHEN: SEPTEMBER 2008
CLIENT: SPORTSGIRL
TOTAL FLOOR AREA (M²):   500

||||||||||||||||||||||||||||||||||||||||||||||||||||||||

FOUNDED IN 1990 AND BASED IN LONDON'S
SOHO DISTRICT, DESIGN CONSULTANCY
HMKM CONSISTS OF SPECIALISTS IN THE FIELDS
OF BRANDING, ARCHITECTURE, INTERIOR DESIGN,
GRAPHIC DESIGN AND ART DIRECTION.
TAILOR-MADE PROJECT TEAMS HELP CLIENTS
TO REALISE THEIR BRAND VISION, NO MATTER
WHAT THE SCALE OF THE PROJECT. THEIR
INTERNATIONAL CLIENT LIST INCLUDES HAR-
RODS, SELFRIDGES, HYUNDAI, SALAM, NIKE
AND LULU GUINNESS.

||||||||||||||||||||||||||||||||||||||||||||||||||||||||

Sportsgirl stores are home to the latest
clothing styles with a strong appeal to young
Aussie fashionistas. The brand asked design
consultancy HMKM to create a super flagship
store in Melbourne, Australia. The store was to
offer its clientele a unique, interactive and
ever-changing retail environment.
Upon entering the store, customers find themselves in an area called 'The Stage'. Inspired
by the changeability of a theatre set, HMKM
designed 'The Stage' as a blank canvas that can
be reinvented time and again to display the latest
trends in art and design: a perpetually changing fashion showcase. Customers find Sportsgirl's
main collections in an area named 'Off the Rails',
where a refined metal space frame allows for an
uncluttered approach to merchandising. Polished
brass, accents in primary colours and timber
with diamond-pattern inlays form the basis
of an eclectic and contemporary furniture mix.
'The Butterfly Garden' fitting rooms radiate
around a central meeting space and are person-
alised with hooks, seating and three-way
mirrors. Butterfly-motif curtains and a mosaic
mirror entrance complete the picture. 'Style Me'
is a personal shopping suite with a constantly
changing collage of inspirational seasonal
magazine and campaign clippings on the walls.
A team of stylists is on hand to help each
customer craft a perfect individualized look.
During the consultancy's visit to the site –
a former movie theatre – they discovered the
opportunity to create an 11-m high atrium at
the back of the store. The atrium creates a
real wow factor and introduces natural light
to the space.

01   Shoe collections are
displayed in the 'Strut' area.

02   A stunning diamond-
mirrored fascia signals the
arrival of Sportsgirl's super
flagship concept.

HMKM
14–16 Great Pulteney Street
London W1F 9ND
United Kingdom

T +44 (0)20 7494 4949
E info@hmkm.com
W www.hmkm.com

Photography: courtesy of Sportsgirl

1 The Stage
2 Strut (shoes)
3 Off the Rails (apparel)
4 The Treasure Chest
   (accessories)
5 Style Me Fashion Studio
6 Butterfly room (fitting rooms)
7 DJ
8 Cash desks
9 Storage

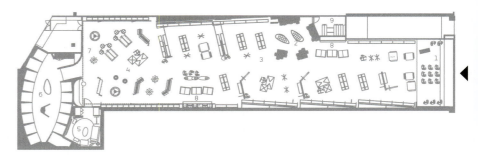

03   In the 'Style Me' section,
a team of stylists helps each
customer to create that perfect
individual look.

04   A DJ area is located in front
of the fitting rooms.

05   In the atrium, diamond—
shaped panels hang from an
open ceiling.

Takeda Truss Trash
No Picnic

WHERE:	GOTHENBURG, SWEDEN
WHEN:	OCTOBER 2008
CLIENT:	WEEKDAY
SHOP CONSTRUCTOR:	NÄSSJÖ INREDNINGAR
TOTAL FLOOR AREA (M²):	1000

SCANDINAVIAN DESIGN COMPANY NO PICNIC WAS FOUNDED IN 1993 BY PARTNERS WHO STILL RUN THE FIRM. THE MULTIDISCIPLINARY TEAM OF ARCHITECTS, INDUSTRIAL DESIGNERS, GRAPHIC DESIGNERS, DESIGN ENGINEERS, STRATEGISTS, TREND ANALYSTS AND PROJECT MANAGERS HAS COMPLETED OVER 750 PROJECTS FOR CLIENTS WORLDWIDE, INCLUDING ASTRA TECH, BOSCH, ERICSSON, OTTO BOCK, SAS, SONY, SONY ERICS-SON, TETRA PAK, UNIBAIL-RODAMCO, UNILEVER, WEEKDAY AND KRAFT.

In 2002, Weekday - a popular Swedish brand that operates a chain of stores - opened its first shop. The brief asked for something that had never been done before. Weekday wanted its style, its fashions, its personality and its history to be transformed into a story so strong and unique that advertising would be unnecessary. That brief remained during years of cooperation between Weekday and No Picnic. Using preliminary studies and workshops, No Picnic develops a 'set design' for each new store, like a storyboard for a Weekday movie. The eighth and latest addition is the 'Takeda Truss Trash' store. All furniture is based on the wire-framed image of an extruded rhombus climbing towards the ceiling. The concept was derived from the crest of the Japanese Takeda clan, which consists of four rhombuses arranged to form a larger one. Window graphics were created in collaboration with Swedish graphic-design studio VÅR.

No Picnic
Ljusslingan 1
120 31 Stockholm
Sweden

T +46 (0)8 556 96 550
E info@nopicnic.se
W www.nopicnic.com

Photography: Rasmus Norlander and Victor Peters (No Picnic)

01

01   All furniture is based on the wire-framed image of an extruded rhombus.

02   Here, as at other Weekday stores, graphics were designed by VÅR.

03   Rhombic frames climbing towards the ceiling are backed by hanging lamps, which were custom-designed in collaboration with lighting-design company Node Ljusdesign.

First floor

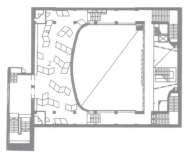

Ground floor

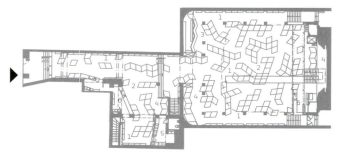

02

03

1 Display hanger
2 Display table
3 Display shelves
4 Fitting room
5 In–store workshop
6 Cash desk

05

04   Stairs behind the fitting
rooms lead to the first floor,
where shoppers find even more
merchandise.

05   Visitors entering the store
find themselves in a dark tunnel
that leads to the light–filled heart
of the retail space.

Timberland
Checkland Kindleysides

WHERE:	LONDON, UNITED KINGDOM
WHEN:	OCTOBER 2008
CLIENT:	TIMBERLAND
SHOP CONSTRUCTOR:	P6
TOTAL FLOOR AREA (M²):	238

|||||||||||||||||||||||||||||||||||||||||

JEFF KINDLEYSIDES ESTABLISHED HIS COMPANY, CHECKLAND KINDLEYSIDES (CK), IN 1979. OVER THE PAST 30 YEARS, THE COMPANY HAS DEVELOPED A UNIQUE CULTURE AND LONG-STANDING RELATIONSHIPS WITH CLIENTS. AT CK CREATIVITY IS DRIVEN BY ROBUST CUSTOMER, DESIGN AND MARKET INSIGHT AND AN ABILITY TO MAKE THINGS WORK AESTHETICALLY, PHYSICALLY AND COMMERCIALLY. CLIENTS INCLUDE CONVERSE, LEVIS STRAUSS AND SONY PLAYSTATION.

|||||||||||||||||||||||||||||||||||||||||

As part of the brief for its new Westfield London store, Timberland challenged Checkland Kindleysides (CK) to bring the brand's iconic tree logo to life and to show Timberland's environmental values in action.

Taking cues from the Timberland logo and the dynamic tree-like roof supports that form the architecture of the shopping centre, CK created a lattice of reclaimed timber branches that wrap the store in the brand's symbolic logo. The façade, with its fret-cut steel signage, creates a strong brand statement and a distinctive endorsement: that you've arrived at Timberland. The structure creates interesting views into the store, with irregularly shaped display windows allowing footwear to be showcased in a simple framework. At the heart of the store is the main footwear display, which has an artistic design enhanced by materials that reinforce the craftsmanship and heritage of the brand. This area incorporates two feature walls. The first, clad in Timberland's original boot leather, is a curved footwear wall highlighting the key footwear display. The second is the 'shoe lath' wall, which is made up of vintage shoe laths set against a panel of hot-rolled steel, allowing for the relaxed and versatile visual merchandising of footwear, clothing and accessories. Display counters and cash desk are made of stacked timber boards. Reflecting Timberland's relationship with the outdoors and nature, a full 85 per cent of the materials used in the retail design served other purposes in a previous life, or are from sustainable sources.

Checkland Kindleysides
Charnwood Edge, Cossington
Leicester LE7 4UZ
United Kingdom

T +44 (0)116 2644 700
E info@checklandkindleysides.com
W www.checklandkindleysides.com

Photography: Keith Parry

01

01 An irregular arrangement of reclaimed timber stretches the full 25-m length of the side elevation, as well as the 11-m-long façade and the 8.5-m height of the store.

02 Enhancing the space, a variety of mid-floor fixtures and furniture of different heights can be mixed, matched and moved around the store to change product displays in both dramatic and subtle ways.

03 An expanse of randomly shaped display windows creates interesting views into the store.

02

03

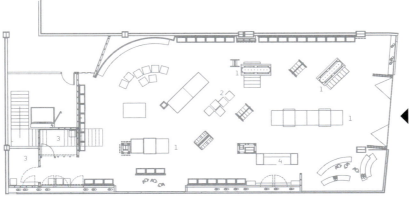

1 Display table
2 Seating area
3 Fitting room
4 Cash desk

04　In the fitting-room area, vintage photographs and graphics adorning the walls pay homage to the 1908 Olympic stadium that once stood on this site.

05　A full 85 per cent of the materials used in Timberland's Westfield store have served other purposes in a previous life. The vintage shoe laths mounted on this wall are a good example.

06　The cash desk - carefully constructed of layers of timber and leather off-cuts - is set against a backdrop of reclaimed doors.

Toxic Explosion
No Picnic

WHERE:	STOCKHOLM, SWEDEN
WHEN:	APRIL 2007
CLIENT:	WEEKDAY
SHOP CONSTRUCTOR:	NÄSSJÖ INREDNINGAR
TOTAL FLOOR AREA (M²):	427

||||||||||||||||||||||||||||||||||||||||||||||||

SCANDINAVIAN DESIGN COMPANY NO PICNIC WAS FOUNDED IN 1993 BY PARTNERS WHO STILL RUN THE FIRM. THE MULTIDISCIPLINARY TEAM OF ARCHITECTS, INDUSTRIAL DESIGNERS, GRAPHIC DESIGNERS, DESIGN ENGINEERS, STRATEGISTS, TREND ANALYSTS AND PROJECT MANAGERS HAS COMPLETED OVER 750 PROJECTS FOR CLIENTS WORLDWIDE, INCLUDING ASTRA TECH, BOSCH, ERICSSON, OTTO BOCK, SAS, SONY, SONY ERICSSON, TETRA PAK, UNIBAIL–RODAMCO, UNILEVER, WEEKDAY AND KRAFT.

||||||||||||||||||||||||||||||||||||||||||||||||

In 2002, Weekday - a popular Swedish brand that operates a chain of stores - opened its first shop. The brief asked for something that had never been done before. Weekday wanted its style, its fashions, its personality and its history to be transformed into a story so strong and unique that advertising would be unnecessary. That brief remained during years of cooperation between Weekday and No Picnic. Using preliminary studies and workshops, No Picnic develops a 'set design' for each new store, like a storyboard for a Weekday movie. The name 'Toxic Explosion' pretty much covers the interior concept of the store shown here. Two damaged columns mark the origin of the explosion, which is also represented by 'light beams' in the form of bright orange rails. Clothes hang on the lower rails, while those overhead support track lighting. Apparently, the big bang has even damaged the heavy columns further away.

No Picnic
Ljusslingan 1
120 31 Stockholm
Sweden

T +46 (0)8 556 96 550
E info@nopicnic.se
W www.nopicnic.com

Photography: Patrik Engquist

01

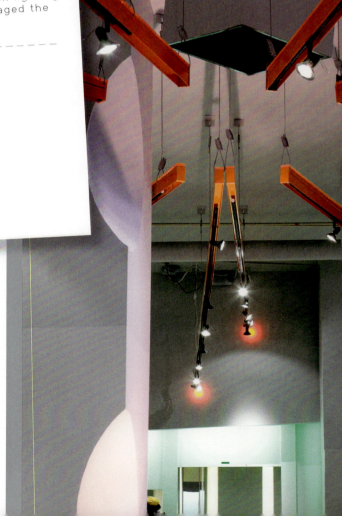

02

03

01   Fitting rooms.

02   Orange rails designed as beams of light hold both track lighting and garments.

03   The 'explosion' that gave the shop its name has damaged the two center columns.

1 Display hanger
2 Display table
3 Display shelves
4 Fitting room
5 Cash desk

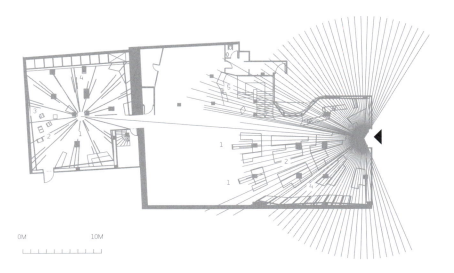

0M   10M

Victorinox
Retailpartners

01

01   Exterior lighting is restrained
and elegant, while vibrantly
illuminated ground-floor shop
windows benefit from the latest
in LED technology.

02   The range of materials and
furnishings has been reduced
to a minimum to create a softly
sensuous quality that gives
the space an intrinsically Swiss
character.

03   Exclusive timepieces are now
part of the brand's product range.

WHERE:	WESTMINSTER, LONDON, UNITED KINGDOM
WHEN:	NOVEMBER 2008
CLIENT:	VICTORINOX RETAIL (UK) LIMITED
SHOP CONSTRUCTOR:	SD SHOP FITTING LONDON
TOTAL FLOOR AREA (M²):	500
BUDGET (€):	2.5 MILLION

|||||||||||||||||||||||||||||||||||||||||

FOUNDED IN 1996, RETAILPARTNERS HAS
A HISTORY OF PROVIDING INTERNATIONAL
RETAIL-DESIGN AND IMPLEMENTATION
SERVICES. IN 2006 THE FIRM JOINED THE
ANDREAS MESSERLI GROUP, A COMPLEMENT
OF COMPANIES CURRENTLY SUPPORTED
BY RETAILPARTNERS' SPECIALIST INSIGHT
IN THE FIELDS OF RETAIL, BRANDSCAPES AND
INTERIORS. MAJOR CLIENTS INCLUDE SUNRISE
COMMUNICATION, JELMOLI GROUP, STARBUCKS
SWITZERLAND, ESPRIT DISTRIBUTION
SWITZERLAND, PHONAK, BATA, NESTLE
NESPRESSO AND PROCTER & GAMBLE.

|||||||||||||||||||||||||||||||||||||||||

The opening of the Victorinox flagship store
marks the beginning of a new era for the brand
that is famous for its Swiss Army Knife. Founded
some 125 years ago in Ibach, Switzerland, the
brand has successfully managed to impart
quality, reliability and iconic design to a wider
range of more contemporary high-quality goods.
The three-level store on New Bond Street in the
London district of Westminster shows the full
range of recent additions, such as exclusive
timepieces, sportswear, men's and women's wear,
fragrances and travel gear.
Design firm Retailpartners and the Andreas
Messerli Group have worked on a number of
Victorinox ventures ranging from points of sale,
shops-in-shops and exhibition designs,
but it wasn't until winning the international
competition for the first European flagship store
that they were challenged with a job of this
scale and complexity. The designers aimed for
a retail environment that would evoke Helvetic
authenticity. To accomplish this they chose a
quiet, sensuous design with features intrinsic
to the character of the Swiss, who often select
colours and textures from their native landscape.
Simplicity and purity distinguish an interior in
which the amount of furniture has been reduced
to a minimum. The design team used technology
to enhance the look and feel of the store and to
underline the contemporary aspect of recently
added merchandise. On 65-in screens, customers
watch specially commissioned films that combine
the scenic beauty of Switzerland with various
Victorinox product stories. To create involvement
and interest in the brand, customized touchscreens in the lounge area illustrate and promote
products while inviting the customer to interact.
Another focus was to achieve a visual connection
linking the three floors of the store.

02

03

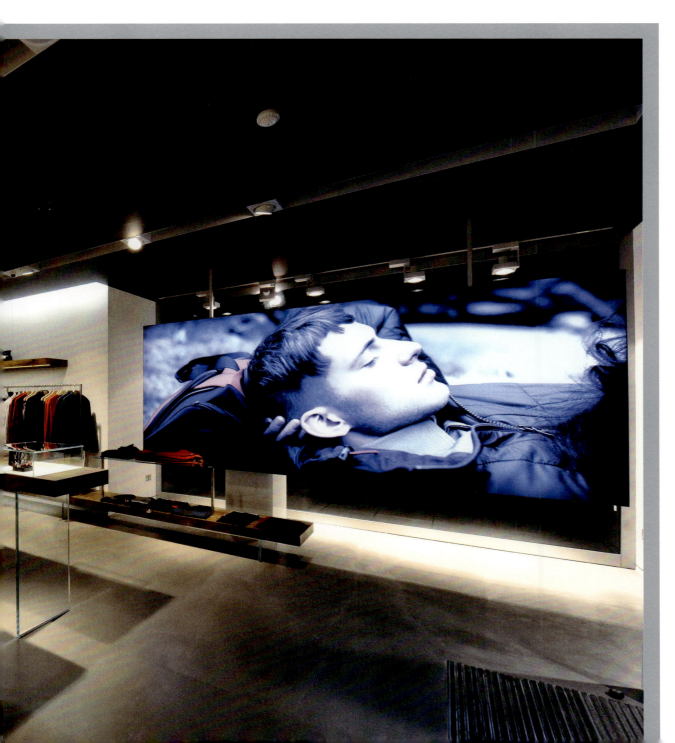

Surrounded by a spiral stairway, a 10-m-high glass case displays models of the iconic Swiss Army Knife. The staircase itself is made from clear glass, providing interesting views as shoppers move from floor to floor and creating an atmosphere of openness and transparency, which reinforces the visual connection that unites the three levels

----

Retailpartners
Motorenstrasse 35
8623 Wetzikon–Zürich
Switzerland

T +41 (0)43 244 7410
E info@retailpartners.ch
W www.retailpartners.ch

Photography: Marco Blessano

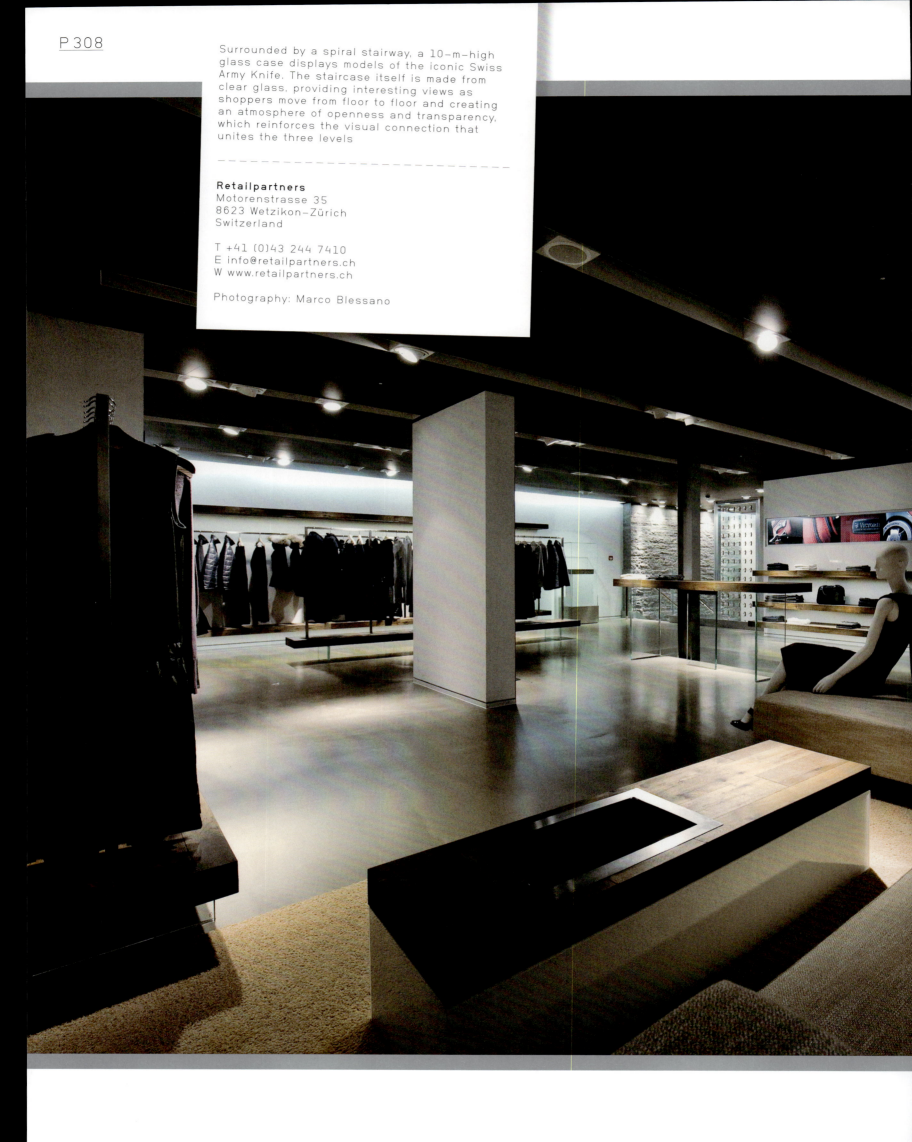

04   Technology underlines the contemporary aspect of recently added merchandise. Multifunctional touchscreens promote products, invite the customer to interact, and create involvement and interest in the brand.

First floor

Ground floor

Basement

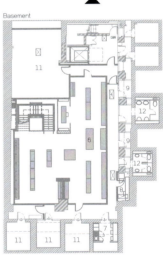

1 Women's collection
2 Men's collection
3 Lounge
4 Info panel
5 Fitting room
6 Cash desk
7 Kitchen
8 Office
9 Locker room
10 Smoking area
11 Storage
12 Lavatories

05   On 65-inch screens, customers watch specially commissioned films that combine the scenic beauty of Switzerland with various Victorinox product stories.

06   Apparel for women is another new addition to the Victorinox product range.

07   A 10-m-high glass display unit links the three floors of the store and showcases examples of the iconic Swiss Army Knife.

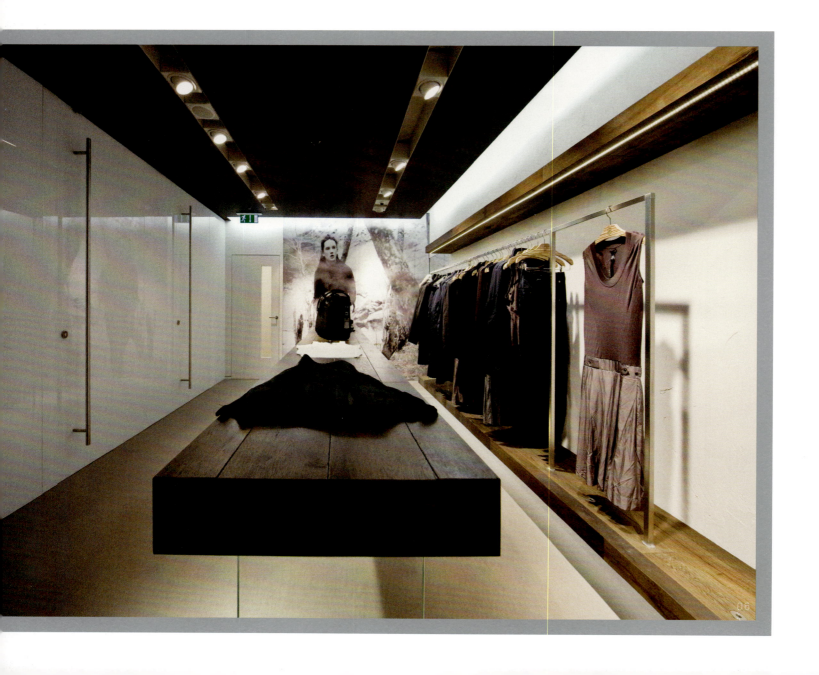

YEShop In House
dARCHstudio

WHERE:	ATHENS, GREECE
WHEN:	OCTOBER 2007
CLIENT:	YIORGOS ELEFTHERIADES
TOTAL FLOOR AREA (M²):	90
BUDGET (€):	10,000

||||||||||||||||||||||||||||||||||||||||||

IN 2006, ARCHITECT ELINA DROSSOU ESTABLISHED DARCHSTUDIO, A DESIGN FIRM BASED IN ATHENS, GREECE. THE STUDIO'S PORTFOLIO INCLUDES A VARIETY OF PROJECTS AT DIVERSE LOCATIONS AROUND THE COUNTRY: FROM PRIVATE RESIDENCES, OFFICE BUILDINGS AND COMMERCIAL SPACES TO TEMPORARY CONSTRUCTIONS, INSTALLATIONS, AND COMMISSIONS INVOLVING SMALL-SCALE DESIGN AND GRAPHIC DESIGN.

||||||||||||||||||||||||||||||||||||||||||

When fashion designer Yiorgos Eleftheriades wanted a new look for his 90-m² shop in the centre of Athens, Greece, he went to dARCHstudio with a special request: please come up with a retail concept that will last one year.
The solution presented by dARCHstudio was 'Papercut', a design based on the union of two disciplines, fashion and architecture. Existing furniture was rearranged, reused and combined with new, eco-friendly, corrugated-cardboard constructions. Tables attached to the wall and lit from behind served as lamps. Bookshelves turned sideways and mounted on the wall became displays, and the wall itself was covered in hand-cut sheets of cardboard, glued together layer by layer. Another addition was a biomorphic construction inspired - like the garments for sale - by the human body. In the same way that people accessorize themselves, this curvy construction was 'accessorized' with boxes featuring built-in lighting and displaying Eleftheriades' collection of accessories.

dARCHstudio
28 Mithimnis St.
11257 Athens
Greece

T +30 (0)21 0823 9484
E info@darchstudio.com
W www.darchstudio.com

Photography: Vasilis Skopelitis

01

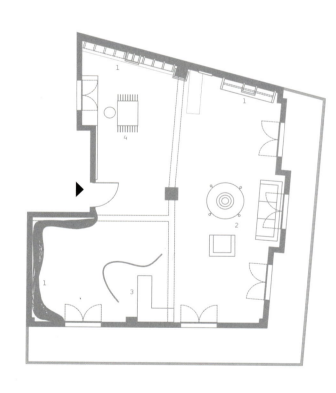

1 Cardboard display
2 Lounge area
3 Fitting room
4 Cash desk

02

01&02   A total of 1500 hand—cut
sheets of corrugated cardboard
were glued together to create
a new look for one wall of the
fashion store.

03   Architect Elina Drossou
gave existing pieces of furniture
new functions.

04   Ten volunteers helped
to create the biomorphic
construction.

Shop Addresses

Double Standard Clothing
p.180
By Propeller Design
Aoyama Plaza Building B1F
2-11-3 Kita-Aoyama,
Minato-Ku
107-0061 Tokyo
Japan
www.doublestandard.jp

EQ:IQ p.186
By AlexChoi design & Partners
Beijing apm
100020 Beijing
China
www.griretail.com

Escada p.190
By CAPS Architecture Interior
Design
9502 Wishire Boulevard
Beverly Hills, CA, 90212
USA
www.escada.com

**Fashion Studio Tamara
Radivojevic** p.196
By Dsignedby.
Strahinjica Bana 59
11000 Belgrade
Serbia

Filippa K p.198
By Aaro Arkitektkontor
Plaats 17
2513 AD The Hague
the Netherlands
www.filippa-k.com

Firma p.200
By Pankrath
Mulackstrasse 1
10119 Berlin
Germany
www.firma.net

Fred Perry p.202
By JudgeGill
Unit 1128 Ariel Way, Level 40
East Central, Westfield
Shopping Centre
London W12 7GD
United Kingdom
www.fredperry.com

Fullcircle p.204
By Brinkworth
1 Western Avenue Business
Park - Mansfield Road
London W3 0BZ
United Kingdom
www.wdt.co.uk

Geometry p.80
By plajer & franz studio
Gipsstrasse 23
10119 Berlin
Germany
www.geometrytheshop.de

Gigalove p.84
By Antonio Gardoni
Viale Italia 31
25126 Brescia
Italy
www.gigalove.it

H&M p.208
By Universal Design Studio
8580 Sunset Boulevard
Los Angeles, CA, 90069
USA
www.hm.com

Heikorn p.88
By atelier522
August-Ruf-Strasse 7-9
78224 Singen
Germany
www.heikorn.de

**Hugo Boss Special
Concept Store** p.210
By Matteo Thun & Partners
401 West 14th Street
New York, NY, 10014
USA
www.hugoboss.com

Icon p.92
By Studio Duo
Nieuwe Graanmarkt 5
1000 Brussels
Belgium
www.icon-shop.be

Intersport Bründl p.94
By Blocher Blocher Partners
Nikolaus-Gassner-Strasse 213
5710 Kaprun
Austria
www.bruendl.at

Irma Mahnel p.212
By d e signstudio regina
dahmen-ingenhoven
Odeonsplatz 12
80539 Munich
Germany
www.irma-mahnel.de

JeansLab p.96
By YalınTan & Jeyan Ülkü
Istiklal Cad. No:115
80060 Istanbul
Turkey
www.jeanslab.com.tr

Jill by JillStuart p.214
By Line-Inc
5-29-8 Jingumae, Shibuya-ku
150-0001 Tokyo
Japan
www.jillstuart.jp

Labels p.100
By Maurice Mentjens
Putstraat 12
6131 HL Sittard
the Netherlands
www.labelsfashion.nl

Laura Zanello p.104
By VON M
Outlet Center
Stuttgarter Strasse
72555 Metzingen
Germany

Laurèl p.216
By Plan2Plus design
Neuer Wall 41
20354 Hamburg
Germany
www.laurel.de

Le Ciel Bleu p.218
By Noriyuki Otsuka
Design Office
Frame Jinnanzaka B1
1-18-2 Jinnan, Shibuya-Ku
150-0041 Tokyo
Japan
www.lcb.co.jp

Levi's® p.222
By Checkland Kindletsides
Kurfürstendamm 237
10719 Berlin
Germany
www.levis.com

**Levi's® Blue Lab
Temporary Store**
p.226
By Liganova
Kettengasse 2
50667 Cologne
Germany
www.levis.com

Mad Child's Dollhouse p.230
By No Picnic
Drottninggatan 65
111 36 Stockholm
Sweden
www.weekday.se

Magazin Zing p.106
By AdaDesign
Sadovaja Street 7
191011 St. Petersburg
Russia
www.ukstyle.ru

Masha Tsigal p.232
By AdaDesign
Pokrovka Street 11
101000 Moscow
Russia
www.mashatsigal.com

McGregor Women p.234
By Conix Architects
Korte Dagsteeg 12
9000 Ghent
Belgium
www.mcgregor-fashion.com

Miffy Shop-in-Shop p.236
By UXUS
Kalverstraat 203
1012 XC Amsterdam
the Netherlands
www.miffy.com

Mode d'Emploi p.108
By Zoom Industries
Driehoekjes 25
2531 AZ The Hague
the Netherlands

Mode Weber p.110
By MAI
Rheinpark-Einkaufszentrum
9430 St. Margrethen
Switzerland
www.modeweber.ch

Mode Weber p.114
By MAI
AFG Shopping Arena
9015 St. Gallen
Switzerland
www.modeweber.ch

Monki: City of Oil and Steel
p.238
By Electric Dreams
Drottninggatan 59
602 24 Norrköping
Sweden
www.monkigirl.com

Napapijri Gallery Store p.240
By Studio DeCarloGualla
Via Manzoni 34
20121 Milan
Italy
www.napapijri.com

Napapijri Totem Concept Store
p.246
By Wagner Associati
Piazza Manzoni 2
6900 Lugano
Switzerland
www.napapijri.com

Roen p.272
By Ito Masaru Design Project /
SEI
Hiroo Office Building 3F
1-3-18, Hroo Shibuya-Ku
150-0012 Tokyo
Japan
www.roen.jp

Rohit Bal p.274
By Lotus
Shop 218-219, 2nd floor,
square one
C-2 District Center, Saket
110017 New Delhi
India
www.rohitbal.com

Röling Import p.122
By Osiris Hertman
Zuidermolenweg 2
1069 CG Amsterdam
the Netherlands
www.roling-import.nl

Romanticism 2 p.276
By SAKO Architects
20 West Huan Cheng Road
310000 Hangzhou
China
www.lmys.com.cn

s.Oliver Selection Store p.280
By plajer & franz studio
Löhr-Center
Hohenfelder Strasse 22
56068 Koblenz
Germany
www.s.oliver.de

She & He p.128
By Architetto Baciocchi
& Associati
Postysheva Street 127
83000 Donetsk
Ukraine
www.shgallery.dn.ua

Sid Lee Amsterdam Atelier
p.134
By Sid Lee with Workshop
Architecture + Design
Gerard Doustraat 72-80
1072 VV Amsterdam
the Netherlands
www.sidleecollectiveshop.com

Sigrun Woehr p.286
By ippolito fleitz group
Herrenstrasse 24
76133 Karlsruhe
Germany
www.sigrun-woehr.de

Siste's More p.290
By Bong Bong
Centergross, Block 6
Via dei Cardatori
40050 Funo di Argelato
Italy
www.sistesmore.it

Son's & Daughter's p.136
By Breil + Partner
Am Läger 1
77694 Kehl am Rhein
Germany

Sportsgirl p.292
By HMKM
283 Bourke Street
3000 Melbourne
Australia
www.sportsgirl.com.au

Takeda Truss Trash p.296
By No Picnic
Kungsgatan 46
411 15 Gothenburg
Sweden
www.weekday.se

Timberland p.300
By Checkland Kindletsides
Westfield Shopping Centre
Ariel Way
London W12 7GF
United Kingdom
www.timberland.com

Toxic Explosion p.304
By No Picnic
Götgatan 21
111 36 Stockholm
Sweden
www.weekday.se

Van Dijk p.138
By Osiris Hertman
Stationsstraat 22
5141 GE Waalwijk
the Netherlands
www.vandijkmode.nl

Victorinox p.306
By Retailpartners
95-96 New Bond Street
London W1S 1DB
United Kingdom
www.victorinox.com

Villa Moda p.140
By Marcel Wanders
Moda Mall
Bahrain World Trade Center
Manama
Bahrain
www.villa-moda.com

Wertgarner 1820 p.144
By BEHF Architects
Schottenfeldgasse 5
1070 Vienna
Austria
www.wertgarner.at

Wigmore Sports p.148
By Portland Design
39 Wigmore Street
London W1U 1PD
United Kingdom
www.wigmoresports.co.uk

YEShop In House p.312
By dARCHstudio
13 Agion Anargiron Street
10554 Athens
Greece
www.yiorgoseleftheriades.gr

POWERSHOP 2
NEW RETAIL DESIGN

ISBN: 978-3-89955-307-9

© 2009 Frame Publishers,
Amsterdam, 2009
© 2009 Die Gestalten Verlag
GmbH & Co. KG, Berlin, 2009

Publishers
Frame Publishers
www.framemag.com
Gestalten
www.gestalten.com

Production
Marlous van Rossum–Willems
and Sarah Schultz

Editors
Marlous van Rossum–Willems
and Sarah Schultz

Contributing editors
Erica Bol, Martijn Frank Dirks,
Jonah Gamblin, Kai van Hasselt,
Lisa Hassanzadeh,
Maaike van Leeuwen, John
Maatman, Cathelijne Nuijsink,
Melle Pama and Katelijn Quartier

Contributor
Peter Kattenberg

Graphic design
Alvin Chan
www.alvinchan.nl

Translation
InOtherWords
(Donna de Vries–Hermansader
and Christine Gardner)

Copy editing
InOtherWords
(Donna de Vries–Hermansader)

Colour reproduction
Grafisch Bedrijf Tuijtel

Printing
Ofset Yapimevi

Cover photography
Leon Abraas

International distribution
Gestalten
www.gestalten.com
sales@gestalten.com

Bibliographic information
published by the Deutsche
Nationalbibliothek.

The Deutsche Nationalbibliothek lists this publication
in the Deutsche Nationalbibli-
ografie; detailed bibiographic
is available on the internet
at http://dnb.d–nb.de

Printed on acid–free paper
produced from chlorine–free
pulp. TCF ∞

Printed in Turkey
978-3-89955-307-9